'The 1922 expedition was [...] ventures. One hundred year[...] the effects of extreme altitu[...] [...] were making it up as they went along, pushing the boundaries of human possibility. With his usual forensic analysis and keen eye for the previously untold anecdote, Mick Conefrey re-illuminates one of the greatest mountain adventures of all time.' – Stephen Venables

....

'A gloriously British failure: The lost story of the tweed jacket-wearing and Kendal mint cake-eating band of eccentrics who were the first to try to conquer Everest is finally told 100 years on ... The story of that first attempt on the mountain is one history has largely erased. Failure tends to be forgotten. But in its centenary year, that 1922 expedition is celebrated in a gripping new book by mountaineering historian Mick Conefrey. Yes, it was a failure – but a glorious one.' – *Daily Mail*

....

'The history of that derring-do, the politics and the drama are wonderfully captured by Mick Conefrey in his new book *Everest 1922* ... it is good to be reminded of its once dark, brooding, remoteness and of the courage which conquered it.' – *Daily Express*

....

'A nuanced, highly readable chronicle of the first attempt on the summit 100 years ago ... The Himalayas were an unknown frontier, and Mr Conefrey captures the awe that adventurers felt in their mighty company.' – *Wall Street Journal*

....

'A renowned author on Himalayan history' – *Trail* magazine

....

'George Mallory's first attempt to summit Mount Everest, in 1922, was more significant than the better-known 1924 expedition that took his life, according to this captivating account from author and documentary filmmaker Conefrey (*The Ghosts of K2*). ... This immersive chronicle restores an overlooked expedition to its rightful place in mountaineering history.' – *Publishers Weekly*

....

Mick Conefrey is an award-winning writer and documentary maker. He made the landmark BBC series *Mountain Men* and *Icemen* and *The Race for Everest* to mark the 60th anniversary of the first ascent. His previous books include *Everest 1953*, the winner of a LeggiMontagna award, and *The Ghosts of K2*, which won a US National Outdoor Book award in 2017.

EVEREST 1922

The Epic Story of the First Attempt on the World's Highest Mountain

MICK CONEFREY

ALLEN&UNWIN

First published in hardback in Great Britain in 2022 by Allen & Unwin, an imprint of Atlantic Books Ltd.

This paperback edition published in Great Britain in 2023 by Allen & Unwin, an imprint of Atlantic Books Ltd.

Copyright © Mick Conefrey, 2022

Maps by Adam T. Burton

The picture acknowledgements on p. 294 constitute an extension of this copyright page.

Every effort has been made to trace or contact all copyright holders. The publishers will be pleased to make good any omissions or rectify any mistakes brought to their attention at the earliest opportunity.

10 9 8 7 6 5 4 3 2 1

A CIP catalogue record for this book is available from the British Library.

Paperback ISBN: 978 1 83895 273 0
E-book ISBN: 978 1 83895 272 3

Printed in Great Britain by Clays Ltd, Elcograf S.p.A.

Allen & Unwin
An imprint of Atlantic Books Ltd
Ormond House
26–27 Boswell Street
London
WC1N 3JZ

www.atlantic-books.co.uk

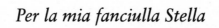

Per la mia fanciulla Stella

Contents

Dramatis Personae

THE EVEREST COMMITTEE

Sir Francis Younghusband   President
Arthur Hinks . . . . Honorary Secretary (RGS)
J. E. C. Eaton . . . . Honorary Secretary (Alpine Club)
Edward Somers-Cocks . . . Honorary Treasurer (RGS)
Colonel E. M. Jack . . . . . Royal Geographical Society (RGS)
Norman Collie . . . . Alpine Club
Captain Percy Farrar . . . . Alpine Club
C. F. Meade . . . . Alpine Club

THE RECONNAISSANCE, 1921

Charles Howard-Bury   . . . Leader
Harold Raeburn . . . . . . Climbing Leader
George Mallory . . . . . . Climber
Guy Bullock . . . . Climber
Alexander Kellas . . . . . . Climber
Henry Morshead . . . . . Surveyor
Oliver Wheeler . . . . . . Surveyor
Sandy Wollaston . . . . . Doctor and Naturalist
Alexander Heron . . . . . . Geologist
Gyaljen . . . . Sirdar
Gyalzen Kazi . . . . Interpreter
Chheten Wangdi . . . . . Interpreter

THE 1922 EXPEDITION

Charles Bruce. . . . . Leader
Edward Lisle Strutt . . . . . Climbing Leader
George Leigh Mallory . . . Climber
George Ingle Finch . . . . . Climber
Howard Somervell . . . . . Climber
Edward Norton. . . . . . . Climber
Henry Morshead . . . . . . Climber
Arthur Wakefield . . . . . . Climber
Colin 'Ferdie' Crawford . . Transport Officer
John Morris . . . . Transport Officer
Geoffrey Bruce . . . . . . Transport Officer
Tom Longstaff . . . . . . Doctor
John Noel. . . . . Photographer
Lance Corporal Tejbir Bura Gurkha Officer
Gyaljen . . . . Sirdar
Karma Paul . . . . Interpreter

Porters (hired in Darjeeling)

Lhakay, Pema, Mingma Boora, Mingma Dorjay, Pasang Tempa, Pema, Norbu Bura, Nima Lama, Pemba Norbu, Tenzing Katar, Dharkay Chopku, Ang Dawa, Little Nima, Dasonna, Leba Tshering, Ang Pasang Lakhpa, Idallo, Karma, Dorjay Sherpa, Rinchen, Goray, Phoo Nima Tendook, Chhetan, Augnami, Kancha, Lakpa, Ang Passang, Pasang Dorjay, Pasang Sherpa, Sangay, Chongay, Augbabu, Phoo Kemba, Lakpa Ptsering, Pemba Dorjay, Gyana, Tobgay, Yeshay, Norbu, Buchay, Dukpa, Tsang Dorjay.

Introduction

In June 2018, an article appeared in the *Financial Times*, entitled 'Everest for the Time-Pressed Executive'. It began with the story of a German businessman who had recently spent $110,000 on a 'Flash' twenty-eight-day commercial expedition, which had got him to the summit with five days to spare, before going on to list several companies offering 'premium' trips to the world's highest mountain. The most luxurious was a Nepali company, Seven Summit Treks, who were selling a $130,000 'VVIP' package that included helicopter flights from Kathmandu to within three days of the mountain, as well as a mid-expedition recuperative escape to a five-star hotel. The VVIP package included a 1:1 mountain guide to client ratio, and the services of three Sherpas, a personal cook and a photographer. It was, as their website proclaimed, specially designed for those 'who want to experience what it feels like to be on the highest point on the planet and have strong economic background to compensate for your old age, weak physical condition or your fear of risks'.

What, you wonder, would Hillary and Tenzing, the first men to reach the summit, have made of Seven Summits' package? Or, going further back, what would George Mallory, the 'Galahad' of Everest, have thought? When in 1923 Mallory was pressed by a reporter from the *New York Times* to explain why anyone would risk their life on Everest, he replied cryptically: 'Because it's there.' Is today's answer 'Because I can afford to', or 'Because I've got two weeks in May between business conferences and a hostile takeover'?

It's quite extraordinary to write a sentence like that, but there's no doubt that over the last thirty years Everest's reputation has changed. Long queues of climbers on the Lhotse Face, lurid tales of frozen corpses and piles of high-altitude trash; even the mountain itself seems to be in rebellion, with the Hillary Step – one of Everest's most famous features – collapsing in 2017. Today, for many mountaineers, Everest has become a symbol of excess and greed, a playground for the rich and occasionally foolish, the ultimate trophy mountain instead of the ultimate challenge.

It was not always thus.

When Everest was first measured in the mid-nineteenth century, it was thought to be so high that no one could survive on its summit. Even in the autumn of 1920, when a reconnaissance expedition was proposed, the respected mountaineer Sir Martin Conway told the *Daily Chronicle* that the climbing difficulties were so great it was unlikely Everest would ever be conquered. 'Its formation is unknown,' he said. 'It has not been mapped. Nothing is really known about it.'

Ten months later, when that reconnaissance was complete, the returning climbers were little more confident. Lecturing at the Queen's Hall in London shortly afterwards, George Mallory told a packed audience that, just before he left Tibet, he'd asked his climbing partner, Guy Bullock, what he thought the chances were of reaching the top. After considerable reflection, Bullock had replied, 'Fifty to one against!'

This book is about what happened next. It tells the story of the very first attempt on Everest in 1922, and the shocking events at its climax. Though in a very literal sense 1922 was Everest's 'Ur' expedition, in recent years it has been overlooked, with much of the historical and literary attention focused on the second British attempt, in 1924, and its still-controversial ending. Arguably, though, the 1922 expedition is more important. It set the style of big-expedition, 'siege'-style mountaineering, with large teams and multiple camps, which would persist for decades to come; it marked the beginning of the oxygen controversy that would dog Himalayan expeditions until the 1970s; it created the link between the Sherpa people and Everest which has turned their name into a global brand; and it elevated George Mallory into an international hero, whose actions and writings have become a crucial part of Everest's mythology.

For principal source material, I have drawn upon the thousands of mostly unpublished documents in the Mount Everest Foundation archives at the Royal Geographical Society (RGS) in London and in several smaller collections, notably at the Alpine Club and the British Library in London – as well as George Mallory's letters at Magdalene College, Cambridge, and George Finch's Everest diary at the National Library of Scotland in Edinburgh.

The climbers and the organizers behind the expeditions of the 1920s were great aficionados of the written word, leaving us with thousands of pages of letters, diaries, reports and Everest Committee meeting minutes, which make it possible to get a detailed inside view on everything from financing to group dynamics. Sadly, there are no first-hand accounts from the Sherpa point of view. At the time, very few Nepalis and Tibetans could read or write; it wasn't until the 1950s, when (ghostwritten) autobiographies of Ang Tharkay and Tenzing Norgay appeared, that you really started hearing the Sherpa voice more directly.

Today, Everest is regarded as an international mountain, with climbers from over 120 different countries having reached the summit by 2019, but until 1921 no foreigner had got anywhere near the mountain. Everest lay on the border of Nepal and Tibet, two nations whose rulers were utterly opposed to any incursions by outsiders. During the nineteenth and early twentieth centuries a steady stream of European and American explorers and missionaries had been unceremoniously thrown out of both countries.

When Everest was first measured in the 1850s by the British Survey of India, it had to be sighted from trigonometrical stations hundreds of miles away, in the hills of Bihar and West Bengal. In an act of cultural appropriation, they decided to name the mountain 'Everest', after Sir George Everest, a previous surveyor general. Good geographer that he was, Sir George didn't like this, and would have preferred the map-makers to have used one of its local names, but the name stuck.

In theory, it was out of bounds, but from the moment Everest was identified as the world's highest mountain, British climbers began pressing their government to seek permission from Nepal or Tibet to stage an expedition. In those days Britain had a huge global empire, and with India as its most important and valuable territory, it was South East Asia's regional superpower. If any country was going to strong-arm Tibet or Nepal into allowing access to its territory and its mountain, it was going to be Britain.

Climbers from Switzerland, Germany, Italy and the United States might have dreamt of attempting Everest, but they knew that British officials would never intercede for them or facilitate their passage across India. The alternative, to go via China, was even more unlikely due to the chaotic political situations and the ongoing conflict between China and Tibet.

Not that it was ever going to be easy for British climbers. While they longed to make the first attempt, Britain's diplomats did not always share that same passion. The Himalayas were in those days one of the most politically unstable regions of the world. As well as the numerous local conflicts between the Himalayan kingdoms of Tibet, Nepal, Sikkim and Bhutan, for many years British officials had feared that Imperial Russia would send its armies south through the crumbling Chinese Empire into Tibet and Nepal, and then right into the heart of British India. In the late nineteenth and early twentieth century, Russia and Britain played the so-called Great Game, dispatching their spies into the Himalayas on illicit journeys, gathering information for projected battles to come. In this febrile diplomatic atmosphere, the pleas of Britain's mountaineers frequently fell on deaf ears. When in 1907 London's Alpine Club, the world's oldest mountaineering institution, sought permission to stage an expedition to mark its fiftieth anniversary, the request never even reached the Nepali or Tibetan courts. It was vetted and rejected by British diplomats – according to Sir John Morley, the Secretary of State for India – for reasons of 'high Imperial policy'.

Official rebuffs did not put off British climbers entirely, however. Six years later, in 1913, the military surveyor Major

Cecil Godfrey Rawling tried again to get official approval for not one but two expeditions, which would climax with the first ascent. His scheme was again supported by the Alpine Club and the equally illustrious Royal Geographical Society, but this time an even greater game intervened: the First World War.

Between 1914 and 1918, all plans for mountaineering were put on hold while the biggest conflict that humanity had ever seen raged across the world. Leading members of the Alpine Club were either killed or maimed in action, as were hundreds of climbers from all over the world and millions of others. C. G. Rawling never made it to Everest; he survived the horrific battles of Ypres and the Somme but was killed by a stray shell as he stood chatting outside his brigade headquarters near Passchendaele in Belgium.

The dream of Everest did not, however, die with Rawling. Barely a month after the guns fell silent on the Western Front, in December 1918 the President of the Royal Geographical Society, Sir Thomas Holdich, wrote once again to the India Office, begging 'to submit to the Government of India proposals for preparing the exploration and ascent of Mt Everest as soon as circumstances permit'. The story of the first attempt begins just a few months later, on a chilly spring night in March 1919.

1

Himalayans at Play

The Aeolian Hall on New Bond Street in London saw several uses in its first fifty years. Built as an art gallery to display the work of the Pre-Raphaelite Brotherhood, it then became the headquarters of a pianola manufacturer, before reinventing itself as a small, intimate venue for opera recitals and concerts. But on the evening of 10 March 1919, the audience crowded in for a very different sort of performance.

For several years, the building had also been one of the main lecture halls for the Royal Geographical Society, one of the great British institutions of the Imperial era – a learned society founded in 1830 'to promote the advancement of geographical science'. That March night, the assembled guests braved the wind and rain to hear a lecture by a young officer in the Machine Gun Corps, Captain John Noel. Tall and thin with striking eyes, Noel had had a very difficult war, like many in the audience, but now he was thinking about the future and a possible return to the adventurous life that he had once lived in India. His lecture took him back to 1913 and

John Noel, self-portrait with movie camera

one of his most memorable escapades: 'A Journey to Tashirak in Southern Tibet, and the eastern approaches to Mount Everest'.

A natural showman, Noel knew how to work his audience. 'Now that the Poles have been reached,' he began, 'the next and equally important task is the exploration and mapping of Mount Everest. It cannot be long before the culminating summit of the world is visited and its ridges, valleys and glaciers are mapped and photographed.'

In the decade before the war broke out, Britain had been gripped with tales of Arctic and Antarctic exploration. The 'Race to the Poles' had made heroes of men like Ernest Shackleton and Robert Falcon Scott, but ultimately Britain had not come out on top. The Norwegian Roald Amundsen had beaten Scott to the South Pole, and the bragging rights over the North Pole had gone to the American Robert E. Peary, even though some disputed his claim. To map and photograph Everest, the so-called Third Pole, had been the lifelong ambition of Noel's friend C. G. Rawling, he declared – invoking the memory of one of Britain's many war heroes – but Rawling had been killed before seeing it fulfilled. 'May it yet be accomplished in his memory!' Noel exclaimed.

It was a sentiment that was bound to chime with many members of the audience, and especially the grand old men of the RGS. As well as Sir Thomas Holdich, the seventy-six-year-old President and esteemed author of *Tibet, the Mysterious*, there was Sir Francis Younghusband, the legendary soldier and explorer, Alexander Kellas, the bespectacled Scottish chemist who was probably the most experienced Himalayan traveller in Britain, and Douglas Freshfield, the geographer who, along with Younghusband, was one of the few Europeans who could claim to have set eyes on Everest. All of them had their own thoughts about future expeditions, but for the moment they were happy to let Captain Noel hold the floor.

The story he told could have come straight out of Rudyard Kipling.

In the spring of 1913, while on leave from his posting in India, Noel had decided to make a private foray into Tibet, aiming to find a route to Everest and, if possible, 'come to close quarters with the mountain'. He knew that Tibet was off limits to all Westerners, and that over the previous decades a series of missionaries and explorers had been captured by Tibetan officials and marched straight back out of the country, but he wasn't going to be put off. Noel had already made several trips along the Tibetan border and was familiar with the territory. He darkened his face, hoping to pass himself off as an Indian, and left his base with three servants: a Sherpa called Tebdoo; a Tibetan called Adhu; and his gun- and camera-bearer, Badri, from the Garhwal mountains of India. His target was the village of Tashirak in southern Tibet, which he thought was the 'gateway' to Everest.

Noel's party travelled light: a pair of A-frame tents, blankets, medicine, a Winchester rifle, a revolver for Noel and automatic pistols for the others. To guide him, Noel brought along a crude map compiled by Sarat Chandra Das, one of the Indian 'pundits' – the local surveyors employed by the Survey of India in the 1880s to make clandestine journeys into the far reaches of the Himalayas, where no European dared to go.

The first part of his journey took Noel from the town of Siliguri, at the foot of the Himalayas, northwards through Sikkim to the Tibetan border. Nominally, Sikkim was a 'princely state' ruled over by a local maharajah, but in reality the British were in control. When Noel reached the small Sikkimese village of Lachen, just inside the frontier, he hired two yak drivers to transport a month's worth of supplies and then split his party to attract less attention, sending the food ahead via a different route. For three weeks, Noel managed to avoid detection in the sparsely inhabited wilderness of eastern Tibet, until eventually at the tiny fort-like village of Mugk, twenty-five miles from Tashirak, he came face-to-face with an angry Tibetan official who demanded to know what he was up to. With supplies running low, and the official refusing to let them buy food or fuel, Noel was forced to turn back and return to Sikkim.

It was a rebuff, but John Noel wasn't finished yet. Having spent so much time dreaming of Everest, he wasn't going to be put off by one hostile official. He reorganized his party, further reduced his equipment, and a month later crossed the border back into Tibet. This time he took more precautions, keeping away from local villages and known trade routes. It wasn't easy though. Even if he and his men were self-sufficient for food, they still had to forage for fuel and water.

Initially Noel and his party managed to travel unhindered, but once again they were spotted at Mugk. This time, ignoring the protests of villagers, Noel pressed on towards a high pass called the Langbu La – which according to Das's map would provide him with his first view of Everest. When he reached the top, the sky was bright and clear, and directly in front of him there was a series of striking-looking peaks covered in snow. Noel had never seen anything so spectacular or dramatic, but there was a problem: the mountains in front of him were, he estimated, around 23,000 feet high, a full 6,000 feet lower than Everest. Had he misread Das's map? Then, gradually, the view changed. A wall of cloud behind the first range broke up and dissipated, revealing a much higher mountain behind. Noel checked his compass: it was Everest, 'a glittering spire top of rock fluted with snow'.

It was the best of moments and the worst. Noel had entered the tiny pantheon of Europeans who had come anywhere close to the world's highest mountain, but in doing so he had discovered that Das's map was incorrect – the mountain range in the foreground had not been included. There was no direct approach to Everest from the east; any mountaineer who wanted to make an attempt would first have to cross the formidable chain of peaks directly in front of him.

Noel knew this was beyond the capacity of his small party and their limited equipment, but he carried on to Tashirak, a large settlement which marked the border between two regions of Tibet. He had now given up all hope of travelling unobserved, and set his sights on reaching a monastery where he had been told the Buddhist lamas worshipped Everest and Kangchenjunga, the world's third-highest mountain.

It was not to be. The officials at Tashirak were predictably hostile, and a few days later the dzongpen, or local governor, arrived at Noel's tent and demanded that he and his party turn back for the second time. The governor had ridden more than 150 miles in three days to confront the intruders – and to make sure they followed his orders, he left a detachment of soldiers to watch over their camp. Noel was not intimidated, even when the soldiers fired a volley of warning shots, but with his food running out and sensing that he had now pushed his luck as far as it would go without causing a diplomatic incident, he was forced to retreat.

A few weeks later, Noel was back in British territory, resting up at a government bungalow and plotting a third and final trip to the nearby mountains of Sikkim, where he would be able to travel and photograph in peace – without the interference of any hostile Tibetan officials. If all had gone according to plan, he would have attempted to return to Everest a year later, in 1914, with C. G. Rawling, but as everyone in the audience at the Aeolian Hall knew, the war had put paid to that hope.

As the lights came up, the great and geographically good prepared to speak. Noel had taken a little longer than expected, but before everyone disappeared, and most importantly before any journalists slipped off to file their copy, the RGS wanted to use the occasion to renew the case for an official British Everest expedition. The India Office still hadn't replied to Sir Thomas Holdich's letter from several months earlier, and the more publicity this event could generate the better – because, as Holdich understood only too well, the fundamental challenge of Everest in 1919 was not coping with the altitude or the cold or the technical climbing difficulty, but something much more basic: securing permission to go there. No one at the Society thought the Nepali government would ever allow a party to approach Everest from the south, because of Nepal's historical distrust of foreign travellers, but the Tibetan government was enjoying better relations with Britain than it had for a long time, and so might just be amenable to a full-scale expedition from its side of the border. The RGS could not communicate with Tibet directly, however – any approach would have to be initiated by the notoriously aloof officials of the India Office.

Douglas Freshfield was first to speak. Tall and bearded with a patrician manner, he was the former President of both the Alpine Club and the RGS, and was no stranger to illegal journeys. In 1899 he had made a clandestine foray from Sikkim across the Nepali border, to photograph and survey the approaches to Kangchenjunga. Freshfield praised Captain Noel for extending their collective geographic knowledge, agreed that Tashirak was probably not the best way into Everest, and called for better roads to be built in Sikkim to make the Himalayas more accessible. He liked to claim that the Himalayas could one day become the 'playground of India', with a network of mountain huts and facilities for walkers and climbers – but only if the colonial authorities took a more active role.

The next speaker, the climbing chemist Alexander Kellas, was not so dismissive of the Tashirak route and thought it might well turn out to be the best way to approach Everest. He had travelled widely in the Himalayas and had thought about Everest for many years. If hostile officials could be placated, he mused, the best approach might indeed be from the East, but good scientist that Kellas was, he also suggested several other possible routes.

Before he could list them in detail – and probably send the audience to sleep – Captain Percy Farrar, the noted climber and President of the Alpine Club, came forward with a direct offer. His club was willing, he said, to put up part of the funds for a future expedition, and more importantly had two or three young climbers who were 'quite capable of dealing with any purely mountaineering difficulties as are likely to be met with on Mount Everest'.

The longest and most animated speech of the evening came from Sir Francis Younghusband, the military explorer who sixteen years earlier had led the controversial British invasion of Tibet in 1903. His travels were legendary, taking him from the Pamir mountains of Russia to the Taklamakan desert of China, and from Ladakh in northern India to the mountains of Kashmir in the far west. Short in stature, with thinning hair and a huge Kitchener-style moustache, even at the age of fifty-five Younghusband remained a force of nature. Ever since his incursion into Tibet, he had been out of favour with the British government, who thought he had been too bullish, but he was determined to regain his place in the public eye and saw Everest as one way to return to the limelight.

Younghusband began by reminding everyone that, long before Noel or C. G. Rawling had dreamt of Everest, back in 1893 he and his friend Charles Bruce had plotted the first ascent on a polo field in Chitral on the North-West Frontier. Nothing had come of it, but a decade later, when stationed at Khamba Dzong in southern Tibet, he had spent three months enjoying a stupendous view of the world's highest mountain. The real problem facing the RGS, he said, was not the Tibetan authorities or the Indian government, but officials and ministers in London. The home government had and was continuing to oppose any travel to Tibet, but, Younghusband added diplomatically, 'If a reasonable scheme is put before them, and it is proved to them that we mean serious business, then they are reasonable and will do what one wants.' With an eye to the next day's headlines, he finished on a patriotic note: 'I hope something really serious will come of this meeting. I should like it to be an Englishman who gets to the top of Mount Everest first.'

Younghusband was genuinely convinced that the diplomatic calculus had changed significantly. Before the First World War, British officials had opposed any thoughts of an attempt on Everest, claiming that it would upset the delicate political balance of the region – and, in particular, antagonize Imperial Russia. But the war had ended with the collapse of that regime. With the Russian tsar dead and a civil war raging between the so-called White Russians and the new revolutionary government, no British diplomat could maintain that Russia was a threat to India, so there had never been a better time to ask permission from the Tibetan government. Any reasonable person would have to agree, wouldn't they?

The press, however, proved not to be quite as enthusiastic as Younghusband might have hoped. There was a rather brief item in *The Times* the next morning about Captain Noel's speech, but it focused more on his suggestion that 'man-lifting kites' could be used for mapping and survey work than on any plan for a British expedition. The satirical magazine *Punch* carried a longer piece, entitled 'Himalayans at Play', in which they lampooned the whole affair, poking fun at the Tibetan names used by Noel and the earnest contributors from the floor. Like *The Times*, *Punch* was intrigued by the kites, adding that trained albatrosses might also be employed for other aspects of the great work.

The 'Himalayans' were not discouraged. Noel's lecture had put Everest back on the national agenda, and as if to prove their point, just over a week later, on 19 March, Arthur Hinks, the Secretary of the Royal Geographical Society, received a letter from a Lieutenant-Colonel Charles Howard-Bury – then staying at the Bath Club in Central London – in which he proposed to make a reconnaissance of Everest that very summer on behalf of the Society, and to negotiate directly with the Tibetan authorities for a larger expedition in the following year. He even offered to approach the Surveyor General and the Director General of Flying in India, to organize an aerial reconnaissance of Nepali territory. It was an extraordinary offer from someone who wasn't even a fellow of the RGS, but the Howard-Burys were a well-known and well-connected aristocratic family, and his letter and offer to go to India was just the boost that Younghusband and his coterie at the RGS needed. Younghusband told Arthur Hinks to write once again to the India Office in Whitehall, to ask if a delegation from the Society and the Alpine Club could come in for a meeting.

A month later, Sir Thomas Holderness, the Under-Secretary of the India Office, finally replied. There was no need to meet face-to-face, he wrote, but the diplomats in Whitehall had not been idle. His office had approached the government of India and put forward the Society's proposal, but yet again they had said no. 'They are of the opinion,' he wrote, 'that until Tibetan affairs are more settled than at present, it is not advisable to relax the restrictions hitherto laid on travel and exploration in that country.' And so concluded the latest British proposal for an expedition to Everest – or at least, that's what the men in Whitehall wanted everyone to believe.

Sir Francis Younghusband begged to differ. A year later he had taken over as President of the RGS, and Everest was still at the front of his mind. On 26 April 1920, he convened the RGS's Expedition Committee and emerged with a detailed plan for a two-year programme, which would start with a preliminary reconnaissance and be followed with an ascent of the mountain itself. When he gave his inaugural address to the fellows of the RGS in May 1920, he reiterated his long-held desire to see Everest climbed. To those who asked what the point was of spending so much time and energy on a project that had no obvious political or financial benefit, he had a simple answer: 'The accomplishment of such a feat will elevate the human spirit.' Climbing Everest might be of no more use than kicking a football about or writing a poem, he admitted, but it would give man 'increased pride and confidence in himself in his struggle for ascendancy over matter. This is the incalculable good which the ascent of Mount Everest will confer.'

Everest might be important for the whole of mankind, but as Younghusband and his supporters at the RGS realized, they would probably get more official help and support in the press if they loudly banged the patriotic drum. 'The personnel of the expedition will be British subjects,' the resolution stated, with no applications from non-British subjects to be 'entertained'. On the following day, Younghusband sent a further request to the India Office which was almost identical to the approach in 1919, asking for a meeting between the Secretary of State and a delegation from the Royal Geographical Society. Younghusband's persistence paid off. This time they said yes.

At 4.55 p.m. on 23 June, as the official stenographer recorded, the meeting began at the India Office on Whitehall. The Under-Secretary of State for India could not attend in person but he sent his deputy, Lord Sinha, a distinguished Bengali lawyer who was one of the first Indians to take a senior position in the British civil service. On the RGS's side, Younghusband had put together an impressive group, including Howard-Bury, Freshfield, and Younghusband's friend General Charles Granville Bruce, but as the official minutes made clear, Younghusband did virtually all the talking.

The Alps had been ascended, he told Lord Sinha, from 'end to end', and elsewhere in the world there had been expeditions to the high mountains of Africa and the Andes, as well as the world's second- and third-highest mountains – K2 in the Karakoram, and Kangchenjunga on the border of Nepal and Sikkim – but still, 'for a great many years past the idea has been in the minds of men to ascend Mount Everest, which is the highest mountain in the world'. He outlined his plan for a reconnaissance followed by a full-blown attempt, and with a flourish pulled out a large panoramic photograph that showed how approachable Everest was from the Tibetan side, saying: 'Compared with other peaks of the Himalayas its form, at any rate, promises well.' Then, to reinforce the point, he produced a second photograph, shot with a telephoto lens, which he said illustrated the 'comparatively fairly even slope' on the northern side.

It was a bravura performance which seemed to win over Lord Sinha. He told his guests that his office had already been in touch with the colonial government in India and that his boss, the Under-Secretary, was entirely in favour of the expedition. They would do everything they could to help, and within a few days would have a reply from the government of India in Kolkata.

It was exactly what Younghusband and his delegation wanted to hear, but when the India Office wrote back to the RGS a full month later, on 31 July, it was as if the meeting had never happened:

> The Government of India have given the matter their careful consideration but though, as the Society is aware, they have every sympathy with the project, they feel strongly that until certain important political questions outstanding in regard to Tibet, are settled, they are not in a position to approach the Tibetan Government with a request for the facilities required by the Society.

It was yet another polite but firm 'no', but Younghusband and his supporters did not despair, because this time round they were no longer willing to wait in their offices and drawing rooms, hoping for good news from on high. Instead, they had a man in the field – the same Lieutenant-Colonel Charles Howard-Bury who had offered to intercede for the RGS back in 1919, and who was at that very moment pounding the corridors of power in India, trying to persuade everyone he could of the rightness of their cause.

Everest was in play.

Charles Howard-Bury looked every inch the archetypal British officer: tall and imposing, with dark thinning hair and a neatly clipped moustache. According to George Mallory he was 'a queer customer', but whether he was hinting at Howard-Bury's sexuality or his eccentric habits it's difficult to know. There was no doubt that Howard-Bury was someone who, despite his conventional exterior, frequently confounded expectations.

He was born in 1881 into the Anglo-Irish aristocracy, went to Eton and then the Royal Military Academy at Sandhurst, from which he graduated as a captain before being posted to the Indian Army. During the First World War he found himself in the thick of the fighting before he was captured and interned as a prisoner of war. In the 1920s he would serve as a Conservative MP before retiring to Ireland after just seven years in Parliament, to spend the rest of his life looking after and restoring the family estate.

So far so predictable, but there was another side to Howard-Bury: a restless fascination with exotic travel and religion, and a refusal to conform. 'The soul of man is never content with what has been attained,' he once wrote. 'The solution of one problem only brings forward fresh problems to be solved.' One of his first acts when he arrived in India in 1905 as a young officer in the King's Royal Rifle Corps was to slip over the border in an attempt to reach Mount Kailash, the holiest mountain in Tibet. In the years that followed, he travelled to Kashmir and the Karakoram, and visited the Buddhist temples of Angkor Wat in Cambodia and the Hindu shrines at Badrinath on the Ganges. He spoke more than twenty languages and filled his home in Ireland with relics and souvenirs from his travels, including a Russian bear called Agu with whom he used to wrestle. He never married but would spend the last fifteen years of his life with Rex Beaumont, a Shakespearean actor nicknamed 'Sexy Rexy'; the pair moved between homes in Ireland and Tunisia. But in the summer of 1920, what mattered to Francis Younghusband was that Howard-Bury had the means and the motivation to put the RGS's case for an Everest expedition directly to the authorities in India.

Younghusband prepared a memo, instructing Howard-Bury to go directly to the British Viceroy of India in Simla and, if all went well, to seek out permission for an aerial reconnaissance of the mountain in advance of the main effort. 'We have some right to expect the Tibetan authorities to grant travellers access to Tibet because Tibetan travellers have been welcomed in England,' Younghusband added, 'and two Tibetans have been trained in surveying by this Society.'

Off Howard-Bury sailed on a two-week voyage, across the calm seas of the Mediterranean and the not-so-placid Indian Ocean, from Marseille to Aden to Mumbai, and then by rail up to Simla in the foothills of the Himalayas. Since 1864 it had been the summer capital of the British Raj, where colonial officials went to escape the heat of Kolkata and Delhi. Simla boasted an Anglican church, a post office, a train station, several British hotels and, most importantly, a host of government offices.

Howard-Bury quickly got down to work. As an 'old India hand', he arranged meetings with the Viceroy, the acting Surveyor General and the head of the Indian Flying Corps. They were all very glad to have someone to deal with in person, but there was no sign of an immediate breakthrough. The main problem – the important diplomatic issue that Whitehall had hinted at – was a small shipment of machine guns and ammunition that had been promised to the government of Tibet but had not yet been delivered. The colonial authorities were in favour, but the India Office in London was hesitating for no apparent reason. Until the arguments could be resolved, Howard-Bury was told, the idea of a mountaineering expedition to Everest could not be broached with the Tibetan authorities. As for any proposed aerial reconnaissance, that was a straight 'no': the Flying Corps had neither the planes nor the inclination to get involved.

It was not a good start, but Howard-Bury refused to be put off. Over the next three months, he travelled ceaselessly to put his case, visiting Kolkata, Dacca, Darjeeling and Sikkim. In the end, he realized that the decision was not going to come down to the Viceroy or even the Secretary of State in London, but to Charles Bell, a semi-retired British official who had been dealing with Tibetan matters for the past decade.

Charles Bell was an unusual man – not a soldier but an intellectual, who spoke fluent Tibetan and had even published an Anglo-Tibetan colloquial dictionary. He was a personal friend of Tibet's religious and political leader, the Dalai Lama, and would one day write his biography. Unlike most British gentlemen of his era, Bell was clean-shaven and had the visionary look of a priest or theologian. His friends in Tibet liked him so much that they thought he was the reincarnation of a former monk. Bell, unfortunately, was known to oppose the Everest venture, and had a reputation for obstinacy. 'He is a most tiresome man to deal with,' Howard-Bury wrote to Francis Younghusband, 'because he is very slow and cautious and does not make any mistakes.'

Britain's relationship with Tibet was tangled, to say the least. According to the government in Peking, Tibet was a province of China, but in 1903 – on the pretext of resolving a frontier issue between Sikkim and its northern neighbour – a British force under Younghusband had invaded, decimated a Tibetan army and marched all the way to Lhasa, the capital city, sending the Dalai Lama into hiding. After occupying the city for several months, the British negotiated a punitive treaty directly with the remains of the Tibetan government, only to renegotiate many of its clauses a few years later with China. When to reinforce their claims the Chinese invaded Tibet in 1910, the Dalai Lama was given sanctuary in British India, and to make things even more complicated, the Indian government helped re-arm the Tibetan military when the Chinese fled in 1913. It was no wonder Bell felt he had to tread carefully, but Howard-Bury refused to take no for an answer.

He tracked Bell down to Yatung, a trading station just inside Tibet. It was a very strange place – a town consisting of two Tibetan monasteries and a British outpost built in the 1890s to facilitate an earlier attempt at commerce between India and its northern neighbour. Initially, the Tibetan authorities had resented what they saw as a British incursion into their territory – so much so that they literally built walls all the way around the residence and trading post. When they followed with substantial fortifications stretching all the way across the valley, blocking the road to Lhasa, the British invaded. In the years since 1903, most of the walls had been dismantled or fallen into disrepair, but the trading post had been reoccupied and revived. The current British resident was David MacDonald, the son of a Scottish tea planter and a Sikkimese mother.

Charles Bell was more hospitable and charming than Howard-Bury had expected. In Bell's opinion, the Tibetans would eventually agree to an Everest expedition, but for the moment he was against it until, Howard-Bury noted, 'the *whole* of the question of the relations between China, India and Tibet had been settled'. Those discussions had been going on for a full fourteen years and, as Howard-Bury wrote ruefully to Younghusband in London, 'may go on as long again'.

Bell gave Howard-Bury permission to go a little further into Tibet but not as far as Khamba Dzong, the famous fort from which Everest was visible. For that pleasure, Howard-Bury had to return to Sikkim and head north up the Teesta valley, following the same route as Captain Noel had taken in 1913. When he got close to the border, he was gifted with magnificent vistas over Tibet. 'The view extended for hundreds of miles over broad valleys, across range upon range of mountains, all touched with the most fascinating changes of light and shade,' he wrote in his diary. 'In the evening far away the peak of Mount Everest stood up against the setting sun.' It was a striking sight, but would he ever get any closer?

As Howard-Bury prepared to sail back to England, for once he was pessimistic. His time in India had not been wasted – he had made good local contacts and won over some of the men in high office – but until Charles Bell retired, he concluded, there would be no progress. And then suddenly, to his great surprise, there was a small ray of hope.

'I think our Everest expedition has advanced a step forward,' Howard-Bury began a letter to Younghusband in late October 1920. Charles Bell, he reported, was on his way to Lhasa for a personal audience with the Dalai Lama, and had been asked by the Indian government to press the case for an Everest expedition. 'I think it is rather a case of kill or cure, for he is not in good health and a journey into the heart of Tibet at this time of year promises to be a cold proceeding.' Either Bell would obtain permission or, as Howard-Bury implied, he would die en route and be replaced by someone more sympathetic to the Society's cause.

Back in London, Sir Francis Younghusband had continued to talk up the prospects of the expedition, even when he knew from Howard-Bury they were far from good. At a meeting of the RGS at the Aeolian Hall in early November, he reiterated his belief that whoever climbed Everest would raise 'the spirit of countless others for generations to come, and give men a firmer nerve for scaling every other mountain'. Then he called onto the stage his friend General Charles Granville Bruce, the jovial and outspoken Welshman with whom he had mooted his first Everest campaign, almost thirty years earlier. Bruce had spent many years in the Himalayas and participated in early expeditions to Nanga Parbat and K2, and if Howard-Bury somehow succeeded, he was expected to lead the future Everest expedition. Bruce was another great banger of drums, telling the audience that 'teams have to be trained and men tested'.

The British press lapped it up. They were now very much on the RGS's side, with articles appearing regularly in both London and provincial newspapers discussing the proposed expedition. General Bruce told journalists that he had been sworn to secrecy about exactly what was going on, but he promised the *Evening News* that the attempt on Everest would be 'BAT'. When their reporter asked what he meant, he replied with a smile: 'British All Through'. However, no amount of patriotic boosting by Bruce or Younghusband would make any difference unless Charles Bell came on side – and persuaded the Dalai Lama to come with him.

On 17 November, Bell reached Lhasa and prepared to visit the Dalai Lama at his private estate, the Jewel Park, on the outskirts of the city. Unlike the Dalai Lama's official winter residence – the monumentally grand Potala Palace, which still dominates Lhasa's skyline – the Jewel Park was low-key and secluded: a series of temples and residential buildings set within an elaborate garden that included an ornamental lake and a small zoo.

Charles Bell had his work cut out. The arms deal was still unresolved, much to the Tibetan government's chagrin. There were many in the capital who, unsurprisingly, did not trust the British, and a few Tibetan generals who even favoured a rapprochement with China. But the Thirteenth Dalai Lama, Thubten Gyatso, was progressive and cosmopolitan in his outlook, and he received Bell in a room that mixed European and traditional Tibetan furniture.

He cut a striking figure: shaven-headed with a broad handlebar moustache and watery eyes, he greeted his British guest dressed in a red silk robe and a yellow jacket. Six years younger than Bell, Thubten Gyatso was born in 1876 into a peasant family in a village in southern Tibet. Two years later he was recognized as the reincarnation of the Dalai Lama and brought to Lhasa. After surviving two invasions – by the British in 1903 and the Chinese in 1910 – he was determined to strengthen Tibet's international relations and modernize his country, holding unprecedented meetings with officials from France, Germany and the USA, as well as Great Britain. He wrote a new national anthem, established the first post office as well as a national institute to preserve Tibet's traditional herbal medical system, and even agreed to send four young Tibetans to London to study electrical engineering and the science of surveying.

Their first meeting was largely ceremonial, but at the end of the second, Bell brought up the proposed Everest expedition. There was no concept of mountaineering as a sport in Tibet. The peaks of the Himalayas, particularly those covered in snow, were thought to be sacred places – the homes of the gods and local spirits. Tibet's most sacred mountains, Mount Kailash and Tsa-Ri, were far away, but very close to Everest there was an important monastery in the Rongbuk valley. Bell knew that many in the Dalai Lama's circle would be sceptical and very suspicious of any British party crossing their territory, but he thought that if he emphasized the scientific and geographical dimensions of the proposed expedition, and the fact that it was so important to so many people in Britain, the Dalai Lama might be persuaded. He left him with a British map showing the location of Mount Everest, but this didn't impress the Dalai Lama or his chief secretary.

The Tibetan name for the world's tallest mountain was Chomolungma, but there were several different versions of its meaning and spelling. Today Chomolungma is generally translated as 'Mother Goddess of the Earth', but in 1921 Bell was told that it meant 'the Snow Mountain of the Bird Sanctuary'. Either way, the British name Everest meant nothing to the Dalai Lama, and the political manoeuvrings over Britain's relationship with Tibet and China continued. At one stage Bell was almost recalled to India, but finally, in early December, he returned to the Dalai Lama's palace to hear his decision on the proposed expedition.

On 10 December, Bell sent a telegram to the Indian government. It took three days to reach Delhi, a further two days for the news to be transmitted to London, and another five before the political secretary of the India Office in London sent a handwritten note to Francis Younghusband. 'You will be interested to know that we have just received a telegram from the Viceroy,' the letter began, 'in which the following passage occurs:—"Bell telegraphs that he has explained to Dalai Lama object of desired exploration [i.e. Mt Everest] and necessity of travelling through Tibetan territory and <u>obtained Tibetan Government's consent</u>".'

The underlining said it all: against the odds, the way was clear. Britain was on its way to Everest. It was the best Christmas present Sir Francis and his friends at the Royal Geographical Society and the Alpine Club could have imagined.

'We May Reach the Roof of the World', thundered the *Evening News*; 'White Silences Where Man Has Never Trod', headlined the *Daily News*; 'The World's Greatest Adventure', declared the *Daily Mail*. There were a few less bombastic reports, but when in early January 1921 the British press heard that, after so much build-up, the first Everest expedition was finally about to get under way, they were almost universally positive. No one questioned the expedition's value or doubted that either this year or next Everest would be 'conquered'; no one pointed out the dangers of climbing at high altitude. A few scientists questioned whether humans could really function in the thin air found at the summit of Everest but, in the popular imagination, the Himalayas were not fundamentally different to the great mountains of the Alps; they were just a little higher.

At 3.00 p.m. on 12 January 1921, Sir Francis Younghusband convened the first meeting of the newly formed Mount Everest Committee at the Alpine Club in Mayfair. Sir Francis was appointed President, and Arthur Hinks, a paid official of the Royal Geographical Society, the acting Honorary Secretary. On the Alpine Club side there were three men present with extensive moun- taineering experience: the former, present and future presidents of the Alpine Club, Captain Percy Farrar, Norman Collie and Tom Longstaff. Over the next twenty years, the members of this committee would play a crucial role in the Everest story. They would select, reject, scheme and machinate. For the moment, though, they had two principal challenges: first, to raise enough money for both a reconnaissance in 1921 and a full-blown expedition in 1922; and second, to choose the climbers who would be given the chance to ascend the highest mountain on earth.

Within a few days of the news of the expedition breaking, letters were coming in from all over the world. There was a Harvard graduate who promised that he was an admirer of 'all things British', a Frenchman who had spent the whole of the First World War on the front lines but was never ill, and a twenty-five-year-old from Geneva who sent in photos of his Alpine conquests. Several American pilots offered to conduct aerial surveys; a couple of men offered themselves as wireless operators, and others as surveyors and 'auxiliaries'. In total, there were over ninety letters from sixteen different countries, but not a single applicant was offered a place.

As General Bruce had confided to the *Daily News* a few months earlier, the organizers had determined that this expedition would be all British. Arthur Hinks threw any applications from Germans or other 'ex-enemies' straight into the wastepaper basket. Even though Britain boasted a very active Ladies' Alpine Club, women were not countenanced. When in early January a French 'sportswoman', Mademoiselle Marring, had the temerity to apply, citing her climbing experience in Italy, France and Switzerland as a well as a balloon flight across the English Channel, Francis Younghusband joked about her at the next meeting of the Royal Geographical Society, sending the tuxedo-clad ranks of gentlemen in front of him into howls of laughter. In fact, not a single woman was invited on any of the 'official' British expeditions over the next thirty years, and it wasn't until 1993 that Rebecca Stephens became the first British woman to climb Everest.

When it came to the leadership of the expedition, there was a surprise. Everyone had assumed, himself included, that General Bruce would be in charge. After all, he was a war hero and a veteran of several previous Himalayan expeditions. He had given numerous interviews to the press about Everest, and as he told Hinks in early January, had in recent weeks been fending off late-night telephone calls from reporters. What he and they didn't realize was that the Everest Committee had chosen another candidate: Charles Howard-Bury.

They had been impressed by his tenacity and diplomatic skills, and on 19 January decided to offer him leadership of the Reconnaissance. Howard-Bury was holed up in Ireland at his house in Mullingar, worrying about the War of Independence raging around him, but he said yes straight away, cabling Younghusband that he was 'most honoured at your confidence'. Over in Wales, Bruce was out of the loop. When he heard, he headed for London to appear in front of a special meeting of the Committee. Even though he outranked him, Bruce offered to serve under Howard-Bury, and suggested that he might even agree to a more limited role – only accompanying the expedition as far as India, where he would train the expedition's Sherpas in the art of mountaineering.

It was a heartfelt offer, but there was a problem with the old general. Whereas Howard-Bury was the heir to a large private fortune and was willing to pay his own way to the Himalayas for the second year in a row, Bruce's finances – 'or want of it', as he wrote in a letter of 25 January – were not so good. He even went so far as to ask the Everest Committee for a £500 annual stipend, a request that did not go down well. After several rounds of correspondence, Hinks agreed to a compromise, offering Bruce provisional leadership of the 1922 expedition but refusing to make any promises about money. The replacement of Bruce with Howard-Bury for the Reconnaissance was a powerful statement: the Committee were in charge, not the climbers. It was the first but would not be the last time that they would behave ruthlessly.

Finding the other members of the team was trickier than might have been expected. In 1921, high-altitude mountaineering was still in its infancy; in the previous fifty years there had been only a handful of Himalayan expeditions. The First World War had stopped everything for several years and had seen several of Britain's leading climbers killed or maimed.

The world altitude record had been set on Chogolisa in the Karakoram mountain range in 1909 by the Italian explorer Prince Luigi Amedeo, Duke of the Abruzzi. He and his team had stopped at 24,600 feet, about 500 feet short of the summit. The highest any British climber had been was 23,360 feet, a record set two years earlier on Trisul by Tom Longstaff, who reached the summit in 1907 along with two Swiss guides and a Gurkha soldier. In January 1921, Longstaff was considered for the role of team doctor on the Everest Reconnaissance, but for personal reasons was unsure whether he could go. By the time he made his mind up and decided to say yes, the job had been offered to someone else. Two men with Himalayan experience who were less hesitant than Longstaff were Harold Raeburn, a Scot, who was nominated as the leader of the climbing team, and his countryman Alexander Kellas, recruited as one of the principal climbers.

Though highly experienced, Kellas and Raeburn were both long in the tooth and crampon – not the bold young mountaineers that the press had expected. Kellas was fifty-two, Raeburn fifty-five. For fresher blood, the Everest Committee turned to a pair of less experienced but more exciting prospects, the two Georges: the schoolmaster George Leigh Mallory and the scientist George Ingle Finch.

Mallory was already well known in the British climbing world, and had all the attributes that would eventually turn him into a national hero and Everest legend. The son of a Cheshire clergyman, he was blessed with a name that conjured up medieval romances and was tall, fit and strikingly handsome, 'with the body of an athlete by Praxiteles', as his friend, the author Lytton Strachey, wrote, 'and a face – oh incredible – the mystery of a Botticelli, the refinement and delicacy of a Chinese print, the youth and piquancy of an unimaginable English boy'. He had many male admirers, both old and young, but Mallory was more than just a pretty face. He was a powerful athlete who had been climbing since his schooldays – in the Alps and on the crags and rock faces of North Wales – and was widely admired for his courage and grace of movement.

When he first heard of the expedition, however, Mallory was not convinced. Though decisive when on a mountain, even to the point of impetuosity, in everyday life he was much less sure of what he wanted and had many other interests. He was a member of the Fabian Society and was friends with the Bohemian artists and intellectuals of the Bloomsbury Group – figures like John Maynard Keynes, the economist, and Duncan Grant, the artist. Mallory's head was full of great schemes to write books, revolutionize education and change the world. Everest didn't immediately fit into his plans, and the idea of leaving home for several months was singularly unappealing.

In 1913 Mallory had met his wife, Ruth Turner, the daughter of the Arts and Crafts architect Hugh Thackeray Turner. Ruth was ravishingly beautiful and shared Mallory's cultural and artistic tendencies. He was smitten straight away. Within a year they were married, and within a few more they had two daughters and a son. Ruth's father provided them with a house in Godalming in Surrey and a generous annual income, and although George never earned much as a teacher, the Mallorys lived very comfortably. During the First World War, after being commissioned as an artillery officer, George had written a long stream of passionate letters to his wife, ruing the conflict that kept them apart. The idea of another long separation was very painful to both of them.

His friend and mentor, the leading mountaineer Geoffrey Winthrop Young, was also enthralled by Ruth, but he did not approve of Mallory's dithering. Young himself would have undoubtedly been invited to join the team if he had not been seriously wounded during the war, so he wrote to Mallory, telling him to seize the opportunity and promising that 'the label of Everest' would serve him well in his future life. When Younghusband invited Mallory to meet for lunch, he finally signed on the dotted line – but, as Younghusband later noted, 'without visible emotion'.

George Finch was an utterly different quantity: a tall, thin, blue-eyed and distinctly self-confident chemistry lecturer. Whereas Mallory had followed the traditional path of the British upper middle classes, going from public school to Oxbridge, Finch was an Australian by birth, who had been educated in France and Switzerland before taking up a post as a chemistry lecturer at Imperial College London. As a climber he was highly regarded on the continent and considered one of the best in Europe by Percy Farrar, the former President of the Alpine Club. When Finch got the call and was invited to appear before the Everest Committee in February 1921, he couldn't contain his enthusiasm, telling Younghusband 'you've sent me to heaven'.

Unfortunately, Finch's eagerness did not win over every member of the Committee, in particular its Honorary Secretary, Arthur Hinks. An astronomer by training, Hinks was a rather portly, bespectacled forty-seven-year-old who had spent most of his life in front of a desk of one sort or another. He was not a mountaineer and had not even travelled very widely, but he was a skilled administrator and someone who liked to get his own way. Unlike the other members of the Committee, Hinks was a paid official of the Royal Geographical Society, so he was able to put much more time than the others into the organization of the expedition. Sir Francis Younghusband might have been the head of the Committee, but on a day-to-day basis Hinks was in charge, and from very early on he took against Finch.

Some of Finch's biographers have seen this as pure prejudice, arguing that Hinks simply did not like his Australian background or the length of his hair. Finch was not a typical British 'gentleman'; he had been through one difficult divorce and was about to go through a second. As Hinks hinted cryptically in a letter to Alexander Kellas, Finch's name was 'doubtful'. Equally though, Finch was a well-regarded academic with a good war record and an MBE for his work in explosives – a member of the establishment, however unconventional.

Whatever the cause, the 'chemistry' between the two men was not good, and over the next two years Finch and Hinks would rub up against each other repeatedly, introducing a level of friction to the Everest project that was invariably destructive.

As for the other side of the expedition – the cartographic and scientific dimensions – it was all a lot more straightforward. The Committee approached the Survey of India and secured the services of two of its officers, Henry Morshead and Edward Oliver Wheeler, and also recruited a geologist based in Kolkata, Alexander Heron. The party was completed with the appointment of Sandy Wollaston, the noted explorer, who was taken on in the dual role of doctor and expedition naturalist.

The other key task for the Committee was to raise funds. In 1921 there were no equipment firms or hedge funds or telecommunications companies to seek sponsorship from, and there was no question of raising money directly from the government, however loudly they banged the patriotic drum. When the Everest Committee put together a tentative budget, they estimated that they would need roughly £4,000 (about £200,000 in today's money) for the Reconnaissance alone, and probably significantly more for the main expedition in 1922. Initially, Younghusband decided to put out an appeal to the membership of the Alpine Club and the RGS, declaring in a circular: 'I am confident that every Fellow of the Royal Geographical Society will take pride in furthering an enterprise which will stimulate mountaineering in the Himalayas – as de Saussure's ascent of Mont Blanc aroused enthusiasm for the Alps.' Early donations, however, were slow and not as generous as Younghusband had hoped, so it was not long before the Committee had to turn to the newspapers for help.

Sir Francis had no qualms about appealing to the press or its readers. He was regularly courted by and quoted in British newspapers, and in 1895 had acted as the *Times* correspondent during the siege of Chitral in modern-day Pakistan. But Arthur Hinks felt very differently. He found the whole idea of publicity and having to deal with journalists and editors demeaning and uncomfortable. Younghusband knew that this was not a moment to dither, though, so he brought in his friend John Buchan, the author of *Prester John* and later *The Thirty-Nine Steps*. As a former head of the War Propaganda Bureau, Buchan knew how to use the press to influence public opinion, arguing for what would today be called a 'broad media campaign'.

As well as making direct appeals to the public via the press, Buchan advocated the sale of expedition dispatches jointly to *The Times*, the *Daily Mail* and the *Glasgow Herald* – or, failing that, the *Daily Telegraph*. The Committee, he advised, should also think about an expedition film, sell the photographs separately, and simultaneously approach the American press to exploit the overseas rights. As if that wasn't enough, he added that his publishing company would be willing to make an offer for an expedition book, although there would not be any commercial value in a purely 'scientific' report. This was all a little too much for Hinks and the more publicity-shy members of the Committee, prompting them to record in the official minutes their anxiety that the Reconnaissance 'should not be exploited as a newspaper expedition'.

Younghusband paid no attention and gave several interviews to the press. In one frequently repeated headline, he conjured up a nameless porter on the London Underground – the 'white van man' of the 1920s – who he had overheard stating with absolute certainty that Everest would never be climbed. Sir Francis was scathing about this kind of attitude. 'If the human race,' he said, 'had always acted in the spirit of the general mass it would never have emerged from the primeval forest... The advantage that would come from ascending Mount Everest was this – that once the highest peak had been climbed men would pluck up courage to ascend all manner of other mountains. Even to the obtuse mass of humanity it would then be evident that men were capable of higher achievement than they had ever imagined.'

Gradually, the coffers did start to fill up. The Prince of Wales donated £50, the businessman Henry Wellcome offered £52, and there were numerous smaller donations from less well-off supporters whose imaginations had been fired up by all the publicity. A. S. Rowe, a self-proclaimed 'workman's son fond of stories of travel and exploration' from Newcastle upon Tyne, sent a postal order for two shillings hoping to gain a 'share in the Mount Everest ascent'. A couple from Muswell Hill in North London donated five shillings – 'a trifle' – which they told Hinks not to acknowledge.

Female climbers might not have been welcome on the expedition, but the Committee were happy to take their money. Mrs Aubrey Le Blond, one of the founders of the Ladies' Alpine Club – the sister organization of the main club – donated two pounds, two shillings; and Mrs Fanny Bullock Workman, the American who held the women's altitude record, offered a very generous £30 (£1,500 in today's money), adding in a note that the money came from her own pocket, not her husband's.

After spending many years in northern India and the Karakoram mountains of today's Pakistan with William Hunter Workman, Fanny was a famous-enough name to be interviewed by London's *Evening Standard* about the forthcoming expedition. She warned that even the strongest men sometimes collapsed at high altitude, recalling the case of a well-regarded alpine guide from Courmayeur in the Italian Alps who she had taken on an expedition to Ladakh. In spite of his reputation, he had fallen ill at 20,000 feet and was unable to join her on the summit of Pinnacle Peak. 'I have studied the effect of mountain sickness,' she finished ominously. '[It] is evidenced by great bodily prostration and a paralysis of the will, which deprives the person attacked of any desire to carry on the work undertaken.'

As the departure date moved closer, Arthur Hinks wrote to Sandy Wollaston, suggesting that all members of the team should undergo a medical before they left. Wollaston booked Mallory and Finch in to see a pair of Harley Street doctors, and organized for Raeburn to be examined closer to home in Edinburgh. In the meantime, Finch liaised with the shipping line and booked berths out to India on the SS *Sardinia,* and met Mallory to discuss clothing and equipment. They had been offered a personal grant of £50 by the Everest Committee, but told by Raeburn that all they needed was 'ordinary Alpine outfit on a liberal scale'. Finch was not convinced. The idea of heading for Everest with nothing more than a tweed suit, a bag full of Shetland jumpers and a pair of hobnail boots filled him with horror, even if no one else seemed too worried. Immediately Finch began thinking about commissioning some specially made items.

In early March, Finch was sent to Oxford University with the expedition's Primus stoves, which were expected to be used extensively on Everest. They were the best portable cookers then available, but Primuses didn't perform particularly well at high altitude so it was hoped that they could be modified for the Everest expedition. In Oxford, Finch encountered Professor Georges Dreyer, a Danish academic and specialist in high-altitude physiology. His department had a hyperbaric chamber where the pressure could be artificially lowered to match the thin air of the Himalayas. Dreyer was happy to test the Primuses, but there were other, more pressing, issues that he wanted to discuss. During the war, he had worked with the Royal Air Force to develop portable oxygen equipment for flying at extreme altitude. Dreyer warned Finch that if the expedition didn't take oxygen sets for the final stages, it would end in disaster. 'I do not think you will get up without it,' he said, 'but if you do succeed, you may not get down again.'

In spite of his own scientific background, Finch hadn't thought about climbing oxygen, but he was intrigued and arranged to return in a few days, along with Percy Farrar from the Everest

Committee. First, though, he and Mallory were called in for their medicals on Thursday, 17 March 1921.

It was a particularly strange day for George Finch. While he was being examined by doctors Graeme Anderson and F. E. Larkins of Harley Street, according to his lawyer he was at the same moment enjoying an illicit tryst with a mystery woman at the nearby Strand Palace Hotel. His love life was anything but simple. Finch had divorced his first wife, Alicia, in September 1920, after she had had a wartime affair with another officer which left her pregnant. He had insisted on keeping the child, the future actor Peter Finch, eventually shipping him off to Australia to be looked after by relatives. Two months after divorcing Alicia, George was remarried on the rebound to a nurse called Gladys May whom he had got pregnant, only to realize that he was in fact in love with a different woman entirely! The only way to obtain a second divorce quickly was to commit an act of flagrant, if fictitious, infidelity. It was no wonder that Finch was looking forward to disappearing from England on a long expedition to the Himalayas.

While the doctors wrote up their reports, the preparations continued. Mallory was asked to bring out some boots for Raeburn and a pile of equipment for Kellas, who was already in India. Gradually, his earlier diffidence was disappearing as the departure date approached. On 23 March, Mallory wrote to Hinks wondering about the results of the medical. He prided himself on his fitness and stamina but he still hadn't heard the verdict. Did he have the 'required number of red corpuscles'?

Mallory needn't have worried. When the reports came in, one doctor called him 'a fit type', the other 'a man in every respect fit'. With George Finch, though, it was different. Dr Graeme Anderson noted that he was 'a determined type' with the right kind of mentality but, he wrote, 'his physical condition at present is poor'. Finch was sallow and out of shape and did not look good. Anderson's colleague Larkins was equally concerned. 'This man is not at the moment fit,' he wrote. 'He has been losing weight... He is slightly anaemic and his mouth is very deficient in teeth'.

When the expedition doctor, Sandy Wollaston, read the reports, he immediately wrote to Hinks to inform him that Mallory had been declared 'excellent in every way' but that a substitute had to be found for Finch. In fact, Finch had not been rejected outright by either doctor, and Larkins had written that he might improve with training, but once again the Everest Committee acted decisively, calling Finch in on 24 March to inform him that he would not be allowed to go to the mountain, on the grounds of ill health.

It was a grievous blow, although George Finch would not be the last Everest wannabe to fall foul of Harley Street. Just six months later, James Wordie – a future President of the RGS, no less – would also be thrown out on medical grounds; and in 1936 a young John Hunt, the future leader of the successful 1953 Everest expedition, would be rejected for a suspected heart complaint by an RAF medical board. But with just three weeks to go for Finch, it was a particularly devastating decision.

With supreme irony, a few days after his rejection on medical grounds, a large photospread appeared in the *Illustrated London News* focusing on Finch, entitled 'Chosen for the Higher Stages of the Mount Everest Expedition'. It showed him climbing in the Alps, demonstrating his skills on Mont Blanc and the Grépon.

Finch's supporters cried foul. Percy Farrar, his champion from the beginning, knew that neither Hinks nor Younghusband liked his protégé. Finch was assertive and demanding and wasn't one of the gang. In 1913, just before the war, he'd written two articles for *The Field*, a well-known magazine, in which he'd lambasted Britain's climbing establishment, calling it aloof and old-fashioned and comparing it unfavourably with what he had found in Switzerland and Germany. Farrar, a distinguished member of that establishment, didn't care. He rated Finch highly as a climber, and although he recognized that Finch needed 'handling', he thought it madness to go to Everest without him.

The crisis escalated when George Mallory heard that Finch's replacement was going to be the forty-eight-year-old William Ling, another Scottish climber who was a close friend of Harold Raeburn. Ling was highly regarded and very experienced, but as far as Mallory was concerned he was simply too old. Mallory briefly threatened to leave, protesting to Arthur Hinks that, as a married man, he had to look after his 'own interests'. Farrar threw fuel onto the flames, arguing that without Finch they could not carry out the same programme on Everest. No one realized that Ling was away in Glencoe with his friends from the Scottish Mountaineering Club. For a week Ling did not reply to Hinks's invitation, leaving Finch in limbo – still supporting the expedition but uncertain of what would happen next.

Finch and Farrar had headed back down to Oxford on Good Friday, 25 March, to collect the refurbished Primus stoves. Farrar returned to London but Finch agreed to stay on for another day to do a series of physiological tests in the hyperbaric chamber. While the scientists watched from outside, he was artificially transported to 21,000 feet and then asked to step on and off a chair while carrying a thirty-five-pound load, first under his own steam and then while inhaling oxygen through a rubber tube. Professor Dreyer was hugely impressed by Finch's performance; he wrote a report praising his 'unusual powers of resistance' and his high degree of physical fitness. Dreyer's assessment made no difference, though, when Farrar presented it to the Everest Committee. Hinks increasingly had come to see Farrar as an irritation and had no plans to invite his favourite back into the fold.

When, on 30 March, William Ling finally cabled back to say that business commitments meant that he couldn't go on the expedition, Finch still didn't get a recall. Instead, Mallory came up with an alternative: Guy Bullock, a former school friend from Winchester who had just returned to Britain on leave from diplomatic service. Bullock was more acclaimed as a runner than a climber, and more recently had restricted his physical exercise to playing a lot of soccer, but he possessed the crucial attribute that Mallory believed would be absolutely necessary on Everest: staying power.

On 31 March, Bullock had a medical and was declared 'powerfully healthy'. A day later he was formally invited to take part in the Everest expedition. Finch returned to Imperial College to lick his wounds and, to add insult to injury, Hinks wrote to him asking for the kit and equipment that he had bought for the expedition so that it could be used by 'some other member of the party'. With amazing good grace, Finch complied. Eight days later, George Mallory sailed from England alone, planning to meet Bullock and the others in India.

The 1921 Everest Reconnaissance expedition had weathered its first major crisis. It would not be its last.

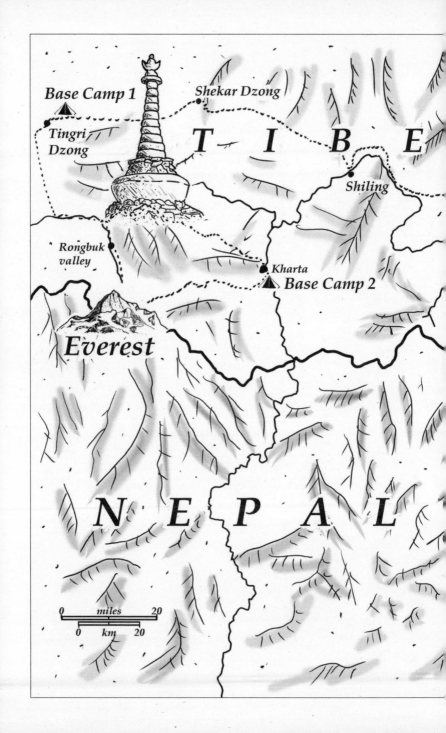

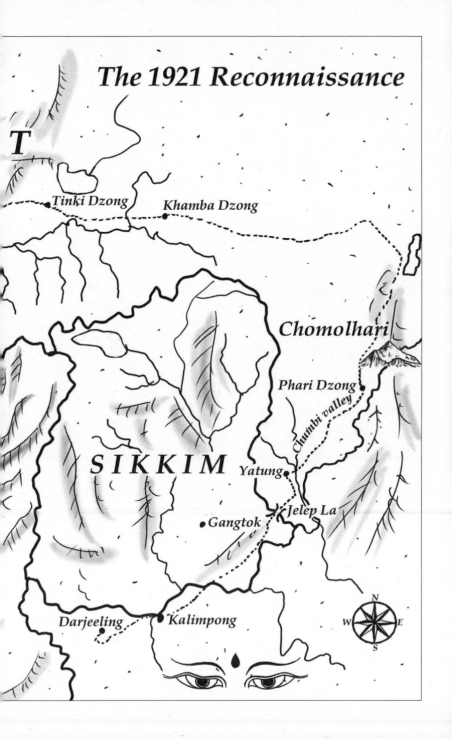

The 1921 Reconnaissance

T

Tinki Dzong   Khamba Dzong

Chomolhari

Phari Dzong

Chumbi valley

SIKKIM   Yatung

Jelep La

Gangtok

Darjeeling   Kalimpong

N
W   E
S

2

No Place for Old Men

It was a tremendous affair in grand colonial style: a printed guest list, embossed invitations, a phalanx of servants resplendent in all their finery, and Lord Ronaldshay, the governor of Bengal, flanked by two soldiers in full dress uniform. In the spring of 1921, the British Empire in India was starting to wobble, with riots and civil disobedience in Bengal and the Punjab, but none of this could be glimpsed on the night of 11 May 1921, when the Everest Reconnaissance party and assorted guests were entertained at Government House in Darjeeling.

George Mallory had only reached town at 3.00 p.m., but various other team members had arrived in dribs and drabs over the previous weeks. Harold Raeburn, the Scottish climbing leader, had been the first to turn up. He'd travelled out first-class on the *City of Lahore*, one of the many British ships that plied its way across the Indian Ocean, before taking a train across the hot dusty plains of central India and then the famous 'toy train', a narrow-gauge track that twisted its way up the hill to Darjeeling.

The Everest Reconnaissance team, Government House, Darjeeling, 1921:
(left to right) Sandy Wollaston, George Mallory, Guy Bullock, Lord Ronaldshay,
Charles Howard-Bury, Harold Raeburn

Raeburn had been put up for free at the Mount Everest, a large
Tudorbethan-style hotel which sat on top of a hill overlooking
Darjeeling, like a Home Counties golf club. On the occasional good
day it boasted outstanding views, but that month Darjeeling was
living up to its reputation for heavy rain and miserable weather,
with visibility down to fifty yards for much of the time.

Charles Howard-Bury had once again stopped off in Simla
before making his way across to Darjeeling. While Raeburn was
busy recruiting porters, he had pounded the corridors of power
trying to hustle up donations for expedition funds. Everyone was
very positive about Everest but, as the Viceroy of India had told
him, money was scarce. The rupee had plummeted in value and
several recent attempts to raise public subscriptions for other

worthy projects had ended in failure. Howard-Bury managed to negotiate reduced rail freight charges for the expedition's supplies and equipment, but that was about all, before he had to leave to join Raeburn.

For the younger members of the team – the two surveyors Henry Morshead and Oliver Wheeler, and Guy Bullock, George Mallory's school friend – Darjeeling had a slightly holiday-like quality when they showed up with their wives hoping to see the foothills of the Himalayas, if the fog ever lifted. Now, as they and the other team members sat around the table in their dinner jackets, making small talk with their neighbours, the idea that within a few weeks they would be sleeping in dust-filled tents, bowing their heads in the face of the vicious wind of the Tibetan plateau, seemed very hard to believe.

And then suddenly, ten minutes after everyone had sat down, the subdued tones of the orchestra were interrupted by the arrival of the final member of the expedition: Alexander Kellas, the Scottish chemist. To George Mallory, Kellas was like an apparition: soaking wet, slightly stooped, sporting crumpled outdoor clothes, huge 'gig-lamp' spectacles and an incongruously elaborate moustache. He looked more like a medieval alchemist than an esteemed lecturer and physiology expert, but for Mallory his arrival was a welcome interruption to a stuffy event.

Kellas was born in Aberdeen in 1868, the son of a shipping agent. He was a gifted student but highly strung, and solitary by nature. As a youth, the two passions of his life soon came to the fore: climbing and science. Both he pursued relentlessly, leaving little room for a social life or anything else. He trained at the University of Edinburgh and University College London, and then spent two years at Heidelberg in Germany before taking up a post at the Middlesex

Hospital in London. In his spare time he had always been a climber and a hillwalker, and gradually his scientific and leisure interests fused into a fascination with high-altitude physiology.

In the summer of 1920, with a small team of Sherpas, Kellas had gone part the way up Kamet, a 25,446-foot peak in the Garhwal mountains of northern India, to conduct a ground-breaking series of experiments on climbing with supplementary oxygen. His aim was to find out whether the benefit gained from carrying bulky oxygen tanks justified the extra burden. Unfortunately, the sets had turned up so late that he had not been able to carry out all of the tests he had planned, so his results were inconclusive, but Kellas had decided to stay on in India.

He had been overjoyed to get his Everest invitation in early February 1921 and said yes straight away, but rather than resting in Darjeeling prior to the rigours of a long trip across the Tibetan plain, Kellas had gone back into the field to tackle two unclimbed peaks: the 19,100-foot Narsing, and then, as if that wasn't enough, an attempt on Kabru, a 24,300-foot twin-peaked mountain on the border of Sikkim and Nepal. Ultimately, Kellas and his Sherpas did not get above 20,000 feet, but he was so taken by Kabru that he vowed to go back after the Everest Reconnaissance to make a further attempt.

George Mallory immediately warmed to Kellas, preferring his 'uncouth' manner to the patrician tones of Howard-Bury. A few months earlier, in the winter of 1920, Mallory had spent a week in Ireland, then in the grips of a bloody rebellion. He had toured the country meeting the families of republicans to write a report for a pacifist organization. Howard-Bury was the kind of Anglo-Irish aristocrat, with a vast estate and huge country house, that Mallory had come to detest – the 'landlord par excellence', as he wrote to his friend Geoffrey Winthrop Young. That evening, as he watched Howard-Bury cosying up to Lord Ronaldshay, his dislike was confirmed.

Howard-Bury, for his part, was utterly focused on leading a successful reconnaissance expedition, and if that meant flattering the local 'bigwigs' then so be it. But it was not going to be easy. He had been sent off to India with a four-page memo from the Mount Everest Committee specifying in detail exactly what they expected of him. It began with a simple, bold statement: 'The aim of the Expedition is the attainment of the summit of Mount Everest, and all activities should be made subordinate to that supreme object.'

After that, it got a little more complicated. Howard-Bury was told to defer to Harold Raeburn on climbing-related matters, and also facilitate the work of Morshead and Wheeler, the two surveyors, as well as Alexander Heron, the geologist, and Sandy Wollaston in his role as expedition naturalist. It was vital, Howard-Bury was told, to preserve good relations with any Tibetans they encountered, but he also had to look after the expedition budget and make sure they didn't spend too much. In addition to sending back photographs, financial accounts and a map, as soon as there was enough data to make one, he was expected to write fifteen dispatches for *The Times* and get these run over to the paper's correspondent in Simla. When the orchestra struck up 'God Save the King' and everyone stood for the national anthem, Howard-Bury knew that he would be returning to his room with a lot more work to do than anyone else at the table.

His main task over the following days was to ensure that the expedition's equipment and supplies were packaged up and prepared for their departure. As well as a mass of items specially imported from Britain, they had purchased large quantities of tea, sugar, flour and potatoes from the local market. Apart from the surveyor Henry Morshead, no one on the team spoke Tibetan, so Howard-Bury had engaged two interpreters: a former Tibetan soldier called Chheten Wangdi, and a Sikkimese nobleman, Gyalzen Kazi, who was planning to meet the British team in Kalimpong, en route to the mountain. Raeburn had hired forty high-altitude porters and the sirdar (head porter) Gyaljen, 'the Mighty One', an old acquaintance from Raeburn's Kangchenjunga expedition a year earlier. Most of their supplies would be taken to the mountain on the backs of 100 mules, provided by the Supply and Transport Corps of the Indian Army, but after that high-altitude porters would take over the carrying.

It was the first time that large numbers of Sherpas had been hired by a British expedition. The Sherpas, or 'people from the East', were ethnic Tibetans who had migrated to the Solukhumbu region of Nepal in the thirteenth and fourteenth centuries. They were predominantly farmers whose livelihoods were based on growing crops and tending yaks. It was a hard, unpredictable existence, so in the late nineteenth century some poorer Sherpas made a second migration, this time to Northern India, to look for work as general labourers. By 1901, there were 3,450 Sherpas in Darjeeling and the surrounding district out of a total population of 265,000. Their closest allies, and rivals, were a second group of ethnic Tibetans, known as Bhotias. They had migrated directly from Tibet to Darjeeling and like the Sherpas they were tough mountain folk, who quickly took to expedition portering.

In the very early days, the limited number of British and European climbers who could afford to visit the Himalayas had tended to arrive with their favourite Swiss and Italian guides in tow, believing that local people were simply not skilled enough to assist them on the mountain. Alexander Kellas was one of the first to reject all this. Apart from the cost of bringing European guides out, he championed the Sherpas as the ideal travelling companions. They might not have had the same technical training as professional Alpine mountain guides, but they were strong and always seemed keen to take on the challenge – and crucially, proved able to carry heavy loads at high altitude.

What the Sherpas and Bhotias really made of their new-found role, it's difficult to know for sure. They left no written accounts of the Everest Reconnaissance or the follow-up expedition in 1922. But if actions speak as loud as words, there was no shortage of recruits.

Many of them were used to carrying goods for local merchants who regularly criss-crossed the Himalayas and its foothills, and even if it only paid twelve annas per day (three-quarters of a rupee), expedition portering was regarded as good employment. With Himalayan climbing in its infancy, there was no real sense among the local community of the risks involved. They knew the religious injunctions against climbing mountains but they were also pragmatic people, and even if many couldn't understand why the foreign sahibs were so hell-bent on climbing for the sake of sport, they were willing to work hard and take all the wages on offer.

During the expedition, the porters addressed the British climbers as 'sahib' or 'sir', the usual terms of respect in British India; the sahibs in their written accounts referred to the Sherpas and Bhotias as porters or 'coolies', the generic term for a labourer. Only very occasionally did they record their names. Though there was always a distance and a power imbalance between the porters and the sahibs, British climbers generally got on very well with the Sherpas and Bhotias and enjoyed being with them, respecting their toughness and good humour. Later, with the expeditions of Eric Shipton and Charles Evans in the 1930s and 1950s, you saw real friendships forming between climbers and Sherpas, but initially the relationships were more formal and business-like.

In recent years there have been several scientific research projects aimed at discovering whether the Sherpas' legendary ability to thrive at high altitude has a simple genetic basis. Perhaps surprisingly, nothing definitive has been found yet. Whether a specific gene will be identified remains to be seen, but back in 1921 Raeburn and Howard-Bury had full confidence that the porters would live up to their expectations.

On 13 May, the surveyor Henry Morshead was the first of the British team to leave Darjeeling. With closely cropped hair and a stocky physique, he was tough and tough-looking – an experienced traveller who had been in India since 1904. Morshead came from a family of bankers but had opted to join the army for a more adventurous life. After graduating from the Royal Military Academy in Woolwich, he had gone out East with the Royal Engineers, but after a couple of years changed direction and joined the Survey of India.

Morshead was perfectly at home in the roughest of weather and wildest of terrain. Fellow climber Edward Norton would later describe him as a 'heart-breaking man to live with', who thought nothing of marching into the wind with barely any protective clothing. Morshead's first task in 1921 was to survey a huge and poorly mapped swathe of northern Sikkim, before crossing the border into Tibet to rendezvous with the main party at Khamba

Dzong. His route would take him through the leech-infested Teesta valley, where the paths were so narrow and overgrown that they were unsuitable for pack animals. He took fifty extra porters instead, to carry his equipment and supplies.

On 18 May, Mallory, Wollaston and the second surveyor, the Canadian Oliver Wheeler, set off by car, followed by the first mule train and half the porters. Their plan was to take the long-established merchant route from Darjeeling through Kalimpong in Sikkim, before crossing the Jelep La pass into Tibet. To guide them, they had a map that had been drawn up after the 1903 invasion, but after Khamba Dzong the main trail turned north to Lhasa and the map ran out. Inauspiciously, the sahibs' vehicle broke down almost immediately, forcing them to switch to ponies and a rickshaw.

The next day, Howard-Bury marched out of Darjeeling with the remaining twenty-odd porters. He, too, did not have a happy start. The heavens opened, the porters argued about the size of the loads they would have to carry, and worst of all, the army mules they'd hired at considerable expense soon showed themselves to be entirely unsuitable. As Howard-Bury wrote in a letter to Younghusband, when in Darjeeling the mules had looked 'fat and sleek and just right for a General's inspection', but once on the trail they showed themselves to be 'completely unfit for any hard work, let alone hard work in the mountains'.

By the time Howard-Bury reached Sedongchen, a small village close to the Tibetan border, the animals were in such a terrible state that he was forced to take drastic action, sending them back home and choosing instead to rely on mules and yaks hired locally. According to the passport issued to the expedition by the Tibetan government, local officials were obliged to provide the expedition with pack animals at mutually agreeable prices – but, in general, merchants and governors were only willing to take the British team to the next town, forcing Howard-Bury to endure lengthy delays in each settlement while he negotiated his onward transport and moved his supplies from animal to animal.

Howard-Bury had no alternative but to press on. On 27 May, Oliver Wheeler became the first member of the British party to cross the Jelep La, the 14,400-foot pass that was one of the main routes from Sikkim into Tibet. On a good day, in the far distance there was a great view of Chomolhari, a striking 23,800-foot peak that was one of the holiest in Tibet, but that morning it was so wet and misty that Wheeler just wanted to get down quickly into the much less hostile Chumbi valley on the other side. The rest of the party followed in dribs and drabs, spending equally little time at the top. It was an important moment, though. When Howard-Bury reached Yatung, the first large Tibetan village, he sent a telegram to the Everest Committee, announcing that the expedition had now passed its first milestone.

The message reached the Royal Geographical Society in London just in time for their anniversary meeting on 30 May. Once again, Sir Francis Younghusband put Everest at the centre of his presidential address, and used the occasion to remind everyone of the spiritual value of climbing. Even if reaching the summit had no direct material benefit for mankind, it would, he said, 'raise the standard of achievement in many other fields than mountaineering'. Then, developing his theme of the search for human excellence, he declared that the men chosen for the expedition were the best that could be found. 'No second best or mediocrity will do,' he declared. 'The Committee had to choose for the party men who would be expected to climb highest, men in the perfect prime of life, in the finest physical condition, and of proved skill and experience in mountaineering.'

Back in Tibet, however, the Everest Reconnaissance team was looking slightly sub-prime. Howard-Bury had hired cooks in Darjeeling but, as everyone soon found out, neither their culinary skills nor their hygiene standards were very high. One by one, the sahibs started to come down with diarrhoea and assorted stomach complaints. Wheeler and Raeburn had a bad dose, but the worst hit was Alexander Kellas.

Unlike the others, Kellas had not been subject to any medical examination, and no one on the Everest Committee realized that he had left Britain for India in 1920 suffering from nervous exhaustion. His closest confidant was his brother Henry, a solicitor who practised in Aberdeen. When Arthur Hinks had written to him in early January enquiring about his brother's health, Henry hadn't mentioned any issues and instead replied that Alexander was 'so interested in carrying out the experiments desired, that I am satisfied the congenial work in which his whole heart lies, has had a most beneficial effect'. Henry Kellas liaised with the Everest Committee and arranged for clothing and equipment to be sent out to India; only months later did he reveal to Hinks that his brother had gone out there after resigning from his medical post in London because he couldn't cope with the stress of his self-imposed workload.

When Alexander Kellas met the team in Darjeeling, he was equally cagey about his health and did not mention that, after his recent trip to Narsing, he had been forced to spend several days in bed and in truth was in no fit state to cope with the cold, blustery winds of the Tibetan plain. Even before joining the Reconnaissance party, he had lost over a stone in weight.

It was Kellas's habit to travel alone with just his small team of Sherpas, so when at an early stage he started to lag behind the others, leaving later and arriving in camp after everyone else, no one had taken too much notice. Kellas always made an effort to appear cheerful and never complained, but as they travelled deeper into Tibet and the weather turned colder and windier, his health visibly began to deteriorate. In Sikkim and for the first few stages in Tibet, the Reconnaissance party had been able to spend their nights in 'Dak' bungalows – rest houses built for travelling officials and officers of the postal service – but at the point where they began encountering the strong and biting wind of the Tibetan plateau, the bungalows ran out and all their nights had to be spent under canvas. Their collective diet improved when Howard-Bury began shooting gazelle and sheep for fresh meat, and Bullock discovered that a butterfly net could be used to catch wild trout, but the team's stomach problems persisted.

On 30 May, the day of the Royal Geographical Society's annual dinner, the Reconnaissance expedition was enjoying the heady delights of Phari, the first large Tibetan town they had encountered. It was, according to Guy Bullock, 'a filthy place', a collection of houses built mainly out of sods and inhabited by people who were 'excessively dirty'. Phari was no place for anyone suffering from enteritis and severe diarrhoea, but the team doctor Wollaston was now so concerned with Kellas's condition that he advised him to stay behind to recuperate. Kellas refused, insisting that he was well enough to carry on and that very soon he would recover fully. It was hard to argue with one of the grand old men of Himalayan mountaineering so, against his better judgement, Wollaston allowed him continue.

They left Phari, pursued by a very strong southerly wind and menacing monsoon clouds, which billowed above them but mercifully chose not to disgorge their contents. Kellas was wrapped in blankets and carried on an improvised litter, but four days later he collapsed and had to be taken to a yak herder's tent far from the expedition's main encampment. Wollaston rushed back and plied him with a mixture of brandy, Bovril and milk, but Kellas obstinately refused to take any medication or stimulants. The life was ebbing out of him but he simply would not admit how ill he was.

The following stage was their most challenging yet. In order to get to the next settlement, Khamba Dzong, they would first have to cross a 17,000-foot pass – 1,300 feet higher than Mont Blanc, the highest mountain in the Alps. Before setting off, Howard-Bury visited the famous Tatsang nunnery. He was shown round by the abbess, who presided over thirty nuns wearing elaborate woollen headdresses over their shaven heads. The building was full of prayer wheels, the largest of which was said to contain 500,000 prayers inscribed on parchment; when turned, it would promote good karma and help rid the world of bad. Howard-Bury didn't mention in his account whether he added a few extra pleas of his own, but afterwards he rode past Kellas, who was being carried on his stretcher. As ever, the ailing Scot picked himself up and tried to appear cheerful, but he continued to insist on travelling separately from the main party. With much to organize, Howard-Bury rode off towards Khamba Dzong.

A few hours later, he arrived to find Henry Morshead encamped on a field below the main settlement. Morshead told Howard-Bury that he and his survey party had enjoyed a good couple of weeks, achieving everything they had intended in Sikkim. They'd been at Khamba Dzong for several days and had almost run out of food, so they were very glad to see the main team and even happier when shortly afterwards the governor came down to their camp with a gift of five sheep and a hundred eggs.

At 4.00 p.m. Wollaston joined them, but there was still no sign of Kellas or his porters. Increasingly worried, Wollaston told Howard-Bury that the time had come to send Kellas back, regardless of his own wishes. From Khamba Dzong there was an alternative, shorter route back to Sikkim, where he could recuperate at a lower altitude. Howard-Bury agreed, but a few minutes later a man ran into camp with devastating news: Kellas was dead.

In a state of shock, Sandy Wollaston mounted his pony and dashed to the other side of the pass just below the crest. But there was nothing Wollaston could do for Kellas; thousands of miles away from his birthplace, the great Scottish scientist had died of a heart attack, the first Western climber to perish on an Everest expedition. When George Mallory heard the news, he was wracked with guilt. 'The most tragic and distressing fact about his death,' he wrote to Geoffrey Winthrop Young, 'is that none of us was with him; it seems so horribly unlike a party of mountaineers.'

Late next morning, they buried Kellas on a slope below the fort overlooking the Tibetan plain, with Everest just visible in the far distance and, closer by, three lesser peaks that Kellas had climbed. Howard-Bury read a funeral prayer from St Paul's letter to the Corinthians, while Kellas's porter team – who had been with him for many months – sat on a huge stone overlooking his grave, which they had decorated with a cross made from wildflowers.

On the same day, Harold Raeburn was ordered to go back to Sikkim. Neither Howard-Bury nor Wollaston wanted another casualty on his hands. Though Raeburn had never been quite as ill as Kellas, he had been suffering from severe diarrhoea for several days and Wollaston was taking no chances. In fact, he was so worried about losing another man that he decided to accompany Raeburn all the way back to Sikkim, even if it potentially meant leaving the expedition without any medical cover for several weeks. In a letter to Arthur Hinks in London written on the following day, Howard-Bury put it succinctly: 'It does not pay to send middle-aged men out to this country.'

Long before the letter arrived, a cable with news of Kellas's death reached London on 8 June, but much to the annoyance of *The Times* and the Everest Committee, the story was scooped by the *Morning Post*. They claimed to have found out via their correspondent in Kolkata – who had probably bribed a telegraph operator somewhere between Phari and India to be tipped off if any interesting news came in. The *Post* even had the temerity to contact Younghusband for a comment. He put Kellas's death down to his 'indefatigable labours', and when the Everest Committee issued a press release, they continued with the theme. The recent events, they said, were a 'grievous loss' to the expedition, but it seemed as if Kellas had fallen 'victim to his own enthusiasm'. Though insisting that they had previously believed him an exception to the rule, they added that 'few men over fifty can stand the strain of prolonged exertion at high altitude'.

Back in Tibet, as Howard-Bury reviewed the progress of the expedition, he had to admit that he was worried. The death of Kellas and the departure of Raeburn meant that the team had lost all of its Himalayan climbing experience. Mallory and Bullock, though young and strong, had never climbed anywhere outside of the Alps. While Henry Morshead seemed in fine form, the other surveyor, Oliver Wheeler, was also suffering from recurrent stomach problems and there was no knowing when Wollaston would return. Howard-Bury was no quitter though, and neither was George Mallory or anyone else on the team.

Although deeply saddened by Kellas's death, Mallory had never really rated him as a climbing partner and had even less regard for Raeburn, whom he described to his wife Ruth as 'rather a worn out factious [grumpy] old person, not at all suitable for the job'. Mallory himself felt supremely fit, and the way was now clear for him to come to the fore with Bullock as his faithful second. On the morning of Kellas's funeral, the two men climbed to a high point above the fort at Khamba Dzong. In the far distance they could see Everest through a layer of hazy cloud. As Mallory later wrote, it looked like 'a prodigious white fang excrescent from the jaw of the world... We were satisfied that the highest of mountains would not disappoint us.' Two days later, on 8 June, they left Khamba Dzong and rode off the map into entirely unsurveyed land. 'It's beginning to be exciting,' wrote Mallory to his friend Geoffrey Winthrop Young.

Ahead lay ten days of hard travelling through the barren interior of Tibet until they reached Tingri, where Howard-Bury hoped to set up the first of two base camps for the exploration of Everest and its approaches. Their route would take them through some strikingly alien landscapes of sand dunes, mud flats and walled towns that clung to cliff faces, but Mallory was really only interested in one thing: a better view of Everest.

On 13 June, he got his wish, when he and Bullock climbed 1,000 feet above the Yaru gorge. Everest was roughly sixty miles away, to the south-west. At first it was hidden by cloud, but gradually the skies cleared, revealing both the North and East faces and the North-East Ridge running directly towards them.

In his diary, Bullock was factual and descriptive, writing that on the East Face there seemed to be a 'very steep slope not far from top' and that 'N Face seems rock with some snow on it', but in a letter to Ruth, Mallory wrote how they had witnessed 'visions of great mountainsides and glaciers and ridges... forms invisible for the most part to the naked eye' until the summit itself appeared. Back in England, when he came to pen his expedition account, Mallory would expand these lines into one of the most lyrical descriptions of Everest ever written:

> Mountain shapes are often fantastic seen through
> a mist: these were like the wildest creation of a
> dream. A preposterous triangular lump rose out of
> the depths; its edges came leaping up at an angle of
> about 70 degrees and ended nowhere. To the left a
> black serrated crest was hanging in the sky incredibly.
> Gradually, very gradually, we saw the great mountain
> sides and glaciers and arêtes, now one fragment and
> now another through the floating rifts, until far higher
> in the sky than imagination had dared to suggest the
> white summit of Everest appeared. And in this series
> of partial glimpses we had seen a whole; we were able
> to piece together the fragments, to interpret the dream.
> However much might remain to be understood, the
> centre had a clear meaning as one mountain shape, the
> shape of Everest.

If George Mallory was already becoming obsessively focused on their main goal, Howard-Bury had a broader vision of the Reconnaissance. He was fascinated by Tibet and its peoples, and continued to visit as many towns and monasteries as he could to witness their unique artwork and religious iconography. When the party reached Shekar Dzong, he encountered some of the most striking sights yet.

It was a large town by Tibetan standards, with most of the buildings at the foot of a low but precipitous-looking mountain. A large labyrinthine monastery was perched higher above, close to an impressive fort. It reminded Howard-Bury of St Michael's Mount, the castle on an island off the coast of Cornwall, although on a bigger and more dramatic scale.

Situated at the crossroads of two major trade routes, Shekar was a well-known commercial centre, but as Howard-Bury quickly came to realize, none of the local inhabitants had ever seen any Europeans. The whole town, it seemed, had turned out to stare at the strange, pale-skinned new arrivals, with their camp followers and odd habit of washing in public. Howard-Bury was so vexed by the crowds that he ordered everyone to retreat into a willow grove, surrounded by a wall.

Once settled, Howard-Bury sent the interpreter Chheten Wangdi to find the local dzongpen. Shekar was considered so important that there were not one but two governors – one ecclesiastical, the other secular. Though no specific instructions had been sent to either man, Howard-Bury had an official warrant issued by the Dalai Lama that ordered local officials to give all assistance to the British party. After several incidences of drunkenness at previous settlements, one of Howard-Bury's first requests was for an edict banning local people from selling alcohol to any of the expedition's porters.

Shekar was most famous for its landmark, the Chö-te or 'Shining Crystal' monastery, and was a major religious centre, with over twenty theological colleges and several hundred resident monks. Howard-Bury was eager to visit the monastery and it did not disappoint. In the main temple there was a fifty-foot-high Buddha, its face covered in gold leaf, as well as rooms full of statues inlaid with jewels and semi-precious stones. With the interior illuminated only by tiny butter-lamps, it was impossible to get a good photograph, but Howard-Bury asked if he could take pictures of some of the novice monks outside – none of whom had seen a camera before, never mind been photographed.

The head lama had lived at the monastery for sixty-six years and was considered a living Buddha. After much persuasion by other lamas, he too consented to being photographed, and was taken outside to a courtyard where, dressed in gold brocade and seated behind a Chinese table carved with an elaborate dragon motif, he sat in regal splendour. Many months afterwards, when Howard-Bury was interviewed by *The Times* at his club on Dover Street in Central London, he said that it was one of the days he recalled most clearly. For months afterwards he felt supremely fortunate to have brought his camera. 'A hundred miles from the monastery we were asked for copies of that portrait,' he remembered. 'No present was so acceptable, for the people worshipped the abbot as a holy man, and the photographs of him we gave them they put in their shrines.'

A few days later, back on the trail, Howard-Bury experienced another and far more exacting aspect of Buddhist religious practice when he met a Mongolian who was making a pilgrimage from Lhasa to Kathmandu. The man was eleven months into his 800-mile journey, which he was carrying out as a series of prostrations in order to purify himself spiritually. He would throw himself

The Abbot of Shekar Chö-te, by Charles Howard-Bury

full-length on the ground, pause for a moment, then get up and
step forward to the point where his hands had touched the soil,
repeating the sequence of actions hundreds of times a day. It must
have been an astonishing, surreal sight, but Howard-Bury had
other things on his mind. Barely stopping to pause, he rode on,
battling his way through clouds of midges towards Tingri, their
home from home for the next month.

They arrived on 19 June, a month after leaving Darjeeling, and set up camp at a former Chinese rest house which had lain abandoned for several years. It was painted with elaborate murals featuring dragons and flying dogs, but the local Tibetans were wary of it, fearing that it was haunted by Chinese ghosts. Though they were tormented by its leaking roofs rather than nocturnal phantoms, it turned out to be the perfect base for Howard-Bury and the British expedition, with its three concentric courtyards: the outer serving as a storehouse, the middle housing the Sherpas, and the sahibs at the centre. Howard-Bury was particularly happy to be able to set up a darkroom and begin processing and printing some of the hundreds of images he had already taken.

Remarkably, the expedition doctor Sandy Wollaston joined them three days later, having taken Raeburn to a small mission hospital in Sikkim run by Finnish nuns before making a series of rapid marches back across Tibet. He found the British team busy but in good spirits, but was almost immediately thrown into work, treating a suspected outbreak of typhoid among the porters.

According to their Tibetan hosts, the rainy season would start within a few weeks, so everyone was keen to get going before severe weather got in the way. As for Everest itself and the best way to reach it, throughout his time in Tibet, Howard-Bury was continually surprised and frustrated by how little knowledge anyone seemed to have of its geography. 'They are strangely ignorant of the country outside the district they live in,' he later told *The Times*. 'You might hear in one spot three different stories of the whereabouts of the same place. This kind of thing added much to our difficulties, especially as our maps were inadequate.' Before any real climbing could take place, there was plenty of work to do.

In the first stage of their plan, Mallory and Bullock would head south to examine Everest up close. The chief surveyor, Henry Morshead, would at the same time make a broad sweep over the land to the north of Everest, aiming to gather enough data for a 1:750,000 map, while his colleague Oliver Wheeler conducted a much closer photographic survey of the glaciers surrounding Everest and its huge faces and ridges.

Wheeler was an expert in a special type of photographic mapping known as the 'Canadian method', which allowed him to move much more quickly than a traditional cartographer and do a lot of the detailed work afterwards. It was not easy for Wheeler and his small team of three high-altitude assistants and the seven-strong porter team, however. His special camera and equipment weighed over 100 pounds, far more than Morshead's surveying kit – and, in addition, his party needed to carry enough supplies and camping equipment to stay in the field for several weeks.

As for the newly returned Sandy Wollaston, once the sick porters had recovered he donned his other cap and began collecting samples of flora and fauna for the Natural History Museum and various other scientific bodies back in London. Wollaston was very pessimistic about the chances of climbing Everest, which he thought looked 'quite unclimbable, it is so terrifically steep', but he enjoyed his role as a botanist – especially when he found an unknown primula, which was subsequently named *Primula wollastonii*. Howard-Bury was also keen on collecting flowers, but as he told Wollaston, he planned to act as a kind of roving leader, travelling between all the various field parties.

On 23 June, shortly after the arrival of the latest consignment of mail, which fortuitously included packets of chocolate and fudge for the sweet-toothed Guy Bullock, he and Mallory left camp at 7.00 a.m. They had a team of sixteen Sherpas, a cook, an interpreter, four local men and their pack animals to transport their equipment, and their sirdar Gyaljen to keep everyone under control. Everest lay approximately forty-five miles to the south, but no one in Tingri seemed to have any detailed knowledge of the best way to reach it, nor did they have anything to say about the huge glaciers and ridges that surrounded it.

Today, Everest is one of the most well-mapped mountains in the world. It has been surveyed from the ground, the air and by satellite. Like many other great mountains, it is not an isolated mass but a massif – a cluster of interlinked peaks – with Lhotse and Nuptse, the fourth- and twentieth-highest mountains in the world, connected to it by long ridges. In shape, Everest resembles a pyramid with three faces: the North, the South-West and the East (or Kangshung). Separating the faces are three principal ridges – the South-East, the North-East and the West – and surrounding the whole mountain are four major glaciers, vast rivers of ice covered in rocks and debris: to the north, the Rongbuk glacier and its tributaries; to the south, the Khumbu glacier and its famous icefall; and to the east, the Kharta and Kangshung glaciers.

In 1921, however, none of this was known to the British team. Everest had been photographed from Khamba Dzong in 1904, and Alexander Kellas had taken some telephoto shots from high on Narsing in Sikkim, but apart from that there were no other reference images. Its height had been measured with a remarkable degree of accuracy from survey stations more than 100 miles to the south, in the Terai region of India, but there were no maps of the approaches to Everest apart from the rough sketches drawn up by the Indian pundits for the Survey of India. Unknown to the

British team, there were Chinese maps of the whole region, but these too had no detail of Everest itself or its environs.

For Mallory and Bullock, the first morning did not begin well, with their newly hired yak men seeming to deliberately take them in the wrong direction – in order, they suspected, to lengthen the journey and extract more pay. In one of his notebooks Mallory had compiled a list of about 150 Tibetan words which he hoped would be useful 'when occasion should arise', but this time round he left their sirdar Gyaljen to sack the first group of yak men and hire replacements at the nearest village. The next two days went more smoothly apart, from a perilous crossing of the Rongbuk river via a distinctly rickety bridge seemingly designed, as Mallory later recalled, 'to offer the passenger ample opportunities of experiencing the sensation of insecurity and contemplating the possibilities of disaster'. When they finally came face-to-face with Everest, they were almost surprised to have found it so easily.

It stood at the far end of what seemed like a relatively benignly angled glacier, which started about halfway up the Rongbuk valley. The North Face looked virtually impregnable, a massive and very steep wall of rock and ice roughly 10,000 feet high, and equipped, as Mallory told Ruth, with 'the most stupendous ridges and appalling precipices that I have ever seen... all the talk of [an] easy snow slope is a myth'. Looking at its sheer monumental mass, Mallory was reminded of the northern aspect of Winchester Cathedral, a view that he knew well from his school days.

Either side of the North Face, there were long ridges stretching to the north-east and west. The West Ridge looked very, very steep; the North-East Ridge appeared to rise more gently towards a high shoulder before continuing on to the summit, but it too was formidable and intimidating.

The whole Rongbuk valley, they soon learned, had for centuries been considered a sacred space where hunting was banned. Guru Rinpoche, the Indian mystic who introduced Buddhism to Tibet, was said to have spent almost a year in a cave in the valley. Tame sheep and gazelle fed close to tiny caves and rough shelters inhabited by up to 400 Buddhist hermits, some of whom had committed years of their lives to solitary prayer.

Just below the meadow they chose for Base Camp was a recently built monastery, which had been begun in 1902. It consisted of a set of several low-walled buildings with an adjacent and slightly unfinished-looking chorten – a tall, roughly cylindrical shrine which rose in a series of steps. The monastery's head lama, Dzatrul Rinpoche, was revered as a reincarnation of Guru Rinpoche himself. When, a few days in, Mallory and Bullock made a brief visit, they were told that he was spending a year in seclusion, though he did send them gifts of salt, flour and milk. Later, in his namthar, or spiritual diary – one of the very few indigenous documents that make reference to the British expedition – Dzatrul Rinpoche wrote how, after a roaring sound and a light appeared from the East, the English sahibs arrived to try to climb the 'snow mountain'. Guy Bullock noted in his rather more prosaic diary that the Rongbuk monastery was simple and austere in comparison with the Shining Crystal monastery at Shekar, though he was impressed by an ornate meeting room. George Mallory didn't even mention the visit in his expedition account.

As Howard-Bury had by now noticed, in spite of the circles within which he moved and his friendship with the painter Duncan Grant and the other artists and philosophers of the Bloomsbury Group, Mallory was surprisingly uninterested in the art and culture of Tibet. Initially he didn't even find the Himalayas beautiful in comparison with his beloved Alps. All that really mattered to him was the mountaineering challenge of Everest; he was here to climb and his excitement was growing. Even though 1921 was billed as a reconnaissance, Mallory thought he might just be able to reach the summit first time round.

His primary mission, though, was to explore the northern approaches to Everest to discover if there was a feasible route onto and up the mountain. In late July, Howard-Bury planned to move operations to the Kharta valley on the eastern side of Everest, so they had about a month to get as close as possible to the North Face and make a proper inspection of all the potential approaches on this side.

Leaving their Base Camp at 15,800 feet, Mallory and Bullock made their first foray up the Rongbuk valley just before dawn on Monday 27 June. Though both men had encountered glaciers in the Alps, they soon discovered the scale of the great Rongbuk glacier was entirely different from anything they had seen before, throwing up entirely new problems. In the Alps, glaciers were vast white highways leading climbers to their goal; the Rongbuk was anything but. At first they saw no ice – instead the whole thing was covered in irregular boulders and rocks of all different shapes and sizes, which were impossible to cross quickly.

After a few hours, they moved to the left-hand side of the valley, climbing a dry stream bed between the glacier and a steep wall of rock. Mallory noticed how difficult the porters were finding it, and Bullock later admitted in his diary that he too found his first experience of a Himalayan glacier utterly exhausting. As well as the awkward piles of rock on either side, in the middle of the glacier they encountered a labyrinth of fifty-foot-high pinnacles of ice that poked up from the surface, interspersed with small glacial lakes – some filled with shale, others with ice-covered water.

By the time they turned back in the late afternoon, the sun was going down but it had done its work, melting any loose snow and turning streams that they had dealt with easily in the morning into miniature torrents which were virtually impossible to cross without getting soaked. When they finally reached their tents at 8.15 p.m., they were very glad to get to the end of a fifteen-hour first day.

Their first foray onto the Rongbuk had taught them several lessons. In the first instance, the glacier was more of an obstacle course than a highway, but if they were careful to scout ahead and accept there would be plenty of dead ends, there was usually a route along one of the edges. As Mallory would later write, the secret of ascending a Himalayan glacier was to breathe very deeply, both on the way up and the way down, and to avoid crossing any snowy sections in the midday sun when a strange feeling of tiredness, which he would come to dub 'glacier lassitude', seemed to take over.

Over the next month, Mallory and Bullock embarked on the systematic exploration of the main Rongbuk glacier as well as the large tributary glacier that peeled off to the west. It was fascinating if sometimes frustrating work, leavened by the feeling that they were the first Western mountaineers to penetrate one of the world's great mountain wildernesses. Bullock was happy to follow Mallory's lead, though occasionally he felt that his partner was asking too much of the porters who were expected to follow them and carry their cameras and camp equipment. The head porter Gyaljen had been on previous expeditions, but the other Sherpas were new to mountaineering.

Mount Everest from the Rongbuk glacier, with Changtse in foreground

There was no hint of any argument in Guy Bullock's diary from 1921, but decades later, when his widow Alice wrote to T. S. Blakeney, the Secretary of the Alpine Club, just after Bullock's diary was published in the *Alpine Journal*, she presented a different story. 'My husband considered Mallory ready to take unwarranted risks with still untrained porters in traversing dangerous ice. At least on one occasion he refused to take his rope of porters over the route proposed by Mallory. Mallory was not over pleased. He did not support a critical difference of opinion readily.'

Back in London, Sir Francis Younghusband had spun the tale that climbing Everest from the north would be relatively easy, but as Mallory and Bullock got closer and closer they quickly realized that it would be anything but. As Mallory wrote in his diary on 28 June: 'The mountain appears not to be intended for climbing... I wish some folk at home could see the precipice on this side – a grim spectacle most unlike the long gentle snow slopes suggested by photos.'

At the top of the Rongbuk glacier, there was a broad basin above which the huge North Face of Everest loomed. There was no question of climbing the face directly; it was just too big and too steep. Instead, their instinct – like most climbers of their era, who tended to avoid mountain faces because of their difficulty and avalanche risk – was to examine the ridges either side. On the left, there was the long North-East Ridge, which rose to a dramatic shoulder at 27,500 feet, 1,500 feet below the summit, and on the right the slightly shorter but steeper-looking West Ridge, which plunged down towards a lesser mountain which is today called Lingtren, marking the border between Tibet and Nepal.

Up close, the North-East and West ridges looked even more intimidating than from afar, but more promisingly in front of them they could now clearly see a secondary north–south ridge which descended from the shoulder to a low col, or strip of ground, before rising again towards the summit of Changtse, a 24,700-foot peak to the north of Everest. If it were possible to get up to that col – christened the North Col by Mallory and Bullock – then it looked relatively straightforward to ascend the

North Ridge up to the shoulder and then carry on up all the way
to the summit.

It was a tantalizing prospect, but there were two significant
problems: the top of the Rongbuk glacier was heavily crevassed
and looked like very dangerous terrain, and even if they could
find a safe porter route across it, just to get up to the North Col
they would have to climb an 800-foot snow slope that looked
very steep and broken. Mallory recognized that Sherpas like Dorji
Gompa were already showing amazing stamina and strength and
their enthusiasm was growing, but none of them had any training
or familiarity with ice axes and ropes and all the other necessary
paraphernalia of mountaineering. Rather than taking too many
risks on this side of the North Col, he decided to wait until the
next stage of the Reconnaissance, when everyone relocated to
Kharta, the valley to the east of Everest, and the Sherpas had
learned a little more mountain-craft. They would then take a look
at the other side of the col, hoping that it was easier to ascend
from that direction.

There was also another, more radical, alternative to consider:
might there be a way to cross over into Nepal, and tackle Everest
from the other side? Though they did not have permission to enter
Nepal, Mallory doubted very much that there were any settlements
or forts nearby, and was intrigued by the idea that there could be
an easier route from the southern side.

Before they could find out, Howard-Bury paid them a flying
visit on 4 July, along with Alexander Heron, the geologist. Heron
informed them that, contrary to what they had expected back in
London, the black rock all around them was hornblende schist;
though lower down there was a lot of granite, an easier type
of rock to climb. Howard-Bury had no particular news but he

was pleased to see that Mallory and Bullock's camp looked in good order, and before leaving he presented them with the leg of a gazelle that he had recently shot. He confirmed that he still planned to relocate Base Camp to Kharta in about three weeks' time, and told Mallory and Bullock that he had learned of a trade route that would get them there quickly.

The next day, Mallory decided to climb an unnamed peak close to the junction of the main Rongbuk glacier and its western arm. It looked like a straightforward ascent over a mixture of snow and rock, and if they could get to the summit he hoped for a good view of the North Col and to see over the West Ridge into Nepal. But once again, their inexperienced Sherpas struggled. Within a few hours, all six had given up and retreated, but Mallory and Bullock persevered and eventually reached the top at 2.45 p.m., 'thoroughly exhausted, and anxious about return' as Bullock later wrote in his diary. Using a portable aneroid barometer, Mallory estimated their height to be 23,100 feet, indicating that they had climbed almost 5,500 feet in a single hard push that morning. When, much later, their barometer was recalibrated in London, it was revised down to 22,520 feet – but it was still a very impressive effort, and far higher than either of them had been previously.

Though they only spent fifteen minutes at the top and the weather was cloudier than they had hoped, it was well worth the effort as much more of Everest's topography was revealed. They were able confirm that the North Face was too sheer to climb but that the North Col did appear to provide a good jumping-off point for a summit bid via the North Ridge. As for the southern approach, they were able to see over the West Ridge into Nepal and were surprised to spot, beyond Everest, two more huge mountains: Everest's so-called twin sisters, the 25,791-foot Nuptse and the

27,940-foot Lhotse, as they are known today. Nuptse and Lhotse were connected to each other by another long ridge parallel to Everest's West Ridge, forming a valley that Mallory called the Western Cwm. They could not see directly into the cwm, however, and could not tell how steep the slope was on the Nepali side of the West Ridge.

For Mallory, who had never really done this kind of exploratory mountaineering before, his excitement and sense of ownership was growing. Some of the names that he wanted to give to peaks and features – notably Mount Clare, after his first daughter, and Mount Kellas in honour of his dead comrade – would not be included in future maps, but the Western Cwm and the North Col are terms that are still in use today.

Was it possible, he wondered, that the western arm of the Rongbuk glacier might be connected to the newly discovered Western Cwm? Could they get into Nepal directly without having to do any difficult climbing? Or, if not, was there a low point on the West Ridge that could be crossed without too much trouble? There was still so much work left to do but already the weather was beginning to turn.

Back in London, no one had been quite sure how the monsoon would affect the expedition. Some had argued optimistically that Everest itself would act like a huge barrier, protecting Tibet from the storms coming up from the south. Mallory and Bullock soon begged to differ as they watched the weather deteriorate significantly from early July onwards, with regular snowfalls and poor visibility.

It took a full two weeks and several false starts before they finally managed to ascend the flank of the West Ridge to a col which looked down over the Western Cwm. It was, they discovered from their Sherpas, known to locals as the Nup La pass, and remarkably – considering how hard it had been to climb – was sometimes used by Buddhist pilgrims travelling between Tibet and the Sherpa homeland in the Solukhumbu region of Nepal.

Mallory was amazed: as he scanned right and left and examined the 1,500-foot ice cliff below him, he concluded there was no chance of getting down easily and nor was there a direct route from the West Rongbuk glacier to the Western Cwm. Even if they could have reached the cwm, in order to get any closer to the South-West Face, they would then have to climb up another very steep glacier, riven by crevasses interspersed with huge blocks of ice that looked as if they might totter down at any moment. It would, as Bullock recorded in his diary, require 'very elaborate organisation for a lengthy expedition. Practically out of the question.'

Perhaps it was a fair assessment at the time, but Mallory and Bullock were wrong. Today, the vast majority of people who climb Everest do so from the Nepali side. The steep broken section of glacier at the beginning of the Western Cwm is the famous Khumbu Icefall, the domain of Sherpa 'icefall doctors' who spend weeks every year fixing rope corridors through it and putting ladders over the most awkward crevasses. In 2019 alone, 660 people climbed Everest from the Nepali side, snaking their way through the Khumbu Icefall and then up the Western Cwm to Everest's South-West (Lhotse) Face. In fact, so many climbers on commercial expeditions regularly use this approach that the local Sherpas have dubbed it the 'Yak route'.

For the moment, though, Mallory was simply pleased to have completed the first stage of the Reconnaissance. The North Col looked possible, but they had ruled out the other northern approaches and dismissed the southern approach altogether. Next, Mallory was looking forward to moving over to the eastern side of the mountain to the reputedly more comfortable Kharta valley, from which they would try to reach the other flank of the North Col. Initially he toyed with the idea of heading there directly over the ridges and valleys to the east of their camp, but continuing snow storms and problems with their sirdar, Gyaljen, who they discovered had been stealing from the other Sherpas, persuaded him that it would be better to withdraw from the Rongbuk valley altogether, rejoin Howard-Bury and make a wider arc around Everest.

Then, on the night of 22 July, just as they were getting ready to leave, a runner reached their camp with some utterly dispiriting news: none of Mallory's photographs had come out. He had been given a quarter-plate camera and had taken dozens of photographs, many from hard-to-reach vantage points, but as Howard-Bury discovered when he processed them, Mallory had put the plates in the wrong way round! In a letter to his wife, Ruth, Mallory complained bitterly that it wasn't his fault and that he had strictly followed instructions from Heron the geologist, but no one was convinced. For all his skill as a climber, Mallory was regarded by his teammates as a slightly chaotic figure who was perpetually losing equipment and having problems with everything technical, whether cameras or Primus stoves. Before he left London, even Arthur Hinks had complained that Mallory was such an innocent and incompetent traveller that he needed an officer from the Survey of India to meet him in Mumbai to make sure he got his luggage off the ship without forgetting anything.

There was no alternative but to delay their departure from the Rongbuk valley. Over the next two days, while Mallory rushed up and down the glacier attempting to retake as many of the photographs as he could, Bullock headed back up to the basin at the top to have a final look at the North Col from the Rongbuk side. Though the glacier basin didn't look as bad as Mallory had thought, the 800-foot slope leading up to the North Col looked impossibly steep and there were clear signs of recent avalanches – channels on either flank that had been carved out by snow slides – making it an even more dangerous prospect. On a more positive note, after scanning the slopes above the North Col with his binoculars, Bullock was able to confirm that the North Ridge ran all the way from the Col to the north-east shoulder and looked 'very promising all the way'. If they could get on to the North Col from the other side, then there did seem to be a feasible route to the summit.

The next morning they broke camp and headed for the village of Chöyling, where they planned to meet Howard-Bury and travel over to the Kharta valley. In spite of his photographic problems, Mallory felt pleased with what they had achieved and was looking forward to continuing their reconnaissance on the eastern side. They had survived a month in the Himalayas, been far higher than anyone on the team had ever climbed previously, and begun the process of training their Sherpas in high-altitude work. Mallory hadn't managed to retake all the photographs, but he'd done his best to rectify his mistake.

As they said goodbye to the Rongbuk valley, however, neither Mallory nor Bullock had any idea that they had made a far bigger error than the photographic 'cock-up' – a mistake which would have a much larger impact on the Reconnaissance, and would take far more time to rectify.

The 1921 Everest Reconnaissance party, September 1921:
(back row, left to right) Sandy Wollaston, Charles Howard-Bury,
Alexander Heron, Harold Raeburn;
(front row, left to right) George Mallory, Oliver Wheeler,
Guy Bullock, Henry Morshead

The Hardest Push

When, several months earlier, Oliver Wheeler heard that he had been posted to the Everest expedition, his first reaction was that it was 'a bit of a bombshell'. The expedition was supposed to leave Darjeeling in the middle of April, but he was due to get married in March in Mumbai to a British fiancée who was coming all the way from Birmingham for the wedding. Wheeler's superiors made it clear that he had little choice but to agree, and fortuitously the schedule shifted a little – allowing him a couple of weeks of honeymoon before he joined the Reconnaissance party in Darjeeling at the end of April, with his understanding new wife, Dorothea, by his side.

Tall and square-jawed, Oliver Wheeler was a handsome, athletic Canadian with a taste for the outdoor life. He was born in Ottawa in 1890; his father, Arthur Wheeler, was one of the founders of the Alpine Club of Canada. Oliver learned to climb at an early age and soon proved himself to be very driven and academically successful. He was head boy at his school in Ontario, and came

top of his class at the Royal Military College of Canada before
being commissioned into the British Army as a Royal Engineer.

Wheeler was first posted to India in 1912, but headed for
Europe two years later as part of an Indian Expeditionary Force
that quickly found itself in the thick of the fighting on the Western
Front. A brave and resourceful soldier, Wheeler was awarded both
the Military Cross and the French Legion of Honour. At the end of
the war, after a long stint in the Middle East, he returned to India
and was quickly seconded to the Survey of India, an organization
which he would come to lead in 1941 – becoming, like George
Everest himself, the Surveyor General.

In 1922, though, Wheeler was just at the beginning of his
career and his ambitions were more tightly focused. His role was
to take enough photographs to produce an inch-per-mile map
of the northern side of Everest and the glaciers that surrounded
it. Mallory didn't rate him initially. Like Kellas and Raeburn,
Wheeler had been stricken by diarrhoea at the beginning of the
expedition, but for him it had eventually cleared.

On 24 June, a day after Mallory and Bullock, he left Base
Camp at Tingri and headed for the small and rather bleak village of
Kyetrak, from which he planned to sally forth to a series of lighter
camps with his three dedicated high-altitude porters to survey the
north-western side of Everest. After a few deceptively good days,
visibility dropped to such an extent that he spent almost a month
in the field without even seeing Everest once. Eventually there were
so many snowstorms and such relentlessly poor weather that he
was forced to retreat to Base Camp at Tingri to rest up and take
time off to develop his first batch of photographs.

Even though he had not been able to capture quite as many
good images as he had hoped for, Wheeler decided to relocate to

the Rongbuk valley, taking his camera in the footsteps of Mallory and Bullock. On 25 July, he and Howard-Bury met them in the village of Chobu, twenty-five miles to the north of Everest. They spent the evening, as Wheeler wrote in his diary, 'gassing hard and swapping lies', though he was a little more formal in an article that he wrote for the *Canadian Alpine Journal*, noting that they had passed the time 'exchanging experiences and extracting information from one another'.

The two parties separated the next morning, with Mallory, Bullock and Howard-Bury heading down towards the balmy pleasures of the Kharta valley, while Wheeler and his porters carried on up to the rather colder comforts of the Rongbuk. In a few weeks, he planned to join them, but only after he had finished his photographic survey. The others, in the meantime, would explore Everest's eastern approaches, and if all went well find a practicable route to the North Col.

Two days later, Howard-Bury, Mallory and Bullock arrived at their new Base Camp. After the dirt and dust of Tingri, Howard-Bury had found a much more comfortable and almost idyllic spot at around 12,300 feet. It was just twenty-two miles to the east of Everest but, as Howard-Bury drily noted in a letter to Hinks, though he had talked to several locals, 'no one seems to know much about it'.

To protect themselves from the wind, their tents were pitched inside a walled enclosure, surrounded by poplars and juniper trees. The Kharta valley itself was split by the Arun river, running from Tibet into Nepal, and all around them were well-cultivated fields and prosperous-looking villages where fresh vegetables, butter and milk were readily available. Mallory wrote to his wife that initially he was so relieved to escape the black-and-white monotony of the Rongbuk glacier that he spent 'half the time in ecstasy'. Howard-Bury was more measured in his response, comparing Kharta to Killarney in Ireland, but he too revelled in the abundance of flowers, which included many varieties that he had never seen before.

For the first few days they rested up. Mallory read and wrote letters; Bullock went butterfly hunting, and then joined Howard-Bury for a social visit to the local dzongpen. Unlike the elderly governors they had met elsewhere, he was a young man of twenty-five, though he told the newcomers via an interpreter that this was in fact his second five-year term. Howard photographed him with his equally young wife, resplendent in a huge 'Lhasa headdress' – an extraordinary confection of false hair and coral-inlaid wood, the whole thing crowned with a pearl. The dzongpen served his guests with bowl after bowl of macaroni, and then a second course of dumplings and mince patties. Fearing that a third might be on the way, Howard-Bury and Bullock made their excuses and fled.

It wasn't long before Mallory was itching to get going. He had two main objectives: first, to examine the East Face and judge whether it was more climbable than the North Face; and second, to find a route to the North Col and then onto the North Ridge. He held out little hope for the former, but thought it likely that they would find an easier way up to the col, which they had failed to reach from the Rongbuk side. A few miles further up the Kharta valley, there was a steep gorge and then another huge glacier, which if it was anything like the Rongbuk, might lead them all the way to their goal.

Mallory set off with Bullock and thirty porters on 2 August. Once again, things did not begin well. This new group of local men, it turned out, were also being tricked out of their pay and rations by Gyaljen and had become increasingly suspicious and demanding. To add to the confusion, Everest shared the same local name, Chomolungma, with nearby Makalu, the world's fifth-highest mountain. When Mallory realized that they were heading for the wrong Chomolungma, he asked their guide to make sure to take them to the furthest version of the mountain.

After a few days, they climbed a high pass and were able to get a good look at Everest's East Face. It did not look any more promising than the North Face, with steep rocky cliffs at its base topped by a line of dangerous-looking hanging glaciers which periodically splintered and avalanched, bombarding everything underneath. 'Other men, less wise,' Mallory later wrote, 'might attempt this way if they would, but emphatically, it was not for us.' When Howard-Bury saw the East Face he was equally pessimistic. 'Everest,' he wrote to Hinks, 'is a formidable proposition from whatever side I have seen it.'

Mallory was not quite so despondent, but he worried that the Kharta glacier might not lead all the way to the other side of the North Col. Once again, he decided to climb a nearby peak – today called Khartse – which he hoped would give a good view of the surrounding area. It was such a difficult ascent that Bullock was unable to make it all the way to the summit, though one of the younger Sherpas, an eighteen-year-old called Nyima, did get to the top with Mallory. He was so impressed that later, in a letter home to Ruth, he briefly fantasized about taking Nyima back to England to work as a general servant. 'He would, if he came, naturally be turned on to all scullery work and floor scrubbing,' Mallory wrote. 'He might either inhabit part of the cellar... or the outside coal shed might be freed by storing coal in the cellar.' Nyima's thoughts went unrecorded.

At that very moment, though, Mallory's attention was focused on what they could see from the summit, and in this respect he felt deeply frustrated. There was too much low cloud to examine anything properly, apart from the occasional tantalizing glimpse of the North Col and the other end of the North Ridge leading up to Changtse.

The next day Mallory fell ill for the first time on the expedition, with what he thought might be tonsillitis. He retreated to a lower camp but, until medicine was brought up from Kharta several days later, he would spend much of his time in his tent tormented by fever and a very sore throat. It was a severe blow for someone who prided themselves on their fitness. Guy Bullock eventually got so bored that he decided to set off on his own with some porters to explore the Kharta glacier. Like the Rongbuk, it had several splits and tributaries. Initially Bullock headed for the northern branch, hoping that it would lead to the long-awaited North Col.

He was sorely disappointed – the glacier ended at another high pass but not their goal. Bullock sent a message back down to Mallory with the bad news; by the time the messenger reached the camp, a not-quite-recovered Mallory was about to set off with the surveyor Henry Morshead, who had finished his main work and decided to join the climbers. They headed towards the other branch of the Kharta glacier. It too, Mallory was soon able to confirm, did not terminate at the North Col, but to his great relief he was able to see the tip of Changtse towering above a different snowy col, which the porters told them was called the Lhakpa La. It was all a little bit confusing, but Mallory reasoned that if they could see Changtse poking up behind the Lhakpa La, then if they climbed up to its crest, they might be able to see the North Col as well.

Back at their tents, while Bullock and Mallory were discussing what they had found and planning how to get up the Lhakpa La, a letter arrived from Howard-Bury with a sketched map, recently drawn by Wheeler, of the Rongbuk glacier and all its branches. It was another distinctly awkward moment.

The sketch revealed what Mallory and Bullock had not noticed: the missing piece to the glacial jigsaw, a second tributary of the Rongbuk which ascended all the way from the main glacier up to the eastern side of the North Col. Early on, Mallory and Bullock had found the western tributary, but though they had noticed a small stream on the eastern side, they had not realized that it signalled the beginning of another huge glacier, today called the East Rongbuk. If they had found it a month earlier, they might have reached the North Col without having to go all the way round to the Kharta valley, and might have already made an attempt on Everest. Wheeler had not gone all the way up the East Rongbuk, but he was a skilled and experienced surveyor and was confident that it would lead to the North Col – the key to the upper slopes of Everest.

Mallory was confused and angry. He couldn't quite believe that Wheeler was correct and that he and Bullock had overlooked such an important feature, but he had a big decision to make. It was now mid-August; they had been in the field for about three months and the monsoon had not quite finished. It would be a logistical battle to get everyone back north and over to the Rongbuk side, and would mean admitting that he and Bullock had committed a huge oversight. The alternative, he decided, was to stick to the current plan and climb up the Lhakpa La pass, hoping that on the other side they would find the elusive route to the eastern flank of the North Col. If his hunch proved correct, they would make an attempt on the summit from the Kharta side. If he was wrong, Mallory would have to swallow his pride, admit his mistake and accept that it was too late in the year for everyone to retrace their steps.

Four days later, Mallory and Bullock struggled to the top of the Lhakpa La, after what Mallory later called the hardest push he had ever made on a mountain. The problem was not just the steepness of the slope but the scorching mist they had to climb through, which made the sky and mountain blend into each other and turned the Lhakpa La into a 'white furnace'. The ever-impressive Nyima matched them step for step, but the fourth member of the party, Henry Morshead, was so exhausted that he reached the crest fifteen minutes after the others.

Fortunately, all the suffering was worth it. Below them was a 500-foot slope which led down into the high basin where the East Rongbuk glacier began. They would need to cross that basin before ascending the flank of the North Col, but the terrain didn't appear to be as heavily crevassed as the other side. Mallory was still reluctant to admit that he could have missed the East Rongbuk glacier, but as Bullock acknowledged grudgingly in his diary, though Wheeler's sketch map might not be entirely correct, 'it is difficult to see how he could be entirely mistaken'. Ultimately, Mallory did not care. 'We saw what we came to see,' he later wrote to Ruth. 'We have found our way to the great mountain.'

Mallory was both relieved and excited. The snow conditions were not good enough to make an immediate start for the North Col, but within two weeks the monsoon was due to end, and by then Mallory hoped to be ready for a full-on attempt on not just the col but the summit itself. Though officially they were not expected to go really high, Mallory had always held to the hope that one way or another, even if it meant crawling on his hands and knees, he would reach the summit.

Three days later, back at Base Camp in the Kharta valley, everyone celebrated the geologist Heron's recent birthday with cake and some whisky punch before hunkering down to rest and prepare for the big push. While Bullock swatted up on Hindustani grammar, Mallory wrote letters to Ruth and Hinks back at the RGS in London. He was full of confidence and fantasizing about the aftermath of the expedition and making a triumphant return to Britain. 'It is a good story, I think, so far,' he told Hinks, 'and I have every reason to expect the climax to be no less interesting... We've a chance of getting up; one can't say more.'

Even if they did not succeed, Mallory had set his sights on coming back with a world altitude record. Bullock was not interested in doing any publicity afterwards; therefore, as Mallory wrote to Hinks, he was putting himself forward as 'rather the obvious person to enlighten the public about the mountaineering part of the reconnaissance'.

After ten days of rest, they sent some of their gear and supplies in advance to a high camp on the Kharta glacier, and then on 31 August, Mallory and Bullock started up with the remainder. The weather was not yet good enough to go a lot further, but they planned to set up one more high camp and have the Sherpas gather firewood and prepare for the big push. Howard-Bury stayed back at Base Camp for the moment, continuing to make forays into the surrounding area to collect samples of flora and fauna and take photographs.

Oliver Wheeler had by then also reached Kharta and was busy developing his photographs. He had some more mapping to do but he planned to join Mallory and Bullock on their attempt to reach the North Col. On the afternoon of 2 September, Wheeler was hard at work in his darkroom when he decided to take a cigarette break. Outside, he saw a figure coming towards their tents. To his astonishment, he realized it was the expedition's former climbing leader and only surviving Scot, Harold Raeburn, who like Banquo's ghost had come back to haunt them.

Raeburn's story was indeed extraordinary. After the death of Alexander Kellas, he'd been taken back to the village of Lachen in northern Sikkim by Sandy Wollaston but, realizing that they had neither the facilities nor the food supplies to look after Raeburn for a prolonged period, Wollaston had arranged to have him carried down to the nearest hospital in Gangtok before leaving to rejoin the others.

It took almost a week for Raeburn's fever to break, and he spent several more weeks convalescing at the British Residency in Gangtok and then at a local doctor's house before he decided to return. Raeburn had no means of getting in touch with Howard-Bury and perhaps out of embarrassment had not contacted the Everest Committee, though to Hinks's annoyance he had been in touch with a firm of instrument makers in London, whom he told of his plans. At the beginning of August, Raeburn had headed back to Darjeeling, where he hired an interpreter, Gyanchen, 'a strong middle-aged man of a somewhat surly temper', and four pack ponies before retracing his route back up the Teesta valley to Khamba Dzong. After paying his respects at Kellas's grave, Raeburn and Gyanchen then set off south hoping to catch up to the Reconnaissance party.

Raeburn remembered that Howard-Bury was planning to relocate to the Kharta valley for the second half of the expedition, but none of the Tibetans he encountered were able to provide information about the precise whereabouts of the British team. At Tingri, the site of the team's first Base Camp, the local governor told him that the expedition party had 'disappeared' and that he had no idea where they had gone. Raeburn pressed on anyway, swapping his ponies for rather slower-moving bullocks.

Following his instincts, they had headed south, but the closer they got to Kharta, the more arduous the travelling became. The monsoon was in full flow by this time and much of the land was flooded. No boats were available because of a local prohibition on fishing, and most of the tracks were submerged under water. There was one key bridge, across a broad river called the Bong Chu, that they had to cross to get to Kharta, but as Raeburn later wrote in a letter to Hinks, when they arrived it consisted of 'a single rope at the time underwater and a flooded torrent of a river which quite forbade all traverse'. One local man told them that he had been waiting for a whole month to cross over to his mother's farm on the other side of the river.

After spending several days searching for an alternative crossing point, Raeburn's interpreter persuaded a group of local men to strip naked and form a human chain. Then, very gingerly, Raeburn made his way across the chocolate-coloured water, carrying his clothes in a bundle above his head. 'It took me up to the shoulders,' Raeburn recalled plaintively, 'and in a small man up to the chin. On getting over I shivered for two hours.' He finally reached their Kharta Base Camp a few days later.

The team made a show of welcoming him, but privately no one was quite sure why he had come and what he planned to do next. Wollaston wrote acidly that Raeburn had 'become quite senile since his illness' and Howard-Bury was furious that he had failed to bring the five bags of expedition mail which had been stuck at

the town of Tinki for over a month, as well as some expedition
stores. In fairness to Raeburn, he was probably worried about
carrying the expedition mail across the floodwaters, but in a letter
to Hinks on 3 September, Howard-Bury was scathing: 'Can you
imagine anyone being such a fool!'

It was obvious by then that Mallory was the effective climbing
leader and that Raeburn was far from completely recovered,
but nevertheless he accompanied Howard-Bury to Mallory and
Bullock's advance base on the Kharta glacier. To Bullock, Raeburn
looked grizzled but otherwise quite well, but Mallory was less
charitable. 'Raeburn arrived at Kharta a day or two after we left,'
he told Ruth, 'a senile, babbling, insignificant, almost a broken
or heartbreaking figure... he plays no part.'

They were playing the waiting game, but there was no sign of
the promised post-monsoon lull, so before attempting to reach
the North Col, Mallory and Howard-Bury made small excursions
to nearby peaks and passes to take photographs. By now all the
delays were taking their toll, both physically and emotionally.
Mallory admitted that he felt 'a certain lack of exuberance when
going up hill' and told Ruth that, as well as intensely disliking
Howard-Bury, he was even beginning to tire of his friend and
partner Guy Bullock:

> We had rather drifted into that common superficial
> attitude between two people who live alone together –
> competitive and slightly quarrelsome, each looking out
> to see that he doesn't get done down in some small way
> by the other. I have been thinking B. too lazy about
> many small things that have to be done – indeed he
> certainly was, at one time, as a result of which I have

sometimes tried to arrange that he shall be left to do them... and so we have both been forgetting Christian decency and even eyeing the food to see that the other doesn't take too much – horrible confession.

Tent fever was setting in.

When the delayed mail finally turned up on 9 September, Mallory found a letter from his friend Geoffrey Winthrop Young, written in July just after he had heard the news of Kellas's death. Back in the spring of 1921, Young had encouraged Mallory to go to Everest, but now he warned him not to push things too far. 'The result is nothing compared to the rightness of the attempt,' he wrote. 'Let no desire for result spoil the effort by overstretching the safe limits within which it must move... Good fortune! And the "resolution to return", even against ambition!'

Mallory's reply started off full of excitement and intention. 'The assault is all prepared and only waiting for the weather,' he wrote. 'We shall have a chance I believe, a bare outside chance perhaps, of crawling to the top.' But by then he had begun to recognize that he was becoming dangerously obsessed with Everest: 'Altogether it is a trying time, while we wait here and try to keep the coolies happy and I begin to feel that sort of malaise one has before putting a great matter as it seems to the touch... Geoffrey, at what point am I going to stop? It's going to be a fearfully difficult decision.'

There was still no sign, however, of anything coming to a climax. The weather remained unsettled, with continual heavy snowfall, which made it hard to climb. On 20 September, with time slipping away, Mallory and Morshead forced a way back up towards the crest of the Lhakpa La with a party of fifteen Sherpas.

At first they moved quickly over hard consolidated snow, but higher up this was replaced by drifts of fine powder which could not be stamped down into firm steps. Only twelve of the porters made it up to the crest before they all retreated back to camp having cached their loads. In honour of the ferocious weather at the top, they rechristened the Lhakpa La 'Windy Gap'.

The plan was to return with a larger party, but Mallory's excitement was tempered by the growing realization that it was all going to be much harder than he'd thought. A two-mile hike separated the Lhakpa La from the North Col, across the basin at the top of the East Rongbuk glacier. The slope leading up to the col he now estimated to be around 1,000 feet, much higher than he had initially thought, and in places it looked as heavily crevassed as it was on the reverse side. The whole thing looked a greater challenge than he had hoped, and would probably be too much for the weaker members of the party.

Nevertheless, two days later, at 4.30 a.m., Mallory set out for the third time for the Lhakpa La at the head of a large party, leaving only Raeburn behind along with three Sherpas who were unfit to start. Once again they struggled up the slope leading to the crest, and once again Windy Gap lived up to its name. This time, however, rather than just dump their loads, they pitched their tents in a shallow snow basin and crawled in for a very uncomfortable night. Several Sherpas had severe headaches and even Mallory felt exhausted. The next twelve hours were purgatorial, as he later wrote in a letter to Geoffrey Winthrop Young: 'We were at very close quarters… but hardly a remark passed from one to another. No cooking, no hand stirred for a thought of comfort, only rest, not sweet but death-like, as though the spirit of the party had died within it.' That night the temperature dropped to –20 degrees Celsius, not the ideal preparation for the great assault on Everest.

The next morning they breakfasted on fried sardines and tea, but it was always hard at high altitude to melt enough snow for cooking and drinking water. Wollaston and Howard-Bury decided they'd had enough and offered to turn back, not wanting to be a burden on the others. Morshead volunteered to accompany them to make sure they got down safely, leaving Mallory, Bullock and Wheeler to soldier on with the Sherpas. There was no question of getting all the way up to the North Col that day, however – the slope leading down to the East Rongbuk glacier was longer and steeper than Mallory had thought, and, with another two Sherpas declaring themselves unfit, the remaining porters had to carry even-heavier loads.

It took four hours to reach the lower slopes of the North Col, where they decided to pitch camp at around 22,000 feet. The wind was relentless, even lower down in the glacier basin, and it continued to torment them throughout the night, making sleep virtually impossible. Mallory was ready to go at 7.00 a.m. the next day, but only three of the remaining Sherpas – Gorang, Lagay and Ang Pasang, Oliver Wheeler's main camera assistants – were fit to continue.

They travelled light, with the Sherpas carrying a little food and the cameras, and the climbers nothing at all. By now, Mallory had abandoned all thought of setting up another camp on the North Col, but he did want to get on to the North Ridge and see how high he could climb, so to conserve energy he let the Sherpas break trail and only took the lead when steps had to be cut at some difficult ground.

The final 500 feet were the hardest, as they traversed leftwards through very soft snow and then gingerly worked their way up and past snow-filled crevasses topped with icy cornices. The wind lacerated them and increased in its violence the higher they got. When Mallory finally reached the North Col, there was no moment of triumph – instead he was almost overcome by breathlessness as he hauled himself up the final few feet through suffocating eddies of snow.

The much-longed-for North Col turned out to be a narrow shelf, roughly split over two levels. There was barely any shelter in the howling gale which roared across from west to east, making it difficult even to stand up. Mallory and Bullock steadied themselves and eyed the North Ridge rising up towards the shoulder 5,000 feet above them. It looked eminently climbable on a good day: a steady thirty-degree slope, some of it bare rock, other passages covered in snow. On that afternoon, however, it would have been impossible to get far; they watched the wind tear across the ridge sending plumes of snow high into the sky, challenging them to go further.

Mallory later maintained that he could have gone on for at least another 2,000 feet, but the others were not at all keen and it was obvious that Gorang, Lagay and Ang Pasang were played out. For the last two hours, Wheeler had lost all feeling in both his feet; any longer on the North Col and he would undoubtedly develop severe frostbite. Bullock was marginally better off, having taken the precaution of donning three sets of underwear and three Shetland jumpers, but he thought it hopeless to continue. As he later wrote laconically in his diary: 'I was prepared to follow Mallory if he wished to try and make some height, but was glad when he decided not to.' After a brief discussion, they climbed a little bit higher up the col, more as a gesture of defiance than anything else, before turning back and retreating to their tents below for another miserably cold and windy night.

The next morning Mallory briefly entertained the idea of returning to the North Col and setting up a proper camp, but the ridge above was still 'smoking' and he knew it would be futile. Neither the climbers nor the Sherpas were strong enough to do anything but continue their retreat. As Mallory wrote to Geoffrey Winthrop Young two months later, it was nothing like how he had dreamt it would be:

> The terrible difference between my visions of myself
> with a few determined spirits setting forth from our
> camp on that high pass, crawling up at least to a much
> higher point where the summit itself would seem
> almost within reach... and on the other hand the reality
> as we found it: the blown snow entirely swept over the
> grey slopes, just the grim prospect, no respite and no
> hope... It was a pitiful party at the last, not fit to be on
> a mountainside anywhere.

There was no alternative but to turn around and climb back over the ever-windy Lhakpa La and all the way to their advance base. In a moment of madness and release, when they found a cache of loads abandoned by the last group of porters, they tossed them down onto the other side and 'stood there laughing like children as we watched them roll and roll 1000s of feet down'. What the Sherpas made of this act of wilful destruction, Mallory did not record.

Back at Base Camp, there was no final celebratory meal to mark the end of the expedition. Howard-Bury left for one last exploratory trip to the nearby Kama valley, where he climbed a ridge which enabled him to look deep into Nepal, the country that he had long wished to visit. It was a thrilling last trip for him, as he wrote to Hinks: 'I wish we had an artist to paint scenes in the Kama valley, it is the most beautiful valley that I have ever seen.' Astonishingly, in spite of his exertions on the North Col, Wheeler accompanied Howard-Bury to complete his survey of Everest's east side.

Mallory's only interest was to get away as quickly as possible. He'd arranged to meet Ruth in Marseille for a brief holiday without their children, and was hoping to take a ship from Mumbai in mid-October. Bullock's American wife, Alice, was also waiting for him, but she was closer by – at Lachen in Sikkim. He didn't want to leave without a few souvenirs, however, so he revisited the dzongpen at Kharta and bought a sword, a prayer wheel, a Buddhist wall scroll and a pen case and, as if that weren't enough, a brass belt from a local woman who was wearing it at the time.

Then, in the early afternoon of 30 September, Bullock and Mallory left camp to begin a very rapid march across Tibet. They didn't wait to say goodbye to Howard-Bury or Wheeler, who returned to their camp at Kharta just a few hours after they left. Howard-Bury was annoyed to see that they had not finished retrieving all the expedition stores from the upper camps. Throughout their six months in Tibet, he had never really felt that either Mallory or Bullock showed any team spirit or were involved in any aspect of the expedition apart from the climbing. As he wrote acidly to Younghusband in London, they had rushed back to civilization 'as they are no travellers and do not appreciate Tibet and the pleasant discomforts of the life here'.

Howard-Bury followed them five days later, after clearing up their camp and presenting the local governor with three sets of unused skis as a parting gift. The dzongpen had wanted one of the expedition's cameras, but Howard-Bury advised him that 'skiing is a much better form of exercise'. He then wrote a brief cable announcing the successful end of the Reconnaissance as well as a longer article for *The Times*, both of which were sent ahead to Phari, the nearest telegraph station.

Howard-Bury travelled quickly on the return leg but he did linger over his final view of Everest, from the junction of the Bong Chu and Yaru rivers fifty miles away. As he stared up towards the East Ridge, he reflected on how much more he understood about the mountain than when they had first arrived, and was delighted to be able to see the site of their camp at Windy Gap – his own personal highest altitude.

The news that the Reconnaissance had finished reached London on 10 October and was published in *The Times* a day later, accompanied by a short interview with Sir Francis Younghusband – who was characteristically positive and keen to remind everyone that the 1921 expedition was only the first stage of their great plan. 'This telegram,' he said, 'shows that the expedition has achieved the object with which it was dispatched... after much careful reconnaissance, the climbing party under Mallory has at last found a route by which it seems possible that a properly organized expedition dispatched next year may reach the top... The news that a way up Everest has been found is the more welcome as it was scarcely expected.'

The editor of *The Times* agreed and was even more complimentary: 'Coming almost at the eleventh hour of the climbing season, that is a great triumph for the members of the expedition, and a notable reward for their perseverance in the teeth of great difficulties and repeated disappointments.'

Raeburn was the first back to London. Mallory reached Marseille on 12 November and was reunited with his beloved Ruth. Morshead and Wheeler returned to their families in Darjeeling, relieved that the expedition was over. As Wheeler later wrote: 'I would not have missed the "show" for anything; but a little of that sort of country goes a long way!'

As for the indefatigable Howard-Bury, he stayed on for a few weeks in India, paying off the expedition bills, meeting the dignitaries that had to be met and sorting out the dispatch of all the photographs that were eagerly awaited back in England. He had every reason to be pleased with himself. The expedition had started badly with the death of Kellas, but ultimately it had been remarkably successful. They had surveyed thousands of square miles of unmapped territory, come back with enough observations to construct the first detailed map of the northern side of Everest and the area around it, and found what looked like a feasible route to the summit. He had established good relations with Tibetan officials and kept within budget, even leaving India with £1,000 to spare. Howard-Bury had every reason to feel pleased with himself – until he looked in the newspaper and discovered that he'd been sacked.

4

Larger than Life

Everyone had a story about Charlie Bruce. How he could tear a pack of cards in half and swear in fluent Nepali. How he introduced shorts to the British Army and used to carry one of his orderlies up a hill each morning to keep fit. How he could lie between two chairs – head on one and feet on the other – and support someone on his belly. He was 'Bruiser' to his friends in the officers' mess, 'Balu' to his Gurkha soldiers. The face of a benign bulldog, the body of an ox, Bruce was the quintessential 'larger than life' character, and in the autumn of 1921 he was on his way to Everest.

Earlier in the year, everyone had assumed – Bruce included – that he would lead the Reconnaissance expedition, but it hadn't worked out quite like that. Officially, 'unavoidable commitments' to the Territorial Army got in the way, but it was clear in his letters at the time that he was ready and willing to go – if the Mount Everest Committee wanted him. Perhaps it was his request for a substantial stipend; perhaps it was the fact that Howard-Bury

Charles Granville Bruce

asked for nothing and even offered to pay his own passage to India; perhaps it was that Arthur Hinks didn't like having a bear in charge of the expedition... either way, the good news for Bruce was that Francis Younghusband thought differently.

On 13 October 1921, the Everest Committee reconvened for the first time since the summer. Hinks was still hoping that Howard-Bury might lead the main expedition, but as Francis Younghusband reminded everyone, that role had been promised to his old friend

General Bruce. Bruce's mountaineering credentials were impeccable: he had been on virtually every major expedition since 1892, when he had accompanied Sir Martin Conway on the first British expedition to the Karakoram and the Himalayas. Three years later he survived the ill-fated attempt on Nanga Parbat which ended with the death of A. F. Mummery, the first British climber to die in the Himalayas. He was also part of A. L. Mumm and Tom Longstaff's much more successful expedition to Trisul in 1907.

The only problem, as Bruce readily admitted, was his health: would he ever get through a Harley Street medical? He was fifty-five and had been invalided out of the army two years earlier, suffering from 'cardiac debility with great enlargement'. A self-confessed heavyweight, he had a huge appetite for life in every sense – once joking to a friend that his liver was so large 'it required two men and a boy to carry it'. Mindful of Finch's rejection six months earlier, Younghusband got Hinks to write to doctors Larkins and Anderson, the Committee's regular Harley Street specialists, advising them that Bruce would not be expected to go much higher than 16,000 feet, apart from a possible foray up to 20,000 feet.

The good doctors played along. The general's body, Larkins noted in his official report, showed 'various scars due to accidents and bullet wounds', his blood pressure was a seriously high 210/110, and there were still heart and liver issues – but ultimately none of this would stop him. 'The above tabulation of defects rather suggests that this man is unfit,' wrote Larkins, 'but summing up the whole Case and taking into account the history and general physique of this man, I consider he is fit to join the expedition.'

When the Committee saw the report on 2 November, it was noted in the official minutes that it was 'not particularly favourable', but unlike six months earlier when George Finch had been summarily rejected from the Reconnaissance, there was no hasty dismissal. Instead they resolved to offer Bruce the leadership 'on the clear understanding that he takes due note of the medical report and runs no unnecessary risks that might impair his health and the success of the expedition'. They also asked him to show the report to his doctor, Claude Wilson, and attend their next meeting. When Wilson saw the report, he congratulated Bruce for getting the job he wanted but warned him to be 'jolly careful' and appoint a second in command – in case he were to 'knock up like Raeburn did'.

Events moved quickly. On 6 November, Bruce wrote to Younghusband telling him that he had secured eight months' leave from his job at the Glamorgan Territorial Association, and two days later he was invited to London to be congratulated on his appointment. On 11 November, the first 'unofficial' report of his appointment appeared in *The Times*. In due course it was picked up by the Indian press, and was spotted by the rather peeved Howard-Bury. He immediately wrote to Hinks that he was 'surprised to read in one of the cablegrams to the *Pioneer* that the President had announced that I had already resigned from the Expedition and that Bruce has succeeded me. He certainly seems to have been in a great hurry to get rid of me.'

In truth, a week earlier the Everest Committee had written to Howard-Bury telling him of Bruce's appointment, but at the time he was in transit and the telegram was not forwarded to him. Howard-Bury was a sensitive man. He told Hinks that the news made him feel like a failure and lost him all standing among the officials he had met in India, but he'd never actually been that keen on going back straight away and had hoped that the second expedition would be delayed until 1923. The Everest Committee, however, wanted to get back to Everest as soon as possible, fearing that the cordial relations between the Indian government and the Dalai Lama might not last. Later on, Hinks mooted the idea of Howard-Bury joining Bruce's party, but he wasn't interested, preferring – as he wrote in December 1921 – to 'sink back once more into quiet obscurity'.

Nobody would argue that Howard-Bury had not done a good job in 1921. His team had found a feasible route to the summit, collected thousands of samples of flora and fauna, and mapped over 16,000 square miles of territory. As a reconnaissance it was exemplary but there had been logistical problems, and as Mallory made clear in his correspondence, the expedition had felt incoherent at times. If they were going to make a serious attempt in 1922, the climbing side of the expedition would have to be much bigger and more tightly organized, and there was no better man to achieve this than Charles Bruce.

In earlier years Bruce had been up plenty of mountains in India and the Alps, but in his mid-fifties he didn't expect to lead his troops up Everest. His role, as he saw it, was to get them to Base Camp in as good a shape as possible, before a dedicated climbing leader took over. Howard-Bury had been tasked with exploring all possible routes into Everest and gathering a lot of other geographical information, but Bruce's focus would be much more singular.

After reviewing all the reports, fieldwork and survey data compiled by Wheeler and Morshead, it was clear that the best way up the mountain was from the north via the East Rongbuk glacier. There would be no stops at Tingri or attempts from the Kharta side. All Bruce had to do was get everyone to the Rongbuk valley as efficiently and painlessly as possible, and maintain them there for as long as was needed.

After all the reports of stomach problems in 1921, Bruce was determined to personally select the cooks and ensure that they got the best Sherpas and sirdars. And instead of indolent army mules that were no good at high altitude, he would use his local knowledge and take full advantage of the mule trains that regularly moved back and forth between Darjeeling and Tibet, carrying merchandise across the Himalayas. On the 1921 expedition, none of the sahibs apart from Morshead had been able to speak any of the local languages, but as a skilled linguist himself who knew the importance of good communication with local peoples, Bruce planned to have at least two British Gurkha officers on the team, and more if he could manage it.

The biggest task for the Committee was once again choosing the team. In theory, for the 1922 expedition the Royal Geographical Society should have handed over the reins to the Alpine Club and accepted a secondary role. The Reconnaissance had been a multifaceted expedition with as much attention given to the surveying and geographical side as to the climbing, whereas 1922 was billed as purely a climbing expedition and therefore should have been the preserve of the Alpine Club.

There had always been a little friction between the two bodies: the RGS was undoubtedly bigger and more prestigious, but although a smaller organization, the members of the Alpine Club had actually donated more money to expedition funds. In the end, however, everything stayed the same. Younghusband offered to stand down as Chairman of the Committee in favour of Norman Collie, the President of the Alpine Club, but Collie declined the offer and Hinks hung on doggedly to his role as Committee Secretary.

When it came to the climbing party, first on the list was George Mallory. He had made mistakes in 1921 but had clearly been the best and most tenacious climber on the team. Once again, though, Mallory was playing hard to get. Hinks wrote to him on 3 November, but instead of rushing back to London to help write the expedition book and prepare for public lectures, Mallory had gone on holiday with his wife to the South of France, leaving their children in England. Hinks was so keen to get hold of him that he had even sent a second copy of his letter to Ruth, asking her to tell George that 'the Committee are just as anxious to see him as the children are'. Mallory didn't take the bait. When eventually he did reply, he told Hinks that in his opinion eight climbers were needed, but he was non-committal about his own availability. 'As to my going out again,' he wrote from Marseille, 'may I leave that over till I see you?... Unless the required number of climbers is forthcoming... I should not be inclined to go out next year, the chances are small enough whatever arrangements are made.'

In November 1921 the idea that they would send out an eight-man climbing team looked over-optimistic. Apart from the cost of supporting so many men in the field, where would they get them from? Kellas was dead and Raeburn was clearly not going to return. Mallory's partner, Guy Bullock, was a career diplomat and had to return to his post in Le Havre in France. The two surveyors, Wheeler and Morshead, had done well, but Wheeler was on his way back to Canada for some long-awaited leave and there was no guarantee that the Survey of India would release Morshead again, especially if there was no need for his services as a cartographer.

The Committee had the pile of application letters that had flooded in at the beginning of the year, but the 'British only' policy still stood and there was never really any chance of a complete outsider being chosen. So the Committee instead turned to their colleagues in the Alpine Club, who over the past few months had been thinking about the future team.

Their first suggestion was Howard Somervell, a surgeon from the Lake District who was known to be a very strong mountaineer. Handsome and stocky with a broad face and an easy smile, Somervell had climbed extensively in Britain and the Alps and was famed for his stamina and his skill on rock. He was also a talented painter and an enthusiastic amateur composer. When the letter of invitation arrived, he was so thrilled that he immediately wrote back offering to pay some of his expenses, and even suggested that he should take his paint box and sketch pad, and hold an exhibition afterwards at the Alpine Club with proceeds going to future Everest expeditions. Harley Street pronounced him 'in every way a fit candidate', and though the Committee initially said a polite no to his artistic offering, Somervell was duly signed up.

Cut from similar cloth, though several inches taller, was Edward Norton, another very capable mountaineer in his mid-thirties. Norton was a career army officer who had served with distinction in campaigns in India and the First World War. His grandfather was Alfred Wills, one of the founders of the Alpine Club, and he had grown up regularly climbing in the Alps. Though Norton claimed to be worried about the medical on account of being 'long and thin', he was known as a great sportsman who excelled at pig-sticking – a popular though dangerous pastime among British officers in India in which participants chased wild boar on horseback, aiming to be the first to spear one with a lance. Military authorities encouraged the sport, according to the 1911 *Encyclopaedia Britannica*, because 'a startled or angry wild boar is… a desperate fighter [and therefore] the pig-sticker must possess a good eye, a steady hand, a firm seat, a cool head and a courageous heart'. Norton wasn't just a good soldier and sportsman, though: he was an avid birdwatcher and a talented watercolourist, and immediately offered his services as the expedition ornithologist and assistant naturalist.

Two slightly older recruits were Edward Lisle Strutt – a forty-seven-year-old former soldier, very much cut in the mould of Howard-Bury – who was taken on as climbing leader, and Arthur Wakefield, a British doctor of the same age, who had been based in Canada for many years. Wakefield was not known as a technical climber but had set the record for the famous Lake District 24-Hour Fell Record endurance event, covering fifty-nine miles and making 23,500 feet of ascent in twenty-two hours and seven minutes. After serving as a military doctor in the bloody battlefields of France and Belgium, Wakefield had come back from the First World War suffering from what his family later described as undiagnosed shell shock, but the members of the Everest Committee were very keen on having him – and after failing to get him to sign on for the Reconnaissance, they were pleased when he said yes. Tom Longstaff, who had also been considered in 1921, was taken on as team doctor and naturalist, when Sandy Wollaston decided that he didn't want to go back for a second time.

To this core of four new members, Bruce added two Gurkha transport officers: his own cousin Geoffrey Bruce, who was famed for his athletic powers, and John Morris, another career soldier who had long been fascinated by Tibet. Eventually, Bruce even managed to swing a third transport officer, securing Colin 'Ferdie' Crawford, an Indian civil servant with experience of Himalayan climbing. The 1922 expedition now had a strong core team, but there was also a pair of very large elephants in the tent: the two Georges, Finch and Mallory.

After his initial show of diffidence, Mallory had quickly come back into the fold. On 16 November, just a week after writing to his sister Avie that he would not go to Everest in 1922 'for all the gold in Arabia', he wrote to Hinks again, this time quietly apologizing for appearing stroppy in his earlier letter from Marseille and making it clear that he was set on returning to Everest: 'I don't know precisely what I may have said in my haste... but please don't tell the committee if the question arises that I don't intend to go unless they do as I wish. That's not my thought.'

Getting the other George back on the team was more complicated. Finch's rejection on medical grounds had not stopped him climbing. In the summer of 1921, while Mallory was slogging up and down the Rongbuk glacier, he had gone to France – where, according to Percy Farrar, Finch's mentor at the Alpine Club, he had taken part in 'the biggest climb in the Alps this season'. Though Farrar was exaggerating a little, Finch's ascent of Mont Blanc's Peuterey ridge with two other British climbers and two Swiss guides had been both daring and demanding. There could no longer be any question of his fitness, and as everyone knew in the British mountaineering world, he was undoubtedly one of the – if not *the* – best climbers in the country.

The problem was Hinks. He simply didn't like Finch, and his immediate boss, Sir Francis Younghusband, was lukewarm about him. The rest of the team was remarkably homogenous, with Hinks noting proudly in the *Geographical Journal* that six members were soldiers, five were from Oxbridge and three were surgeons. Finch was none of the above.

It would be wrong, however, to portray Finch as some kind of Australian roughneck. Like Edmund Hillary, he was born into a well-to-do family and was highly educated, having attended one of the best technical colleges in Switzerland. Undoubtedly, though, Finch was different from the others, a maverick spirit with a rigorously scientific mind. He could appear arrogant and dogmatic and was very much his own man. The other members of the British team, Charles Bruce excepted, were compliant and undemanding, but Finch was busy and assertive. He would never offer to pay his own way or meekly kowtow to the Committee's demands, so Hinks would always feel uncomfortable around him. To add extra spice, Finch was Percy Farrar's favourite and Hinks liked nothing more than to annoy Farrar, whom he regarded as irritatingly outspoken and rude.

If they were serious about getting up Everest in 1922, however, there was no question that Finch should be with them, and so, undoubtedly gritting his teeth, Hinks wrote to him on 10 November inviting him to join, subject once again to a medical exam. On 21 November, Finch dropped in on Dr F. E. Larkins of Harley Street, who that same day had examined new boy Howard Somervell. This time, Larkins was unequivocal in his report to Hinks and the Everest Committee: 'I also re-examined Finch today. He is now absolutely fit and has lost his glucosuria. In my first report on him I stated that I thought all he wanted was to get into training.'

The fact that Finch had been declared fit did not get him immediately accepted onto the team, however. First, Younghusband wrote to Strutt, asking him whether or not to include Finch. In reply, Strutt was positive, if not quite enthusiastic: 'I think that Charles Bruce and I should be able to handle him. At the same time if the other members dislike him, which I fear is the case, it rather alters the situation. However in reply to your question I should like Finch to go. He is the one man I would back to reach the summit and we should always remember that!'

On 3 December, Hinks wrote to Finch again, to ask if he was available for 1922. A week later Finch replied that Imperial College had approved eight months' leave, and finally, on 15 December, he was formally invited to join, though not without yet more finger-wagging from Hinks. Recalling the *Illustrated London News* article from earlier that year, he reminded Finch: 'It is also important that we should continue the practice which has been so successful of abstaining from any dealings with the press, either directly or indirectly; and should not be allowed to appear in anything which looks like an individual advertisement.'

Five days later, Finch attended the Everest Reconnaissance's reception at the Queen's Hall, in front of the assembled members of the Alpine Club and Royal Geographical Society. It was, as *The Times* noted the next day, 'a worthy tribute to their fine success in the first stage of the great Everest adventure'. The Duke of York attended on behalf of the royal family and 'decorations were worn' by the esteemed attendees. Younghusband delivered a predictable homily to the success of the expedition; Howard-Bury gave an overview of their achievements; and Mallory read a paper which focused on the expedition's struggles at high altitude. He talked for so long that there wasn't time for Sandy Wollaston's planned speech about the team's activities on the natural history front, though during questions at the end Sir Francis was able to inform the audience that a new species of whistling hare had been discovered in Tibet.

Though there was a celebratory air to proceedings, no one was making any rash promises. Mallory said the odds were against them, warning that it would require a huge effort from the climbers and their porters. On a slightly more optimistic note, he added that if they could set up a top camp at 26,000 feet, then the final 3000 feet 'might be accomplished'. It was a big if.

Part of the game for the expedition's organizers, of course, was to manage expectations. They did not want to look foolish by talking up the chances of success too much. Equally, if they wanted to keep up the momentum on the diplomatic and fundraising fronts, they had to appear positive. But the fact was that, even if they had identified a potential route up Everest, they had not got above 23,000 feet in 1921 and had not really needed to face up to the key question Mallory discussed in his presentation: just how high could a climber get before they were overcome by the altitude?

Today, the term 'death zone' is one of the familiar tropes of Everest writing, but in 1921 the phrase – and the concept – did not exist. The science of high-altitude physiology was in its infancy, and very little was understood about the effect of altitude on the body. When the world record was set at 24,600 feet by the Duke of the Abruzzi on Chogolisa, he and his guides had been stopped from reaching the summit by heavy snow, not breathing difficulties. The official expedition report had concluded that 'if there is a physical limit, we are still far from reaching it'. Everest, however, was 4,500 feet higher than Abruzzi's high point, and there were many scientists who believed that its summit lay above the threshold for human life.

Over the previous century and a half, the sport of mountaineering had developed in parallel with the emerging science of aeronautics, and in both fields the physiological impact of high altitude was a key question. In 1786, during the first ascent of Mont Blanc (at 15,771 feet, the highest mountain in western Europe), the two climbers Michel-Gabriel Paccard and Jacques Balmat reported no particular ill effects apart from extreme exhaustion, but in the following year, when the Swiss geologist Horace Bénédict de Saussure made the second ascent, he reported that several of his companions were stricken by vomiting, palpitations and fever, all of which disappeared when they descended to lower altitude. In Paris four years earlier, in 1783, Jean-François Pilâtre de Rozier and François Laurent had made the first manned balloon flight. They only ascended to around 2,500 feet and did not suffer any ill effects at all, but as their fellow balloonists rapidly 'pushed the envelope' of balloon flight higher and higher, extreme reactions were reported.

In September 1862, the British meteorologist James Glaisher and his partner Henry Coxwell, a practising dentist, took a balloon to an estimated 37,000 feet, at which point Glaisher fell unconscious. Fearing that he too would collapse, Coxwell attempted to open the valve that would let the air out, but he couldn't move his hands and, fittingly, had to open it with his teeth.

Thirteen years later, in 1875, a trio of French 'aeronauts' attempted to repeat their feat, but when they reached around 29,000 feet all three fell unconscious. By good fortune, the balloon soon started descending by itself, but when the basket hit the ground with a crash, only one man, Gaston Tissandier, was still alive. His former teammates, Joseph Crocé-Spinelli and Théodore Henri Sivel, had blackened faces and mouths full of blood. It was a very dramatic and brutal demonstration of the dangers of rapidly ascending to high altitude.

The problem, as scientists began to realize, was the higher the altitude, the lower the air pressure – and therefore the greater the effort required to fill the lungs with air. At the summit of

Everest, air pressure is approximately a third of its value at sea level, making it much harder to breathe without considerable effort. Oxygen deficiency causes hypoxia and hypoxemia, two very uncomfortable and potentially fatal conditions in which the blood and the tissues are starved of oxygen, causing headaches, erratic heartbeats, coughing and, perhaps most dangerous of all, mental confusion.

The solution was to carry containers of compressed oxygen, but it wasn't until the early twentieth century that portable cylinders became available. Initially they were very heavy and cumbersome but, as ever, military conflict spurred technological advances. In 1914, when the Great War started, neither the Allies nor the Axis powers had significant numbers of planes or airships, but by the end of the war, aviation was playing an increasingly significant role in the fighting and planes were flying higher and higher – their pilots sometimes equipped with breathing masks and supplies of oxygen. In September 1918, a six-foot-four American test pilot, Rudolph 'Shorty' Schroeder, reached almost 29,000 feet – the height of Everest – in a Bristol biplane, breathing oxygen in the final stages of his flight via a rubber hose.

Of course, there were significant differences between climbing and flying at high altitude. Whereas it took Schroeder just over an hour and a half to get from ground level to his ceiling altitude, a climber would take much longer, allowing for the possibility of acclimatization. Like the 1921 Reconnaissance team, the prospective members of the 1922 expedition were committed to a month-long trip across India and Tibet, which would entail a steady rise in altitude until they reached the Rongbuk glacier at 16,000 feet, allowing their bodies to gradually adjust to the thin air.

The other key difference between a pilot and a climber was the issue of weight. Carrying an extra thirty-five pounds of equipment in a plane or a balloon would affect its performance to a small extent, but the burden was shouldered by the machine, not the man. On a mountain, though, there was always a trade-off between the weight of an oxygen set and the boost it gave. The first person to do a cost/benefit analysis of climbing oxygen was Alexander Kellas. In the summer of 1920, six months before he joined the Everest Reconnaissance expedition, he had conducted a series of experiments in the Garhwal mountains of northern India, getting his Sherpa porters to climb a premeasured slope and then comparing their performance with and without oxygen sets.

Kellas's initial conclusion was that there were no significant benefits, but as his critics pointed out, he had particularly heavy oxygen cylinders which weighed twenty pounds each, and he had conducted his experiments at 18,000 feet – a comparatively low altitude, where the additional weight might not be offset by the benefit. Kellas had been planning to conduct further experiments in 1921 on Everest, but when he died his equipment was left behind at Khamba Dzong and was never used as intended.

The question of oxygen had also been broached earlier in 1921, when Finch had met Professor Georges Dreyer, the altitude expert who had worked extensively with the Royal Air Force during the First World War. Dreyer had convinced Finch of the value of portable oxygen sets, but there hadn't been enough time to get him involved in the Reconnaissance, and after his rejection on medical grounds, Finch had taken no further part in the expedition. The oxygen question, however, had not gone away, and with the focus of 1922 shifting firmly to reaching the summit of Everest, Finch went back up to Oxford to see Dreyer in January 1922 to talk further. He was joined by Percy Unna, the engineer and Alpine Club member who had accompanied him on his first visit, as well as Howard Somervell, one of the new recruits. Somervell, a practising surgeon, had read Kellas's reports and was interested in finding out more about oxygen.

When they reached Oxford, Dreyer invited Finch to take part in a further series of tests in his hyperbaric chamber, in which he and Somervell would be taken to a simulated altitude of 23,000 feet and asked to perform various tasks. Finch went first, climbing on and off a step while carrying a thirty-pound load. He was slow but steady, and able to repeat the task twenty times. When Somervell took over, he started off at a faster rate, but collapsed after just five steps. He regained consciousness when he was given oxygen through a mask but bad-temperedly denied suffering any ill effects – a classic sign of hypoxia.

When they returned to London, the trio of Somervell, Finch and Unna attended a meeting of the Everest Committee to report back on their discussions with Dreyer and the experiments they had taken part in. They were so convincing that it was agreed that as much as £400 (£23,000 in today's money) would be put up to fund the development of oxygen sets. Finch took the lead, over the next two months working hard to get a basic set together. The Air Ministry supplied face masks and the rest of the set was manufactured by Siebe Gorman, a British company that specialized in breathing equipment for miners and firemen.

Today, the vast majority of climbers who reach the summit of Everest do so with the aid of supplementary oxygen. There are a variety of different mask designs available, but most use Russian-made Poisk oxygen cylinders manufactured from a lightweight titanium alloy covered in Kevlar fibres. The cylinders used in 1922 were made from high carbon steel and much heavier, weighing in at around five and three-quarter pounds each when fully loaded.

The eventual design was based around a metal frame which could carry four narrow cylinders painted white, in order not to warm up in the sun. The flow of oxygen was controlled by a regulator worn at chest level and then fed to the mask through a rubber tube. Though the cylinders could theoretically withstand 150 times atmospheric pressure, it was decided to compress the oxygen inside to just 120 atmospheres in order to reduce the likelihood of leakage.

On 23 February, with a week to go before they left for India, the team was invited to the Air Ministry on Kingsway in Central London to try out the new design. Not all the climbers were looking forward to it. As Mallory wrote to his friend Geoffrey Winthrop Young on the day before the oxygen test: 'I found Wakefield no less gloomy than myself... 29lbs to carry on one's back and what will happen when one takes off the mask no-one seems to know.'

When the climbers arrived they were invited to don a set and then run up four flights of stairs to the roof garden, but as Percy Unna wrote in a report to the *Alpine Journal* afterwards, they soon discovered that the mask 'as originally designed was not intended for hard exercise'. Arthur Wakefield collapsed and had to have his mask ripped off his face before he asphyxiated. When an alternative arrangement was tried, in which the mask was replaced by a rubber tube held between the teeth, the glass cover of the flow meter broke because it wasn't strong enough to cope with increased pressure on exhalation. Clearly there was still a lot of work to do, but with the main consignment of oxygen cylinders already on their way to

India, the show had to go on. Ten sets were prepared and sent out in advance, with an eleventh set retained for 'oxygen classes' to be held on board the ship during the voyage.

As everyone could see, portable oxygen sets were essentially a novel technology which, aside from Kellas's experiments on Kamet, had never been tried before on a mountain. Tom Longstaff, the old hand who had been brought in to replace Sandy Wollaston as the expedition doctor, wrote a formal letter to the Committee, advising them that the current oxygen sets were just too primitive and underdeveloped to be used on Everest. What would happen to a climber, he asked, if something malfunctioned and the flow of oxygen was interrupted at high altitude? Could anyone survive if they were suddenly deprived of gas? Others pointed out that the oxygen sets were heavy and awkward – not ideal for the tricky manoeuvres they would have to execute on the world's highest mountain.

To add to all these pragmatic considerations, a more personal element was becoming part of the oxygen debate. Hinks, the Chairman of the Everest Committee, had never accepted Finch and was increasingly irritated by his main backer Percy Farrar, who was also in favour of using supplementary oxygen. Nominally, Hinks was just the Committee Secretary, but on a day-to-day basis he was in control of the expedition planning. Even though he had no experience of mountaineering, Hinks began to loudly object to the use of oxygen on 'sporting grounds'. Was it really fair to use 'un-natural' technology in this way? Shouldn't climbers operate under their own steam? The fact that George Finch had become so associated with the development of the oxygen sets added to his disdain.

Hinks wasn't the only one to object on principle, though: George Mallory memorably labelled oxygen a 'damnable heresy', and after his experience at the Air Ministry, Arthur Wakefield was even more hostile. Actively encouraged by Hinks, a rift opened up between the pro- and anti-oxygen factions on the expedition and on the Committee which would run and run, and would dog British Everest expeditions for the next thirty years.

Charles Bruce largely stayed out of the argument, having left for India at the end of January. The only 'equipment' that he seemed to have really strong feelings about was food. The 1921 Reconnaissance had been minimalist when it came to provisions. Some tinned goods had been taken out from Britain, but a lot of their supplies were bought locally, and supplemented by game shot by Howard-Bury or other members of the team. There would be no hunting in 1922, following religious objections by the Tibetan government, and the fresh vegetables and fruit that Howard-Bury had found so abundant in the Kharta valley would be much harder to come by on the Rongbuk side of the mountain.

Bruce's solution was to go straight to the Army & Navy Stores catalogue and put in a very large order. For quick and easy high-altitude food, for example, he ordered forty-five tins of Heinz Spaghetti and fifty tins of Irish stew; to excite jaded palates when the going got tough, they would have forty-four tins of quail in foie gras and twenty-five tins of mock turtle soup; and to make their breakfast more appetizing, there were fifty-six tins of marmalade. Other expedition requisites included dozens of tins of sweets, from butterscotch to peppermint bulls-eyes, but – evidently fearing that this would not be quite enough – Howard Somervell put in a personal order for ten slabs of Kendal Mint Cake at a cost of two pounds, five shillings. With several birthdays to celebrate during the expedition, Bruce also took twenty-four half-bottles of Champagne and one regular case of Montebello 1911, a prized vintage.

In total, the Army & Navy Stores packaged up and shipped out no less than 813 cases of provisions, tents and equipment for the 1922 expedition. It was significantly more than the previous year, but compared with the British expeditions of the 1950s the overall approach was relatively laissez-faire. Once again, individual members were offered a large clothing grant, but there was no real guidance as to what to purchase, and most of their climbing gear was individually tailored. In 1953, when Hillary and Tenzing made their famous ascent, virtually every item of clothing and equipment had been rigorously examined and frequently redesigned to make sure that the British team had the best possible gear; but, apart from the design of the oxygen set, there was no special attention paid to clothing or climbing equipment in 1922.

This is not to say that that everything was utterly inadequate. As on the Reconnaissance, they wore the tried-and-tested clothing and footwear that had been used in the Alps for years: hobnailed leather boots and high-quality wool and tweed that was both warm and wind-resistant. There was none of the obsessive fetishizing of 'technical' clothing that characterizes modern expeditions. Equally, though, there was no recognition that the peculiar conditions at extreme altitude required specialist gear. The Irish writer George Bernard Shaw had famously remarked on seeing a group photograph of the 1921 team outside their tents, dressed in a varied selection of Norfolk jackets, army greatcoats, scarves and waistcoats, that the entire scene resembled a 'Connemara picnic surprised by a snowstorm'.

The only exception was, unsurprisingly, George Finch. Back in March he had been appalled at Raeburn's advice that all they needed for their trip to the Himalayas was standard Alpine clothing. Since then he'd had plenty of time to think and had come up with a new concept: lightweight garments made out of balloon silk lined with eiderdown. Finch went to a specialist outdoor clothing manufacturer, S. W. Silver and Co., and commissioned a coat, some trousers and some gauntlets. These were prototypes of the duvet jacket and trousers that have become staple items on modern-day expeditions, and perhaps predictably the other members of the team made fun of him – until they reached the Tibetan plain and saw that Finch's outfit was much warmer and more effective than anything they had brought.

Finch also had the foresight, or the impertinence, to write to Hinks asking if he could take his own photographs, anticipating that in the future he might use them for lectures and books. The Everest Committee had once again sold the rights to official expedition dispatches to *The Times* and the rights to photographs to the *Illustrated London News*, but did this preclude ordinary members taking their own 'snaps', he asked? Hinks immediately wrote back telling him that the copyright of all images taken on the expedition would be owned by the Committee, including any photographs that Finch might take. It was not the answer that he wanted to hear, but Finch went ahead anyway and took several cameras and enough photographic film and chemicals to come away with over 800 images.

Sensing that this would be a historic expedition, the Committee had decided that, in addition to all the newspaper coverage and an expedition book, they would both commission a film and send the well-known landscape painter Cecil Arthur Hunt as official artist. Hunt's Everest expedition, however, didn't get any further than Harley Street. Even though Hinks had sent another pre-emptory letter promising that he would not go high and that he would be given 'as comfortable a time as possible', Hunt was rejected on the grounds of a weak heart and borderline emphysema. For the official cinematographer and photographer, the Committee chose someone younger and fitter: that old Everest hand, John Noel.

In the three years since he had given the lecture at the Aeolian Hall that had revived interest in Everest, Noel had had a busy time as a trainer in the Machine Gun Corps – but there was little chance that he would say no to a return trip to Tibet. He had become increasingly fascinated by photography and was very happy to be offered the role of cameraman in 1922, especially when the Committee were willing to make a significant investment in the latest equipment. In the early 1920s there was a real public appetite for travel films in exotic locations, and Noel had high hopes that he would bring back footage of Tibetan life as well as dramatic coverage of the British expedition.

This time round there weren't the same diplomatic hurdles to cross, but nor were things absolutely smooth. In December 1921 there were rumours in India that the Everest Committee had decided to postpone the expedition. These were quickly quashed, but at around the same time bona fide letters were received in India from the Tibetan government listing a number of problems on the Reconnaissance. As well as complaints that Howard-Bury had hunted on sacred land and had not always paid a fair price for pack animals, the local governors at Shekar made a much more serious charge against Alexander Heron, the expedition geologist. According to a letter sent from the Viceroy in Delhi to the India Office in London, the Tibetans believed that he had used the expedition as 'an excuse for digging earth stones from the most sacred hills of Tibet' and that, not only had he pocketed rubies and turquoises, but he had also disturbed 'fierce demons, the very guardians of the soil', potentially prompting 'fatal epidemics [to] break out amongst men and cattle'. When he heard that he had been accused of larceny and disturbing demons, Heron pleaded innocence, replying to Hinks that: 'I did no mining and the gentle hammer tapping which I indulged in was, I am sure, insufficient to alarm the most timid of the fraternity.' Clearly he didn't take it seriously, but the Tibetans did and they refused to allow Heron to return.

Apart from these last-minute complications, Bruce was able to go off to Everest confident that his hosts would once again be very helpful to the British team, and that good relations had already been established with most of the local officials en route to the mountain. Never missing an opportunity to assert its importance, the Committee drafted a new four-page memo detailing Bruce's responsibilities as the 'father' of the expedition. Everything was specified, from how to ensure that the climbers had 'scope for personal initiative and resource' to a detailed checklist of the dispatches that he would be expected to send back to *The Times*. Though various members of the team were still expected to collect samples of the flora and fauna for Kew Gardens and the British Museum, this time the focus of the expedition would be much more singular. The time for reconnaissance was over: 'The object of the Expedition this year is to make a determined effort, with every available resource, to reach the summit.'

With Mallory, Finch, Somervell and Norton, Bruce realized that he had a very strong team of climbers capable of mounting a real challenge. Norton and Somervell were both raring to go, and Mallory, who was still writing his account of the 1921 Reconnaissance, already regarded Everest as unfinished business.

For George Finch there was a sense of everything finally coming together. A few months earlier he had married for the third time, to one Agnes 'Bubbles' Johnston, the woman with whom he would share the rest of his life. His department at Imperial College was thriving, but fully supported his departure for Everest. With good weather and a little bit of luck, it was quite possible that he or one of the others might go all the way to the top. But even as Finch joined the others for the voyage out to India on the SS *Caledonia*, the tensions within the expedition were clear: Finch wanted to conduct regular oxygen training classes, but no one else seemed to be keen. Team bonding, he realized, would not be as easy as he had hoped.

The Everest Team, March 1922:
(back row, left to right) Crawford, Norton, Mallory, Somervell, Morshead,
Wakefield; (front row, left to right) Strutt, Bruce, Finch

5

Oxygen Drill

In the summer of 1902, the fourteen-year-old George Finch and his younger brother Max found themselves in the middle of their toughest challenge yet: the ascent of Notre-Dame in Paris. George had recently discovered Edward Whymper's famous book *Scrambles Amongst the Alps*, an account of his early years as a climber and the first ascent of the Matterhorn. The Finch brothers had already completed Whymper's route up the famously dangerous cliffs at Beachy Head, and now they were following their hero up one of the world's most celebrated cathedrals – not realizing, or perhaps not caring, that Whymper had climbed Notre-Dame from the inside not via the sheer west wall.

George and Max were two wild young boys, born from an unlikely marriage between a middle-aged Australian widower and his much-younger second wife. Charles Finch was a landowner from a well-to-do and well-connected family. Laura was twenty-five years his junior, a self-styled 'Bohemian' and a disciple of theosophy, a popular New Age philosophy that mixed Eastern

mysticism with European esotericism. She persuaded her husband
to take the family to Europe on what was supposed to be a
year-long Grand Tour. Charles eventually returned but Laura
never went back, settling first in France with her children before
eventually moving to a theosophist commune in India. Their
parents never formally divorced but neither George nor Max
saw their father again.

As a single parent, Laura Finch veered between strictness and
a laissez-faire attitude which occasionally allowed her to leave
George and Max on their own while she disappeared for days on
end with her artistic friends. When it came to climbing, a sport
that both brothers came to excel in, she took a tougher line,
insisting that they limit themselves to peaks below 10,000 feet
and employ professional guides. As Laura was footing the bill,
the Finch brothers initially at least complied, and learned their
craft from Christian Jossi, a well-respected Swiss guide. George's
skill and obsession with mountaineering only grew when he went
to Zurich to study chemistry. When Max eventually joined him,
the pair forged a reputation as two of the best young climbers in
Switzerland, storming through the Alps and eventually climbing
Whymper's Matterhorn themselves in 1908.

The strangeness and emotional dislocation of his childhood
left its mark. George would eventually lose touch with both his
mother and his brother, and would marry three times before he
found his soulmate. Throughout his life, climbing would remain
a constant for him, however, and in many ways he would come
to resemble Edward Whymper. Both men were very strong and
lithe, and both were independently minded and self-reliant to
the point of abrasiveness. Whymper worked as an engraver but
would have liked to have been a scientist; Finch was a scientist

but would have liked to have been a musician. In spite of their frustrations, both men achieved much in their lives, but there was one ambition that Finch would realize that Whymper never quite managed: to climb in the Himalayas.

When Finch and the other members of the team boarded the SS *Caledonia* in early March 1922, they were committing themselves to a climbing trip that was expected to last at least six months. The voyage to India alone would take about two weeks, with a further week of overland travel to get to Darjeeling, and then a month's trek across Tibet before they and their two tonnes of luggage were expected to reach Base Camp at the beginning of May. There was no point in arriving much earlier because it would be too cold to climb, but equally they could not afford to arrive much later knowing that the monsoon would hit the Himalayas in early June and put an end to their ambitions. For the expedition to succeed, they would have to show great patience at the beginning and great alacrity at the end.

For the moment, though, as their ship puffed its way out of Marseille harbour into the warm waters of the Mediterranean, no one was in a particular rush. The SS *Caledonia* was typical of the ships that regularly plied their way across the Mediterranean and the Indian Ocean in the early twentieth century. During the First World War it had been used as a troop ship and had almost been sunk by enemy mines, but it was repaired, refitted and returned to service. It had a crew of 294 to support 315 first-class and 175 second-class passengers; though not quite luxurious, the British team and the other upper-deck passengers could amuse themselves playing deck tennis and were expected to dress formally for dinner, summoned by the sound of a bugle.

For George Mallory, who had gone out to India on his own in 1921, the opportunity to meet and bond with the other members of the British team was much welcomed. Though he liked to spend time alone, meditating in his deckchair or working on his chapters of the official book about the 1921 Reconnaissance, he especially enjoyed getting to know Howard Somervell and Edward Strutt, the team's climbing leader who, contrary to expectations, proved not stiff and dry but 'a chatterbox and quite entertaining'. As for Finch, though they had met in North Wales and climbed together in the Alps just a year earlier, there was no sense of a pre-existing bond. Mallory told Ruth that he found him a little bit humourless and was struck by the shape of his head, which he said 'seems to go out at the sides where it ought to go up'.

Like everyone else, Mallory was expected to take part in Finch's equipment drills, but though he was not quite as hostile as Arthur Wakefield, who had not forgotten his experience at the Air Ministry, he remained distrustful of supplementary oxygen. He even added an aesthetic dimension to the whole controversy, writing to Ruth how repelled he was by the thought of 'the saliva dribbling down' when a climber had an oxygen tube in their mouth. Though he admitted to feeling proprietorial over Everest, he was less explicit about the rivalry that he clearly felt towards Finch.

Finch, for his part, though outwardly bullish, would later confide to his new wife, Bubbles, how empty and forlorn he had felt at the beginning of the expedition. He came to distrust Mallory and Somervell, and though he liked the other members of the team, he was ill at ease. Finch had been drawn to Everest as a climbing challenge, not a scientific one, but from the moment he had gone down to Oxford in the spring of 1921 to talk about the team's Primus stoves, he had become associated with the 'oxygen faction' on the Everest Committee, and latterly had become its standard-bearer. Initially, Finch had thought that the surgeon Howard Somervell would be his main ally, but Somervell quickly bonded with Mallory and was soon drawing caricatures of men in oxygen sets and composing doggerel verse mocking Finch's oxygen training sessions:

> Are you lounging at ease, are you trying to sleep?
> Are you watching the porpoises play in the deep?
> Are you busy increasing your beverage bill?
> Come away, for it's time for the oxygen drill.

Finch took it all with apparent good humour but it was not easy for him. It was one thing to battle against Hinks and the men in suits – quite another to feel estranged from the men he would have to climb with and to whom he would be entrusting his life.

On 17 March, the SS *Caledonia* arrived in Mumbai. It was a highly charged moment in Indian history. Just a week earlier, Mahatma Gandhi, the prominent politician and lawyer, had been arrested for sedition after supporters of his non-cooperation movement became embroiled in a demonstration in Uttar Pradesh that ended with the deaths of twenty-two policemen and at least three protesters. Though Gandhi was a lifelong and vocal advocate of non-violence and had not been present at the event, he was tried and convicted a day after the Everest team arrived and was sentenced to six years in prison.

No one on the British team was remotely sympathetic. When the expedition doctor, Tom Longstaff, heard the news of Gandhi's arrest, he wrote in his diary how it was 'greeted joyfully by everybody'. Though George Mallory could be called a proto-socialist and was certainly sympathetic to Irish independence, he does not seem to have felt the same towards India – his only reaction being to worry that rail services might be disrupted by the political instability. Fortunately they weren't, and a few days later the British climbers took the 'toy train' up the hill to Darjeeling, only to spot their leader, Charles Bruce, on his way down in an open-top car. He greeted them exuberantly and turned round straight away.

The general had been in India since late February, glad-handing officials, begging further assistance and getting ready for the approach march. As well as procuring pack animals and extra stores, his main task had been to personally choose about forty high-altitude porters who would accompany the expedition across Tibet and do the carrying on the mountain. With unemployment high there were plenty of candidates, and with his fluent Nepali and general bonhomie, Bruce quickly made friends in the local community. After decades commanding Gurkha troops, Bruce had a high regard for the peoples of Nepal. To a much greater extent than Howard-Bury, he recognized that the Sherpas and Bhotias would play a vital role on the expedition. Besides which, they were his kind of men: gambling, drinking, enjoying practical jokes and occasionally a fight – what wasn't there to like?

On the day before Mallory and the others arrived, Bruce had been the guest of honour at a pre-expedition send-off for the porters and the sahibs organized by Laden La, an important local official who was one of the very few Tibetans who had visited England. Bruce impressed everyone by making a speech in Hindi, and the local Buddhist and Hindu priests were there to hand out ceremonial scarves and garlands.

On the following evening, the British team held a rather more restrained dinner at the Mount Everest Hotel. Everyone was there apart from Edward Norton, who was in hospital in Kolkata with a sudden, but fortunately fleeting, flare-up of haemorrhoids – the 'riders' curse' – after taking part in the Kadir Cup, the most important pig-sticking event in the calendar. For the climbers from Britain, the dinner was an opportunity to meet their three transport officers: the Gurkhas Geoffrey Bruce and John Morris, and Alpine Club member Colin Crawford, who after a lot of pressure from Charles Bruce had been given leave to join the expedition by the Indian Civil Service.

Crawford was an experienced climber, but neither Morris nor Geoffrey Bruce had done any mountaineering at all. Like General Bruce himself, though, they had both done a lot of hard travelling as soldiers stationed in the frontier regions of the British Empire. Initially, as Morris noted in his dramatically titled memoir, *Hired to Kill,* the Alpine climbers were rather sniffy about the non-mountaineers, who they regarded as 'slightly superior servants', but within a few weeks they came to realize how much they depended on their linguistic skills and general ease around the Sherpas and Tibetans. General Bruce had also managed to prise Henry Morshead from the Survey of India, this time to act as a full-blown climber – further increasing his reserve of climbers and local language speakers.

Even though London was now thousands of miles away, there was a brief reminder of the previous year's controversies when a bundle of newspapers turned up at the hotel from the RGS. For some inexplicable reason, in among the more recent press there was a copy of the *Illustrated London News* from several months earlier, with the photospread showing George Finch climbing in the Alps. Whether this was another little bit of mischief instigated by Arthur Hinks, it's impossible to be certain, but it had that effect. When the article was read by the expedition's climbing leader, Edward Strutt – another arch-traditionalist who disliked publicity – he declared loudly, 'I always knew the fellow was a shit.'

Finch himself was much more concerned with the late arrival of the expedition's oxygen. The 120 cylinders had not travelled with them on the *Sardinia* but had been sent out on a cargo ship, the SS *Chilka*. Unfortunately it was running very late and was not due to dock at Kolkata until the end of the month. If the *Chilka* arrived that late, the cylinders might not reach them until 15 April. The thought of this threw Finch into an utter panic: he had been told to wait in Darjeeling with Colin Crawford until the oxygen arrived and then attempt to catch up with the main party. If it turned up two weeks late, he worried, he and Crawford would undoubtedly be delayed in Tibet and would struggle to find pack animals to carry everything.

As Finch wrote pessimistically in his diary on 21 March, 'we shall not see the Rongbuk glacier Base Camp before the 20th of May', leaving them with just a few weeks before the monsoon hit. To make things even worse, if he was separated from the main party, he would not be able to conduct any more oxygen drills until they reached Base Camp, and because they would be travelling without the expedition's toolkit he would not be able to do any work on the oxygen sets. The more he thought it through, the worse it seemed, but Finch had the magical ability to work himself up into a lather and then pull back. The odds against the oxygen party succeeding were growing, but ultimately events were out of his hands, so he resolved to stop worrying and not risk turning himself into a nuisance.

There was better news for everyone on 21 March when Norton turned up in Darjeeling, looking a little weak but much recovered from his brief spell in hospital. A day later Captain Noel arrived with his photographic equipment, and to Finch's great delight, a spare developing tank and extra chemicals. With departure set for the 26th, there was plenty for Bruce and his transport officers to do, leaving Strutt to come up with a plan for how to climb the mountain once they reached Base Camp.

Mallory was impressed by Bruce and thought he would lead a much happier party than Howard-Bury had the previous year. He hoped that the general would not be too rigid about planning, but worried that they had not hired quite enough porters for the high-altitude work. Though Strutt was the nominal climbing leader, it was already assumed that Mallory would lead the first attempt and that, because of the shipping delays, it would be made without supplementary oxygen. Not that this bothered Mallory at all – he remained unconvinced of its value and was very pleased to be able to lead the first attempt before Finch turned up with his 'heretical' oxygen equipment.

Leaving Finch and Crawford rattling around the Mount Everest Hotel, on 26 March the main party set off for Kalimpong, where they were due to meet the first of several trains of pack animals that would carry their equipment through Sikkim into Tibet. Though Arthur Hinks frequently complained about the cost of transporting all the oxygen sets and cylinders, John Noel's photographic equipment was equally bulky: three film cameras, two panoramic cameras, four glass-plate cameras, one stereoscopic camera, six small Kodak cameras, a portable darkroom, and all the necessary chemicals and gadgets to develop and print in the field.

Before they left, the British expedition even received an unexpected telegraphic blessing from an Italian priest, Abate Achille Ratti, better known as Pope Pius XI. He had recently been elected pontiff, but in his youth he had been an avid climber and had even published a book on his Alpine exploits, *Climbs on Alpine Peaks*. His cable to the Everest team arrived on the day of their departure: 'May God who lives in the heights bless this expedition.' Thus protected, staunch Roman Catholic John Noel recorded the first stage of the approach to Everest by setting his camera up on the roof of the train to take daring point-of-view shots as it snaked its way through the rainforest.

A few hours later, the train reached Kalimpong, a bustling trade centre which was a melting pot of different ethnic groups from all over the Himalayas and northern India. It was also home to several schools and the famous St Andrew's Colonial Homes – set up by the Scottish missionary J. A. Graham for the mixed-race orphans of the British Raj. General Bruce had agreed to deliver a speech to the children and to local Scout groups on behalf of Baden-Powell, the founder of the Scouting movement. Having done his duty, the next day Bruce split the Everest party into two in order to avoid overcrowding on the trail into Tibet, and set off with the first party for the Tibetan border.

The approach march first took them through the damp, sweaty rainforests of Sikkim. The trail was reasonably good and punctuated by Dak bungalows every ten or so miles, but it was hard work – and the higher they got, the colder it became. By day four, as Norton declared in his diary, it was 'three blanket weather'; General Bruce was very disappointed by the continual misty haze which hung over the valleys, denying the party a view of the high mountains that surrounded them.

All the sahibs had an expedition pony, but Charlie Bruce often preferred to dismount – in order, he said, to walk off his belly. The new members of the expedition were captivated by the dense, brightly coloured foliage, but as in the previous year Mallory found much of the approach tedious and the landscape disappointing until they started hitting the real mountain country. Though he admitted in a letter to Ruth that he occasionally felt the altitude, he was happy to sleep above 12,000 feet and keen to get to Everest as quickly as possible.

The first stage of the journey ended on 2 April when they crossed the Jelep La from Sikkim into Tibet. Old hands Mallory and Morshead had made the crossing before and were not particularly impressed, but for the others it was a thrilling moment – especially when the sky cleared to reveal Chomolhari, the 23,800-foot peak to the west that overlooked Phari. Though not wishing to spoil the party, Bruce was quick to point out that, though Chomolhari might have looked very high, their proposed advance base on the North Col was in fact only 600 feet lower than its summit, and that there was considerably more to go before the top of Everest.

Riding past the remains of a Chinese wall that had once attempted to keep outsiders at bay, they descended into the lush Chumbi valley. As in 1921, the expedition was greeted by David MacDonald, the British trade agent, but this time he'd also brought a long guard of honour: ninety splendidly dressed Punjabi soldiers who were there to protect, albeit symbolically, the British trade posts at Yatung and at Gyantse, Tibet's second-largest town. As fellow soldier John Morris later wrote, being stationed in Tibet was not considered a good posting, so the arrival of the British team was one of the few events to break up the monotony of garrison life.

The next two days were spent at Yatung with MacDonald, resting and repacking. Longstaff and Norton took the opportunity to begin amassing a large collection of birds and small animals for the Natural History Museum back in London. As per their agreement with the Tibetan government, they were not allowed to shoot any game, so they had packed catapults instead for bird hunting expeditions.

For Charlie Bruce it was his first real opportunity to catch up with his correspondence. Like Howard-Bury in 1921, he had committed to write fifteen expedition dispatches for *The Times*, but though very witty he was not quite as assiduous a correspondent. He was pleased to find a typewriter in the expedition stores and even more pleased when John Morris offered to act as his secretary, but writing dispatches was never high on his priority list – a problem that would grow as the expedition progressed, much to the annoyance of Arthur Hinks.

Bruce's dispatch from Yatung was characteristically cheerful and positive, though he warned readers that the clock was already ticking and that, once the expedition reached Base Camp on the Rongbuk glacier, they had a maximum of six weeks to get to the top of Everest before the monsoon hit. While Morris had his fingers poised, Bruce also dictated a letter to Hinks asking for another £1,000 for expedition funds. It was a lot of extra money considering that they had already spent more than the Reconnaissance, but Bruce was unabashed, arguing that as this was a much bigger expedition, costs were inevitably higher. He finished the letter in characteristically ebullient fashion: 'Please note that I am doing my best for this Expedition. I have interviewed the Viceroy, I have preached to Boy Scouts, and I have emptied the poes [latrines] in a Dak bungalow. This is the meaning of the term General. They are cheap at home, they are more expensive out here. Hurry up with that thousand please.'

On 5 April, Bruce's party left Yatung heading for Phari, the first major Tibetan town. En route, to everyone's surprise they crossed paths with one of four Tibetan students who had recently returned from Britain, after spending the previous two years being taught the art of surveying. The equally surprised young man told them that he was on his way to Kalimpong to buy the equipment and materials needed to build a new telegraph line between the capital city, Lhasa, and Gyantse. The unexpected encounter was another indication that Tibet was tentatively starting to open itself up to the outside world.

Two days later they reached Phari, very much an image of old Tibet and famous for its livestock breeding and its malodorous drains. Thomas Manning, the scholar and orientalist who in 1812 had been the first Briton to visit Lhasa, had stopped briefly at Phari and described it scathingly in his memoir: 'Dirt, dirt, grease, smoke, misery, but good mutton.' Charlie Bruce was not quite so critical and was more interested in drink than meat. It was 7 April, his fifty-sixth birthday, so to celebrate he ordered the cook to unpack a bottle of 120-year-old rum that he had been looking forward to for several weeks.

While Bruce and most of the team stayed at the bottom of the hill at the comfortable, British-built Dak bungalow, with its incongruous flagpole and Union Jack, Captain Noel was the first to venture upwards to the town proper, taking the opportunity to meet and photograph local people and explore what he saw as an 'amazingly interesting' town. Most of Phari's houses were built out of what he called 'Tibetan reinforced concrete': mud strengthened with assorted horns and animal skins. Outside most houses, there were huge piles of offal and mounds of yak dung, the only local source of fuel. Inside, Noel noticed that the walls were greasy and stained black with soot. The local children were equally rough and ready, but cheerful and ever-inquisitive about the new arrivals.

Howard Somervell paid a visit of a very different kind, as he was called in to minister to a rich lady who had broken her arm. Back home in London he was a surgeon at University College Hospital on Gower Street, but there were no hospitals or purpose-built operating theatres in Phari. Instead Somervell was taken to a rather wealthy-looking house where, surrounded by three priests who prayed throughout the procedure, he removed a poultice – which to his amazement was made of bear's bile – and then did his best with the traumatized arm. As a reward he was given two carpets and a fox fur, before being escorted back out to the road.

Though there was still no news of Finch and Crawford and the oxygen, General Bruce was determined to press on. After Phari they would swap their Tibetan mules for a rather slower and slightly motley selection of horses, cattle and 200 yaks. Like the camels of the Arabian peninsula, the yaks were the 'ships' of the Tibetan plateau, huge lumbering creatures that moved at around a mile an hour. They appeared virtually impervious to the cold and seemed to be able to find grass even in the most desolate-looking landscapes. Their handlers tied large bells around their necks and small ones around their tails.

As it left Phari on 8 April and moved onto the Tibetan plateau, the British expedition resembled a small army, with the sahibs and the Sherpas in front accompanied by dozens of assorted pack animals, followed by the larger but slower-moving party of yaks and their handlers, with the whole caravan sometimes spread out over a distance of up to five miles.

The plateau was a vast, seemingly empty expanse of parched land, over which the wind roared and screeched. Everything appeared frozen hard, and soon after midday a blizzard descended, making it even more difficult to follow the trail. George Mallory called the wind 'a taste of the diabolical'; John Noel was more poetic, comparing it to 'a thousand knife points that pierce all and any clothes you may wear'.

When they stopped, they were not quite the 'pukka' sahibs of old. Edward Norton had taken a tumble from his pony and been dragged fifty yards. The others had alternated brief spells in the saddle and longer periods of walking, which seemed to keep them marginally warmer but still left them cold and bedraggled. From Phari onwards, there was no firewood available at all and they had to cook with yak dung, which gave everything a distinctly unpleasant smell. That night, however, there was so much snow on the ground that initially it was impossible to find any dung. Morshead, who had been out in front, came in for a lot of abuse for not finding an earlier camping spot, prompting Bruce to announce that he would be in charge of route-finding the next day.

The snowstorm cleared up overnight but the next morning's march was, if anything, even harder. The temperature never got above zero and the wind was utterly merciless. In front of them lay three high passes, each over 17,000 feet. Charlie Bruce and Tom Longstaff rode ahead across what Longstaff called 'a weird desolation of red and yellow hills'. Far from finding a good camping ground early on, it took them a full twenty-five miles before they stopped at a suitable place. By the time everyone was in, it was past 10.00 p.m. – though three of their yak drivers did not arrive at all, forced to take shelter at the nearby Tatsang nunnery after getting lost in the darkness. 'Travelling in Tibet in the early spring', as Bruce would later write in a dispatch for *The Times*, 'is no picnic.'

For George Finch and Ferdie Crawford, who were now not-so-hot on the heels of Bruce and the others, the poor weather was not making things easier. The missing oxygen had arrived at

Kalimpong in early April and they had got under way immediately afterwards. Finch realized that the cylinders and oxygen sets were too fragile to be carried on yaks so they hired forty porters, but on their third march out he noticed an ominous rubbing sound coming from the packing cases. With the expedition toolkit many miles ahead of them with the main party, the only implements they had at hand were their penknives. Once the wooden crates were opened up, Finch saw straight away that the oxygen cylinders were rubbing against each other, hence the grinding sound. If they did nothing, the metal would be worn out by the time they reached Everest, with potentially very dangerous consequences to man and morale. Ever resourceful, Finch sent for a drum of rope and as much cloth as was available, and set about repacking the cylinders so that their metal exteriors did not touch.

On 8 April, on the same day that the main party endured their first really difficult march, Finch's party crossed the Jelep La into Tibet in the middle of a snowstorm – only, to their great surprise, to bump into a fellow Brit shortly afterwards, at Yatung. It was Sir Henry Hayden, a famous geologist from the Survey of India, accompanied by his long-serving Swiss guide, César Cosson. Hayden was on his way to see the Dalai Lama in Lhasa before setting off into the interior to begin a survey of Tibet's mineral wealth. It was another uncanny moment: 'Tibet the Mysterious' now seemed to be overrun by British scientists and mountaineers.

As Finch and his party raced along trying to catch up with the main expedition, it remained very cold and blustery, the wind scouring their faces with dust and sand. Finch was very pleased to see that his specially made duvet jacket and padded trousers were keeping him warm, but the tweed-clad Crawford and the porters were not so blessed and suffered in the cold.

Like Mallory, Finch found the seemingly endless Tibetan plateau rather dreary but he was impressed by the sunsets. Unlike Mallory, who at a low point in the 1921 Reconnaissance had described Tibet as a 'hateful country inhabited by hateful people', Finch warmed to the Tibetans he met along the trail, finding them hard-working and good-humoured. His most memorable encounter came on 12 April when, like the lost yak drivers from the main party three days earlier, Finch and Crawford were forced to seek shelter at the Tatsang nunnery.

Though it was good to get out of the wind, Tatsang was rather different to the Dak bungalows they had grown used to. Finch and Crawford were quartered in the main temple area, in a roofless room. One elderly nun set a yak-dung fire going to cook their supper while another laid out Finch's sleeping bag on top of an altar. When later that evening Finch wriggled inside, he noticed the decaying corpse of a goat hanging from the ceiling above, but he was so tired that rather than fret he fell asleep almost immediately.

A day later, Finch and Crawford caught up with Bruce and the others at Khamba Dzong, the large Tibetan fort where the principal trade route turned north towards Lhasa. The last stragglers from the main party were only just arriving themselves when Finch and Crawford came in 'showing evident signs of wear and tear', as Bruce put it in his expedition account. Finch was very relieved to hear that to celebrate their arrival, Bruce had decided to halt the convoy and take an extra rest day. He was made even happier when, after a short walk, he managed to bring down a pigeon with his catapult. 'Something for breakfast!' Finch wrote gleefully in his diary.

For General Bruce, there were dignitaries to meet and presents to hand over while the rest of the team completed their expedition chores and wrote letters home. Henry Morshead's personal servant,

Munir Khan, cropped his sahib's hair with some portable clippers, but few others decided to avail themselves of his services. As in the previous year, the sahibs who had not visited Tibet before were shocked by how pungent the towns and their inhabitants were – the product of what they snobbishly considered to be low standards of hygiene. John Morris, the team's transport officer who had spent a lot of time soldiering in the barren wastes of the North-West Frontier, was not so critical. With no firewood available, the only way to get hot water was to boil a pot over a yak-dung fire, so for Morris it wasn't surprising that local people were reluctant to waste precious fuel on unnecessary social niceties. For their part, the inquisitive Tibetans laughed at the strange habits of the invading sahibs and were particularly amused to see them washing and shaving.

Like Howard-Bury, Morris was a committed Tibetophile who had read widely and attempted to learn the language. He even managed to find a way to cope with yak-butter tea, the local delicacy that so many outsiders found revolting. It was made from brick tea which had been mixed in a churn with salt and yak butter – frequently of the rancid variety – and was served boiling hot, often with a buttery scum on top and crowned with yak hair. One tactic for a reluctant guest was to knock a cup back in a single gulp, but the problem was that hosts then immediately filled it back up. The solution, Morris realized, was to think of it as a bowl of soup, not a cup of tea, making its savoury strangeness a little more palatable.

Khamba Dzong, as well as being an important Tibetan town, was the final resting place of Alexander Kellas, the Scottish scientist who had died a year earlier on the Reconnaissance. Longstaff visited his grave and reported back that it looked well tended, with inscriptions in English and Tibetan still visible. It was also the first spot where there was a really good view of Everest. Longstaff was impressed, describing it as having the 'brutal mass of the all-in wrestler'. Mallory, however, had seen it all before and was frequently bored with the journey – and the sights and smells of Tibet.

As in 1921 he was not really interested in encountering Tibetan culture or appreciating the harsh beauty of the landscape. All that really excited him was the prospect of climbing. On 20 April, with Everest still over a week away, he persuaded Bruce to allow him to break the monotony of the journey by making an attempt on Sangkar Ri, a rock peak just over 20,000 feet high, close to the next major town, Shekar Dzong. Howard Somervell would be his partner, with Finch and Arthur Wakefield making up a second pair. Even though Wakefield violently disagreed with Finch over oxygen, he was happy to climb with him.

The four sahibs set off in late afternoon with six porters to carry their tents and cooking equipment, aiming to set up camp and make a rapid climb the following morning. Mallory and Finch were keen to show off. They argued about the best way to approach the peak and then raced each other to get to the spot where they were going to set up their tents. After another bitterly cold night, the sahibs set off at dawn the following day, only to find their way seriously blocked by a vast moraine. By the time they got onto the peak itself, it was 9.00 a.m. Finch started to feel ill and vomited. Eventually he was forced to turn back with Wakefield, leaving the others to carry on.

Mallory felt on top form, but having lost Finch and Wakefield, he was soon worrying that his own partner did not look so good either. Here he underestimated Somervell: with characteristic

stamina and good cheer, Somervell insisted on carrying on and
soon the two men found themselves engaged in difficult climbing
on exposed rock. In order to reach the summit they would have
to overcome a tall spike blocking the ridge, called a 'gendarme',
but thirty feet up, they found themselves on a dangerously smooth
slab of rock. In North Wales or the Alps it would have been an
exciting challenge, but at 20,000 feet in the Himalayas, for two
men on their first day climbing at altitude and carrying limited
amounts of rope, tackling the slab would not have been a prudent
move. Instead they traversed out onto the west side, only to find
the shaded rock so cold that it felt sticky and blistered their fingers.

Then, after regaining the main face of the gendarme some
way above, they arrived at a tricky overhang, which required
all their strength to overcome. With 500 feet more of the ridge
to go before the summit, Mallory realized that it was time for
discretion to become the better part of valour. Even if he and
Somervell could have made the first ascent of Sangkar Ri, they
had promised Charlie Bruce not to spend more than a night away
from the main party, so reluctantly they turned back.

Catching up with the others was not so easy. Two ponies had
been left for them, but the next camp had been set up ten miles
away on the other side of the notorious quicksands at Shiling,
which were reputedly very dangerous. Mallory could just about
remember a safe route from the previous year, but by the time they
reached the last river, it was so dark that he found it impossible to
pick out the fording point. It was an awkward situation until he
spotted a light on the other side, gradually coming closer. Mallory
assumed it must be one of the nomadic yak herders who lived
on the plateau, and was very glad when someone shouted from
the other side and then waded across the river with an offer to

carry everyone back over. Cold and tired, it was not a moment to be bashful, and to further add to Mallory's good luck, once the man had carried them to the other side it emerged that he was actually one of the expedition's camp followers, and was able to guide them all safely back to the mess tent where supper was prepared and waiting.

They hadn't reached the top of Sangkar Ri, but Mallory was pleased with his performance and Somervell's staying power. Even though he had suffered from a severe headache towards the end of the climb, Mallory hadn't expected to do so well on his first outing. Longstaff was less charitable, writing acidly in his diary: 'Mallory and Somervell decided to go for a peak and Bruce consented hoping the experience would teach them "scale". It did and they returned peak-less and wiser.'

The next morning, a few miles down the trail, the whole team was gifted with its first really good view of Everest. The mountain was still about fifty miles away and shrouded in snow, but in the clear air it looked much closer. John Noel unpacked his movie camera and filmed Everest's reflection shimmering in the frigid waters of the Yaru river, which flowed through the valley below. Edward Norton was equally captivated, immediately taking out his sketchpad, but George Finch was slightly underwhelmed. 'A great and stirring sight,' he wrote rather formally in his diary, 'which renewed the enthusiasm of all, perhaps a little dulled by our lengthy trek.'

Before they could get close to Everest's slopes, there was one more major stop: Shekar Dzong, home of the famous Shining Crystal monastery, a long string of brilliant white buildings rising up a steep slope, set against red-brown hills. Shekar was the religious centre where, eleven months earlier, Howard-Bury had photographed the elderly lama known as a living Buddha to his monks. Tom Longstaff called it 'the most picturesque town I've seen in Tibet' and John Noel was even more enraptured by Shekar's architecture: 'They are Dream Towers of the air, and at times, caught in the light of dawn or of sunset, are unbelievably beautiful.'

Bruce was very aware that they needed to move on, but he also knew how important it was to pay his respects to local officials. Cooperation with dzongpens was vital if they were to get resupplied with food and the pack animals necessary for the final stage of their trek to Base Camp. The previous year Howard-Bury had presented officials with pocket torches, but Bruce's gift of choice was a Homburg hat. Knowing how popular these were with Tibetan officials, he had stocked up on twenty-four Homburgs at Whiteway and Laidlaw outfitters in Darjeeling. As he expected, they were very gladly received.

Bruce had also been given several albums of photographs taken by Howard-Bury during the Reconnaissance. The most lavish of these was intended for the Dalai Lama and had its own silk bag, sewed specially by Sir Francis Younghusband's daughter. The governor of Shekar Dzong was not in quite the same league, but as Bruce knew, the Rongbuk valley where they intended to set up Base Camp lay within his jurisdiction. In the autumn of 1921, it was he who had complained to Lhasa that the British had underpaid for pack animals and that Heron, the expedition geologist, had carried out unauthorized digging. In order to bring him firmly on side, Bruce presented the governor and his wife with a roll of much-prized brocade, along with photographs of the Dalai Lama and the Tashi Lama, the second-most important religious figure in Tibet. The goodwill offensive worked: not only did the governor provide them with all the transport animals they needed, but he also attached his agent, Chongay La, to the expedition, instructing him to assist them in whatever way he could.

After three days of unpacking and repacking, Bruce set off with fresh yaks and a new set of drivers and camp followers. Howard-Bury had made a further stop at the town of Tingri, where he had set up his first Base Camp, but Bruce took a different route and headed straight for the Rongbuk valley. As they crossed the Pang La, the last high pass on their route, they had another striking view of Everest's huge North Face, now apparently stripped of snow by a recent storm. It looked so different from the last time they had seen it properly that, to the bemusement of Edward Norton, a huge argument arose as to whether it was Everest at all. The row was only settled when the clouds lifted from the skies behind it, revealing with certainty that there was nothing else taller. It was a slightly absurd moment – but after all, they were the first mountaineering team to pass this way. They had no photographs to reference and no GPS to check; the 1922 team were pioneers – the first Westerners to cross this pass, the first European mountaineers with Everest firmly in their sights.

But why had they come so far just to climb a mountain?

This was the question posed to General Bruce by the Rongbuk Lama, Dzatrul Rinpoche, three days later at the Ronbuk monastery. He was regarded as one of the holiest men in Tibet, the incarnation of Guru Rinpoche, the legendary Indian mystic who had introduced Buddhism to Tibet. Ten months earlier, when Mallory and Bullock had visited the monastery for the first time, he'd been in the midst of a year of seclusion, but when General Bruce arrived on 30 April 1922, the lama graciously offered the British team an audience.

It was a strange encounter. After several days travelling through the austere, primal landscape of southern Tibet, where everything that was not covered in snow or ice tended towards drab brown, the interior of the monastery looked dark and mysterious with a slightly unfinished air. Yak-butter lamps illuminated religious paintings on brightly coloured silks, and inscriptions disappeared into the shadows.

The porters and the team's main interpreter, Karma Paul, were clearly overawed by the head lama, and everyone on the British team recognized that there was something special about this man with a huge head and serenely benevolent expression who seemed to command so much respect. What, though, did he make of their mission? There are two different accounts of the encounter: one published in General Bruce's expedition book, the other in the Rongbuk Lama's spiritual biography.

According to Bruce, after exchanging pleasantries, the lama asked directly: 'What is the good of an exploration of Everest? What can you get out of it?' to which Bruce replied that the team regarded 'the whole Expedition, and especially our attempt to reach the summit of Everest, as a pilgrimage'. George Finch expanded on this in his own Everest account, remembering how Bruce told the head lama that because it was the highest point on earth, the summit of Everest was also the closest point to heaven, so it was only natural that they would try to get there at least once during their lives. These explanations apparently satisfied the lama, and he offered his guests rice and glasses of yak-butter tea, a drink detested by Bruce. Once again, the old general rose to the occasion, this time wryly telling the Rongbuk Lama that he had sworn never to touch butter until he reached the summit, at which point he was offered tea with sugar and milk.

Dzatrul Rinpoche remembered it rather differently. According to his namthar, when asked why they had come, Bruce replied: 'This mountain is the highest in the world. If we can ascend it and reach the summit, then the British government will give us big pay and a title.' Quite why there is such a discrepancy, it's difficult to know, but it's possible that Karma Paul translated each man's replies more liberally than they had hoped. Either way, the British team left the monastery with the Rongbuk Lama's blessing, beginning a tradition that would be kept by many expeditions to come.

Initially, Bruce had not planned to spend a night close to the monastery and had sent the cooks further ahead down the valley to pitch the mess tent, but seeing that the weather had deteriorated again, he recalled his staff and told them to set up camp nearby. The next morning they moved off, aiming to reach the junction of the main Rongbuk glacier and its eastern spur: their highway to Everest.

It was wishful thinking. When they reached a point close to the snout of the main glacier, the yak men stopped and began unloading their animals, demanding their fees. Bruce wanted them to carry on, following the path between the glacier and the lateral moraine that Mallory and Bullock had found during the Reconnaissance, but they refused – and no amount of threats or bribes could persuade them to go any further. There was absolutely no grazing further on, and the yak herders were worried for the safety of their animals. As Bruce wrote ruefully, 'There was promptly a strike among the local transport workers, but the employers of labour were wise enough to give in to their demands.'

After several noisy hours, the yak men were paid off and given their baksheesh. Then at 4.00 p.m. the sahibs sat down for 'five o'clock tea', and watched the yaks and their handlers disappear into the distance. Later on they would toast Bruce with vintage Champagne to congratulate him for getting everyone there in one piece. It was 1 May and, by Bruce's reckoning, they had five or perhaps six weeks to reach the summit before the monsoon arrived to blow away all their hopes and desires. The real work was only just beginning.

The head lama, Dzatrul Rinpoche, of the Rongbuk monastery, April 1922

6

News from the North

Arthur Hinks hated publicity. He advised Charles Bruce to get rid of his telephone when he complained that reporters were pestering him in the evening. 'The telephone is a great mistake,' he wrote, 'and you will do well to be rid of it. I would not have one in my house for anything.' When in May 1921 a newspaper editor had the temerity to ask for biographical information on Howard-Bury and the others, Hinks initially refused to send anything, explaining that the Everest Committee had been 'rather anxious to avoid these personalities and I am sure the members of the expedition would rather preserve their freedom from publicity which they have up to the present happily achieved'.

Hinks's position, though, was untenable. As he grudgingly came to realize, without publicity there would be no Everest. Donations could cover part of the expenses but without significant newspaper sponsorship, lectures and books, it was impossible to fund a major expedition. The only way to feel good about it was to avoid the common press and stick with a 'newspaper of record' like *The Times*, which could be relied upon to provide dignified, unsensational reporting. It still came at a price. Like the *Illustrated London News*, which had bought the photographic rights, and the Philadelphia *Public Ledger*, which had bought the US rights, *The Times* needed feeding with regular dispatches and photographs, and that meant the expedition leaders had to keep the words flowing. Howard-Bury had done a good job in 1921, but Hinks was not so confident about Charles Bruce.

He was right, of course. When Bruce and his team pitched their tents on the Rongbuk glacier on 1 May 1922, delivering a full set of dispatches was not at the top of the expedition leader's priority list – and even if it had been, communications were never going to be easy. After the invasion of 1903, the British had set up three outposts of the Indian mail service inside Tibet, but once the Everest expedition was in the field everything depended on runners provided by the dzongpens, who carried letters and dispatches to the outside world. The most important and pressing messages were transmitted by telegraph from the nearest station at Phari; the rest went into the regular post.

The 1922 expedition had come equipped with official letter-headed paper and a Remington typewriter, but these trappings of modernity didn't get letters and cables home any more quickly. There was invariably a lag between something being written and it arriving at Fleet Street or the RGS, and the further the team got from Phari, the bigger that gap became. By the beginning of May, Bruce's most recent dispatch had been typed out by John Morris on 12 April, just a few weeks into their trek across Tibet. It was published in London on 24 April, but after that there would be no further dispatches until 9 June, a break of almost seven weeks.

Charlie Bruce's main concern was logistics. If they were ever going to succeed, he would have to ensure that a mass of supplies got all the way up to an advance base at the head of the Rongbuk glacier. He had not envisioned setting up Base Camp so low down the Rongbuk valley or having to build an extra camp at the junction between the East Rongbuk and the main glacier. In addition to the forty-three Sherpas and Bhotias recruited in Darjeeling, another dozen or so had attached themselves to the team, but Bruce had always intended to reserve most of the Sherpas for high-altitude duty later in the expedition, not to exhaust them early on with extra carries.

To add to the uncertainty, although back in 1921 Oliver Wheeler had gone part way up the East Rongbuk glacier, he had stopped early, so no one knew quite how difficult it would be to ascend. It was unlikely that any heavily laden porter would be able to get all the way up in a single day, so Bruce plotted an extra camp somewhere in the middle and then a large camp at the foot of the North Col. After that they would set up the advance camp on the col itself, and if all went well pitch one further light camp on the North Ridge before making their final dash for the summit.

Quite how they would get all the necessary gear up the col, Bruce had not quite figured out, but first things first, on 2 May, he sent out Finch, Strutt and Norton to find the best site for Camp 1. The others stayed back to organize Base Camp and make everything as comfortable as possible for what would undoubtedly be at least a month-long stay.

Base Camp was located on a broad strip of ground at around 16,500 feet – twelve horizontal miles and 12,500 feet below the summit of Everest. It was very close to Mallory and Bullock's much smaller camp in 1921, but whereas Mallory remembered a grassy meadow next to a clear spring, in early May the ground was still frozen hard and apart from a few miserable tufts there was little grass to be seen. For fresh water, there was the nearby Rongbuk Chu, a small stream flowing from the glacier that would grow into a roaring torrent as the weeks wore on and the temperature rose.

Much camp life centred around the cook tent and a large mess tent where they ate their meals. They had brought folding chairs and a large collapsible table, but as Mallory wrote in disgust, its top soon became filthy with spilled cocoa and soup. Before long, the table had been largely abandoned, with most of the climbers preferring to sit on a tarpaulin, using the numerous wooden packing cases as ad hoc tables. The Sherpas, needless to say, ate separately from the sahibs, subsisting primarily on a diet of a coarse barley called tsampa, supplemented with dried or occasionally fresh mutton.

Around the main mess were the smaller tents where everyone slept. Most of them were classic A-frame Whymper tents, designed by the great Victorian mountaineer. They were built to hold four men, sleeping on a six-foot-square groundsheet in reasonable comfort. At the higher camps they would use smaller Meade and Mummery tents, again based on designs by famous climbers of the past. In the 1950s, portable air mattresses became standard-issue on Himalayan expeditions, but the pioneers of the 1920s made do with a bed of Hudson's Bay Company blankets on top of their groundsheets, whenever they were available.

Though they were many miles away from the nearest town, in one of the most inaccessible countries in the world, Base Camp was not quite as isolated as you might think. Local Tibetans came and went, selling dried yak dung and occasionally offering to work for a few days as expedition porters. There was a limited amount of local fresh food for sale, but at one point a Chinese merchant arrived with a vast consignment of Favourite Horse cigarettes, which he sold at two rupees for a thousand. John Noel bought dozens of boxes for his camera porters, after they got through the first batch of 20,000 cigarettes that he had brought for them from India.

Noel had his own dedicated darkroom tent, to develop his film and photographs, and Finch too was able to process and print his photographs. As if that weren't enough, both Norton and Somervell had brought sketchpads and art equipment and were soon producing numerous drawings and watercolours of Everest and the area around Base Camp. Though they weren't expected to bring back as many specimens as the Reconnaissance team, Tom Longstaff and Edward Norton took their roles as expedition naturalists very seriously, and used their time at Base Camp to collect specimens and to skin and preserve what they had gathered en route.

The main focus of Bruce's attention was Everest and its ever-changing weather. From the very beginning the expedition was a race against time, or to be more precise against the arrival of the monsoon. No one knew quite when it would hit, but they had at most six weeks to get to the top, provided bad weather didn't interrupt their supply build-up.

In the late afternoon of 2 May, Strutt and his party returned, having chosen the site of the first camp at around 18,000 feet near the snout of the eastern spur. They had pressed on for several miles up the East Rongbuk glacier, but though they had not found a site for Camp 2, they were able to report that conditions on the first part of the route were not too bad.

For the next three days, everyone stayed at Base Camp while Bruce planned and organized the stores and equipment that would have to go up the mountain. Finch checked out the Primus stoves that would be used for cooking in the higher camps and then lectured the team and the Sherpas on how to get the best out of them. George Mallory, who was notoriously untechnical, baulked at Finch's lectures – whether on oxygen or cooking equipment – and was so uninterested that he persuaded Howard Somervell to go on another training climb to a nearby 21,000-foot peak on the other side of the valley. It was not a great move: they got to the top, but in doing so Mallory gashed his hand and inadvertently caused a boulder to drop on his boot, injuring one of his big toes.

George Finch meanwhile gave John Noel a different kind of shock, when Noel complained that his photographic tent was very airless. Why not try some Oxylithe, Finch suggested, handing him one of the tins that had been sent out along with their oxygen cylinders. Oxylithe was the trade name for a compound, made from powdered sodium peroxide, that had been used in early breathing sets for miners and firemen. When it came in contact with water or moisture, the sodium peroxide liberated oxygen, but as Noel discovered, Oxylithe had to be handled carefully. Ten minutes after he had opened a tin, there was a loud bang and a bright flash, and Noel ran out pursued by a cloud of noxious caustic soda.

On the following morning, 5 May, the second stage of the campaign began with Norton setting out, this time accompanied by Strutt, Longstaff and Morshead, supported by sixteen porters and enough food for several days. Their aim was to find sites for the next two camps before the advance base on the North Col. Strutt was considered an expert in travel over glaciers, but like Mallory and Bullock a year earlier, nothing that he had seen in the Alps could prepare him for the huge rivers of ice that flowed out of Everest, and the vast heaps of rocky moraine that accumulated either side of the main flow.

Tom Longstaff, the third sahib on the team, was an elder statesman of the British climbing world. Short, with a bushy beard and an impish smile, he had already climbed all over the Himalayas and the Arctic, and was famous for his ascent of the 23,360-foot Trisul in 1907, the highest summit reached at that point. In 1921, Longstaff had been present at the first meeting of the Everest Committee and had later offered to accompany the expedition, but by then Sandy Wollaston had been chosen as expedition doctor, so Longstaff had gone on an expedition to Spitsbergen with a student team from Oxford.

Though nominally the expedition doctor for 1922, Longstaff wasn't exactly keen on medicine. He had graduated from St Thomas' Hospital in London in 1903, but he had never actually worked as a GP or in a hospital, instead spending his time travelling and climbing. In his account of the 1922 expedition, John Morris remembered how, before they started, Longstaff issued a stark, if tongue-in-cheek, warning: 'I want to make one thing clear... I am, as a matter of fact, a qualified doctor, but I feel it my duty now to remind you that I have never practised in my life. I beg you in no circumstances to seek my professional advice, since it would almost certainly turn out to be wrong. I am however willing, if necessary, to sign a certificate of death.' On the approach march across the Tibetan plateau, Longstaff had fallen ill with dysentery, requiring Arthur Wakefield, the expedition's other – and rather more experienced – doctor to take over on occasion. Aged forty-seven, Longstaff wasn't expected to go really high, but he willingly signed up for the reconnaissance of the East Ronbuk glacier. It was a decision he would come to regret.

Just a few days after their first foray up the Rongbuk, slightly warmer temperatures had already caused the topography to change. The stream that flowed down from the East Rongbuk glacier was no longer frozen, making it much more awkward to cross. Eventually they reached the site for Camp 1, and left the porters there to build a stone shelter. While Strutt and Longstaff rested, Norton and Morshead carried on, looking for a location for their next camp. They didn't find anything suitable and would not occupy their next site, Camp 2, until 7 May.

By then, Longstaff was starting to feel ill, felled by the influenza that would later infect several of the Sherpas. While the others pressed on to find the third and final campsite, he stayed behind at Camp 2, languishing in his tent. The others found the going increasingly hard, their progress blocked by another huge glacier which joined the East Rongbuk from the south-west. At the 'crush zone' where the two bodies of ice collided, the surface was riven with crevasses and bizarre clusters of icy towers, or seracs, which looked like giant flakes of blue ice breaking through the surface.

As they climbed higher and higher, they were afflicted with the same glacier lassitude that Mallory had reported on the 1921 Reconnaissance expedition: a sudden drop in energy and the weird feeling that, as Norton noted in his diary, 'one hadn't a bone in one's body'. In the end, the combination of hot sun and bright white glacier was so debilitating that they decided to turn back and spend another night at Camp 2 at 19,000 feet.

The next morning they made swifter progress, and within a few hours were in sight of the lower reaches of the North Col. At first there was no obvious place for their final camp, but eventually they spotted a flattish-looking shelf underneath some cliffs leading up to Changtse, the satellite peak connected to Everest by the North

Col. They were at 21,000 feet – 2,000 feet below the crest of the col. Standing in the midday sun it seemed like the ideal spot for an important camp – a suntrap that would be sheltered from the wind – so without more ado, they deposited three lightweight tents and a sack of sleeping bags and turned around, reaching their second camp in two hours, half the time it had taken on the upward journey.

It was too late to go all the way down, so they spent another chilly night at Camp 2, leaving the following morning in glorious weather. Longstaff insisted on accompanying them, but when they reached Camp 1 he was too weak to continue, so he spent an extra night there – supervised by the travel officer John Morris, who had just come up from Base Camp with a group of porters and a large consignment of supplies. Morris was so alarmed by what he saw that he sent for a stretcher from Base Camp to help Longstaff descend the following day. It was a humiliating moment for the veteran climber, but he would not have made it down under his own steam. In a letter home, Henry Morshead labelled Longstaff 'another Kellas case' and, seeing him so badly laid up, promised his wife that he would give up climbing when he reached forty. Mallory was a little more sympathetic, writing to Ruth that Longstaff was 'a great heart in a frail body'.

Back at Base Camp, Bruce was getting ready to move on to the next phase of his plan. Now that the three supply camps had been located and established, he would send up relays of porters carrying all the supplies and equipment necessary to reach the North Col and pioneer a route up the North Ridge. The problem was manpower.

After the yak drivers had refused to go all the way up to the East Rongbuk glacier, Bruce had tried to hire Tibetans from the local villages to do the carrying. He wanted them to hump the supplies as far as Camp 2, leaving the better-equipped Darjeeling Sherpas to cover the more difficult ground between Camp 2 and Camp 3. Bruce had hoped to recruit ninety casual porters but was only able to get forty-five men and women, and even then they only signed on after he had offered them a considerable 'war bonus'. His newly hired hands worked hard for the first two days, but then to Bruce's dismay and frustration, most of them disappeared on the third, telling him that they needed to go home to replenish their stocks of food. Very few returned. It was ploughing season, and there was plenty of work to do on their farms. Over the next month there would be a steady but unpredictable flow of local labour, making planning very difficult.

Bruce's porter problems had a significant impact on the climbing: the logistical challenge of getting the heavy cylinders and oxygen apparatus up the Rongbuk glacier meant that the first attempt would have to be made without supplementary oxygen, by a two-man team. Mallory and Somervell were chosen as the spearhead, leaving Finch to make the second – oxygen-powered – attempt with Norton. Mallory had hoped to lead a larger party, but as ever he was keen to get going and pleased to be chosen for the first attempt.

The big news, however, was that for the first time since they'd stopped at Khamba Dzong over a month earlier, a mail runner had reached Base Camp. Several packages had been damaged after being dropped in a river, but this did not dampen anyone's excitement. George Mallory was overjoyed to receive dozens of letters from his friends and family, and immediately wrote back to his wife to tell her how much he missed her. Edward Norton was equally thrilled with his letters from home, though saddened to read that one of his uncles had just died and that his father had suffered a seizure. George Finch received two letters from his new wife, Bubbles, but there was one less-welcome item in the postbag that he hadn't anticipated: an article from the *Geographical Journal*, written by his old tormentor Arthur Hinks.

Though the Everest team was thousands of miles away from the RGS on Kensington Gore, Hinks couldn't help interfering, especially if he could do something that would irritate Finch and Farrar. When earlier that spring Hinks had heard that the engineer Percy Unna had written an article for the *Alpine Journal* on the development of the team's oxygen sets, Hinks had decided to use the May 1922 edition of the *Geographical Journal* to counter what he saw as the oxygen faction's propaganda. Unna's piece was actually a rather dry, scientific tract which implicitly made the case for using supplementary oxygen but was not in any sense strident. Hinks's riposte was much more of a polemic, in which he questioned the sporting legitimacy of supplementary oxygen, and mocked the complexity of the equipment and the admittedly tortuous scheme that Unna had come up with for laying a series of oxygen caches up Everest before the final summit dash. The Committee had not been unanimously in favour of oxygen, Hinks wrote, but had done everything they could to help the team, some of whose members 'had convinced themselves, or had been convinced that they would never reach the summit without it'.

Before publication, Hinks had sent the article to the Alpine Club asking for any comments. Farrar had come back immediately, complaining about Hinks's satirical tone and some of the financial estimates he had quoted, but Hinks refused to give any ground. 'If some of the party do not go to 25,000 feet to 26,000 feet without oxygen they will be rotters,' Hinks wrote to Farrar, knowing that he would disagree.

Quite why Hinks, a Cambridge-educated scientist, decided to take such a strong position is not absolutely clear. He was neither a climber himself nor a sportsman of any kind, yet here he was, stridently objecting to the use of oxygen – and not for pragmatic reasons but on the grounds of 'sporting ethics'. The answer is probably more personal than he would ever have admitted. For all his serious airs, Hinks was a gossip, and someone who always wanted things to go his way. He could be kind and supportive to the people he liked and approved of, but could be equally unpleasant to anyone who had the temerity to disagree with him.

Even if Hinks had been genuine in his opposition to oxygen, his behaviour was extraordinarily destructive – not only had he published the article but he had sent a copy to Base Camp. In the official memo that the Everest Committee had given to Bruce, it had stated quite explicitly that the expedition was to make a determined effort to reach the summit 'with every available resource', but in the final paragraph of Hinks's article, he effectively set a different goal: instead of making an all-out attack, their new mission was 'to discover how high a man can climb without oxygen'. This, he argued, was more important than getting 'to a specified point, even the highest summit of the world, in conditions so artificial that they can never become "legitimate" mountaineering'.

As Finch had already discovered, there were plenty of members of the team who were sceptical about oxygen. Hinks's article only reawakened the arguments, and confirmed their doubts at the very moment when the team should have been pulling together to make a concerted attempt on the mountain. As Finch later wrote: 'The author of the aforementioned article, campaigning against the use of supplementary oxygen… had shaken our group's belief in its mission… I remained the only one firmly believing in the power and indispensability of oxygen.'

Hinks's intervention was not Finch's only problem, however. Though the expedition as a whole had so far been much healthier than the 1921 Reconnaissance, Finch had by this time joined Longstaff on the sick list, confined to his sleeping bag on Wakefield's orders because of a bad stomach. Though he rallied briefly after a few days, Finch spent about a week in his tent, so ill that he could barely make a diary entry.

While he was stuck at Base Camp, Mallory and Somervell left on 10 May with a detachment of porters and spent the night at the stone shelter at Camp 1. Presumably in honour of its frigid temperature and draughty interior, one unknown wit had christened it 'Villa Never Sweat' and hand-painted a sign on the outside. In spite of the cold, Mallory was glad to be able to sleep for once in a solid shelter, having spent all of the previous month in a tent. A large cache of supplies had already begun to accumulate around Camp 1, allowing Mallory and Somervell to choose the gear and the foodstuffs they would take higher up the glacier.

On the following day, they hiked up to Camp 2 and then, leaving their porters at the tents, climbed up to a point from which they could see the Lhakpa La –Windy Gap – though Everest itself was obscured from their view by Changtse. The next morning, following a line of cairns built by Strutt's party a few days earlier, they set off to ascend the upper part of the East Rongbuk glacier to Camp 3. The ice was much smoother and harder than lower down, causing the porters to slip and slide. Though they had proper boots, the nails were already worn and they hadn't yet been issued with crampons.

Camp 3 was not quite Shangri-La, nor even the windless spot that Mallory had been promised. When Strutt and Norton had first reached it, the sun had been shining and the wind becalmed, but arriving in the early afternoon it soon became obvious to Mallory and Somervell that by 3.30 p.m. the camp would be in shadow, causing the temperature to plummet. Strutt's party had left tents and sleeping bags, but before any of them could be pitched, first they had to clear the sharpest stones and try to create level platforms on which to sleep. Once the work was done, Mallory sent most of their porters back to Base Camp – to their evident relief – holding on to a cook and their two 'personal' Sherpas.

While Mallory tucked himself into his sleeping bag to keep warm, the indefatigable Howard Somervell took his sketchbook and crossed the glacier, aiming for a high point from which he hoped nearby Makalu would be visible. His keenness was misplaced; Somervell came back with the beginnings of a sketch, a roaring headache and little appetite for supper. Both Mallory and Somervell needed to take a rest day, but knowing that time was of the essence, they agreed that the next morning they would climb the North Col to find a site for Camp 4.

They were awake early, but one of their porters was ill, so taking just one Sherpa, Dasno, to carry a small tent, they shuffled out of camp towards the steep slope that led up to the col. Their challenge was not just to reach it, but to find a safe route that could be used multiple times by porters. Mallory was able to pick out the line that he had followed the previous September, but whereas then it had been covered in snow, this time round the surface was bare, revealing hard blue ice below. It looked difficult to ascend without cutting a lot of steps and would always be dangerous, so Mallory led them up a new line which, though more complicated, appeared safer. On the most exposed parts, they stopped to fix ropes and hammer in wooden ice-anchors, but for the most part it was easy-enough going.

Eventually they reached the icy shelf just below the crest of the North Col, where they planned to set up camp. Though they didn't admit it at the time, both Mallory and Somervell had found the ascent harder than they had expected, but before turning back, Mallory wanted to go a little further – if possible, onto the North Ridge itself.

He remembered a crevasse higher up from his visit with Guy Bullock at the end of the Reconnaissance the previous year, but as he soon discovered, in the intervening months it had grown enormously and was too wide to safely jump over. Eventually they found a snow bridge, but on the other side there was a very tricky-looking wall of ice that would need to be fixed with a rope ladder, if it was going to be used regularly. For a brief moment Mallory worried that it might be too difficult an obstacle to conquer. As he later wrote in his expedition account: 'It seemed rather a long way to have come from England to Mount Everest, to be stopped by an obstacle like this.' Fortunately, his anxiety was unfounded. After retracing their steps, they discovered a way to avoid the large crevasse entirely and soon found themselves standing right on the crest of the North Col.

It was a terrific moment – 'the most amazing spectacle I have ever seen', as Mallory later wrote to Ruth. Whereas in September 1921, the wind had been so ferocious that they had spent most of their time bent double, for a few minutes it was calm enough to survey all the peaks and ridges around them. Below, they could see the head of the main Rongbuk glacier, and then, stretching away into the distance, Everest's huge West Ridge, and going further, the summit of Pumori – 'Young Girl Mountain' in Sherpa – the elegant 23,000-foot mountain that Mallory had wanted to name after his daughter Clare.

Just before the wind picked up, they were able to walk to the edge of the cliff and look down upon the Sherpa Dasno, who was resting on the shelf below them. It was 4.00 p.m. Mallory had developed a vicious headache that would last well into the evening, so without more ado, they returned to Dasno, unpacked the tent he had carried up, and cached it on the shelf as a symbol of their future intentions. Then they descended to Camp 3, where soup and aspirin awaited.

Down at Base Camp, the logistical battle continued. In 1922 there were no sat-phones or portable radios. Bruce had no idea how well or otherwise Mallory and Somervell were doing, but he knew that in order for them or anyone else to get high on the mountain, a considerable amount of food and equipment would have to be carried up to Camp 3. Whenever local farmers appeared offering their services, he would get them to join the parties shuttling between Base Camp and Camps 1 and 2, after which the Darjeeling porters would take over. At one stage, to Bruce's amazement, some Sherpa families arrived who had come all the way from the Solukhumbu region, having trekked over the Lho La without sleeping bags or any shelter, but the numbers of workers were unpredictable and inconsistent, and the clock was counting down.

Bruce's other worry was Finch. He had not quite warmed to him, but he respected him as a climber and recognized that he was a key member of the team – and the only one who really knew how to operate the oxygen sets. Right now, though, Finch remained confined to his tent with what looked like a bad case of dysentery. Oxygen drills had stopped and the equipment had not been checked. With the monsoon expected within weeks, Bruce and Strutt were forced to make a significant change to the plan. Instead of waiting until Finch was fully recovered, on 14 May, Bruce sent Norton up with Morshead to be the follow-up party to Mallory and Somervell. They would make the second attempt without supplementary oxygen.

It was an intensely difficult moment for Finch. With Norton gone, the only other experienced men left at Base Camp were Ferdie Crawford and Arthur Wakefield, but Finch had little regard for either man's mountaineering skills, regarding Crawford as 'tending to hysteria' and Wakefield as 'distinctly hysterical'. Finch did not admit it in his diary at the time, but he later wrote: 'When I saw the last mountaineers of the expedition leave the Base Camp, my hopes fell low.'

The only good news was that his stomach bug did seem to be clearing up. When the second party left camp on 14 May, Finch spent the day experimenting with an alternative type of oxygen set, designed by a British scientist, Leonard Hill. At one end, there was a breathing tube and a mask; at the other there was a tightly sealed bag containing Oxylithe, the same substance that had given Noel such a shock a week earlier. When water was added to the bag a chemical reaction ensued, causing the sodium peroxide to release oxygen. The whole set-up was much lighter than a typical oxygen set – but as Finch soon discovered, the system was, in his own words, 'useless'. The oxygen liberated was contaminated with crystals of sodium hydroxide formed during the chemical reaction, which caused anyone who breathed from a Leonard Hill bag to cough and spit.

Far more successful, but with a shorter-lasting benefit, was to fill a Leonard Hill bag with oxygen from a cylinder. The ever-helpful John Noel – 'St Noel of the Cameras', as Bruce called him – played the guinea pig, climbing up a nearby moraine with and without an oxygen bag while Finch stood close by with a stopwatch. He was pleased to discover that Noel could get up his chosen slope a full one minute and twenty seconds faster on a full bag, proving yet again the value of supplementary oxygen.

Tom Longstaff, the official expedition doctor, was sceptical. He had always been wary of oxygen sets on the grounds that, if something went wrong at high altitude, a climber might find themselves suddenly deprived of air, with potentially catastrophic consequences. In order to test this, Finch offered to go up to Camp 3 a few days later and deliberately interrupt the oxygen supply while climbing up to the North Col, to see what would happen. Both men agreed that this was a safe-enough altitude in which to stage the experiment, but Finch was actually hoping to go a lot further.

Up at Camp 3, Mallory and Somervell were stuck in their tents, waiting for Crawford to arrive with the porters who would accompany them to the North Col. Mallory had decided to make two trips: the first to carry up most of the supplies, the second to get the Advance Base Camp properly established. After that, he envisaged setting up just one more lightweight camp at 25,000 feet, from which they would make their attempt on the summit. They could do nothing, though, until reinforcements arrived.

Fortunately, Mallory and Somervell had already developed a strong friendship and were very happy whiling away the hours playing cards and occasionally reading aloud to each other. Their small library included a collected works of Shakespeare and an anthology of the Christian poet Robert Bridges, *The Spirit of Man*. Somervell also continued to sally forth on sketching expeditions, while Mallory composed a three-page letter to Ruth, noting that it always took longer to write at high altitude. He was excited about the prospect of making the summit attempt, but knowing how slow the mail was, he warned her that she would probably hear the news of their success or failure in *The Times* or via a telegram before any letter from him reached her. 'Isn't it a venture?' he finished.

Then, late in the afternoon of 15 May, much to Mallory's surprise, thirty-six porters arrived at Camp 3, accompanied by Morshead, Norton and Strutt – but no Finch. Mallory had not heard of the change of plan or of Finch's continued sickness. After a rapid two-day march from Base Camp, the new arrivals looked distinctly weary. Strutt – by almost ten years the oldest man in the party – was feeling the altitude particularly badly. Crawford, it transpired, had also come up, but he was even worse off and lagging far behind the others. Fortunately Morshead and Norton were both in good shape, and as they told Mallory, pleased to have the opportunity to make the second attempt.

The next day, the weather was bitterly cold, so instead of going straight away to the North Col, they all went on a training climb to a nearby pass called the Rapiu La, hoping to be able to look down on Makalu and the Kama valley – a view that Howard-Bury had been so enthralled by on the 1921 Reconnaissance. When they reached the top, Makalu was only just visible and the atmospheric conditions looked distinctly menacing. In the distance there were thick grey clouds – presaging, they feared, the early arrival of the monsoon.

There was no time to wait. At 9.15 a.m. the following day, Mallory and Somervell made their second ascent to the North

Col with their ten strongest Sherpas, some carrying up to sixty pounds. Morshead, Norton and Strutt accompanied them, leaving Crawford to escort the remaining porters back to Base Camp.

Strutt had spent the previous day in his tent and knew that he was close to his personal limit. He found the ascent exhausting, and only after a monumental effort managed to reach the crest. He later wrote that he wished that Noel had been there with his film camera to witness just how beat up a climber could be. The others coped better and, after pitching their tents and dumping their supplies, everyone left at 2.20 p.m., making it back down to Camp 3 in less than half the time it had taken to climb up.

Bruce had given Strutt permission to organize things as he saw fit, so with the monsoon at the front of everyone's mind he decided on a radical change of plan: instead of making two separate attempts, they would switch to a single attempt by four men, supported by their best Sherpas.

Mallory approved. He had always believed that a four-man party was the ideal. If one climber got ill, someone else could take him down, leaving the other pair to carry on. Recognizing that he was the weakest sahib in the group, Strutt announced that he would stay at Camp 3 in reserve, leaving Mallory, Somervell, Norton and Morshead to form the climbing party.

On the night before they left, Mallory composed what he hoped would *not* be a final love letter to Ruth. He was clearly very excited but also keen to manage her expectations. 'Well it's all on the knees of Gods,' he wrote. 'We shan't get to the top; if we reach the shoulder at 27,400, it will be better than anyone here expects.' He finished with a heartfelt declaration of love: 'Dearest one, you must know that the spur to do my best is you and you again – in moments of depression or lack of confidence or overwhelming fatigue I want more than anything to prove worthy of you.'

Down at Base Camp, Tom Longstaff was not quite so emotional, but he was keen to get a letter off to Sir Francis Younghusband in London before the mail runner left for Darjeeling. 'They are facing the utmost limits of endurance,' he wrote. 'It's harder than Polar work. And the climbing is none too easy: it's not an easy peak.' On a more ominous note, Longstaff added that, for the first time, he had noticed a heat haze over Everest and that it was clear to everyone that the weather was changing.

On the morning of 19 May, the stage was set for all the efforts of the previous years to come to a climax. A fully recovered Finch was on his way to Camp 3, accompanied by the untried transport officer Geoffrey Bruce and a promising Gurkha soldier, Lance Corporal Tejbir Bura. Mallory and Somervell were on their way out of Camp 3 with Norton and Morshead, heading back to the North Col. They would aim to get onto the North Ridge the next morning and see how high they could climb. Would it be their magic line to the summit, or would everything be much harder than they anticipated? As Strutt later said in a lecture to the RGS, 'It was better to try and fail than never to have tried at all.'

The Camps of the 1922 Expedition

West Rongbuk glacier

Rongbuk glacier

Camp 2
19,000 ft

Camp 1
18,000 ft

Base Camp

7

We May Be Gone Some Time

They were a remarkably homogenous group – middle-class professionals in their thirties. All four were public school educated: Mallory and Morshead at Winchester, Somervell at Rugby, and Norton at Charterhouse, the same school where Mallory had worked for several years. Two had gone to Cambridge – Mallory to study History, Somervell to read Natural Sciences. The other two had gone to military college – Norton to join the Royal Artillery, Morshead the Royal Engineers. All of them had served in the First World War, with Morshead and Norton both winning Distinguished Service Orders. Two were already married with children – Morshead and Mallory; Somervell and Norton would each be wed within a few years.

Like many men of their class, Mallory, Norton and Somervell had been introduced to climbing in their teenage days. Mallory had begun at Winchester supervised by Robert Irving, the schoolmaster and author of *The Romance of Mountaineering* who had also introduced Guy Bullock to the sport. Somervell had grown up in Kendal, surrounded by mountains; he was inspired by a book by George Abraham, the well-known Lake District climber, and joined the local branch of the Fell and Rock Club. Both Mallory and Somervell climbed in Britain but also holidayed in the Alps, where Edward Norton had learned the ropes – literally. His grandfather Alfred Wills owned a chalet near Chamonix where Norton and his brother were introduced to climbing.

Henry Morshead was the exception. Before the 1921 Reconnaissance he had never been involved in recreational mountaineering, but his job with the Survey of India had turned him into a very able mountain traveller.

Climbing wasn't the only passion for any of them. Mallory read widely and dreamt of one day becoming a writer; Somervell was the team's Renaissance man, who in addition to being a highly regarded surgeon was a gifted artist and enthusiastic amateur composer; Norton was a great sportsman but was also very dedicated to his sketchpad and a keen ornithologist. Again Morshead was the slight exception, having no particular hobby of note, except perhaps exploration which was in a way an extension of his day job.

As they left camp at 8.45 a.m. on 19 May, accompanied by nine porters, they were confident that even without oxygen they would still be able to get high up on Everest – and one way or another would make history. For Mallory and Somervell it was their third ascent to the North Col and each time it had been easier. For Norton and Morshead it was their second ascent, but they too were in good shape and excited to get on with the attempt.

By 1.00 p.m., after an uneventful climb, they reached the platform below the col. While Mallory and Norton pitched the tents, Somervell and Morshead carried on up, aiming to fix ropes up a difficult section. They had five tents: two for the climbers, three for the porters. For safety's sake the entrances were positioned facing inwards, towards the ice cliff that split the col in two, to protect sleepwalkers and anyone who had to get up at night.

For their evening meal, the sahibs enjoyed pans full of 'hoosch', a kind of stew championed by Morshead which had become an expedition favourite – perhaps because it was so easy to make. Its base was pea soup, into which he would add ship's biscuits and meats of varying descriptions; the whole thing was usually washed down with lashings of cocoa.

After downing their supper at around 4.30 p.m., everyone slipped into their sleeping bags and got ready for the night. Higher up they would share two-man 'flea-bags' in order to keep warm, but on the North Col they were all able to enjoy a modicum of comfort in single-person bags. As was the practice of the day, the tent entrances were not closed too tightly, to encourage the air to circulate. When in the middle of the night Mallory looked outside to check the weather, he was pleased to see a black starry sky, which he hoped presaged fine weather.

In between bouts of fitful sleep, Mallory thought through the plan for the following day. Down at Camp 3, the porters had prepared four loads for the top camp. Each was around twenty pounds, light by Sherpa standards, and would be even easier to transport if the men doubled up and took turns with the carrying. Mallory's aim was to get everyone to between 25,000 and 26,000 feet and pitch two small Mummery tents, each with one double bag and enough provisions and cooking implements for one meal, plus two thermos flasks and a little food. The Sherpas would then go down, unchaperoned, leaving the sahibs to make a dash for the summit the following day. Just by sleeping on the North Col they had already set a new world record for the highest camp on a mountain; if everything went their way, they would reach the summit or at the very least set a new world altitude record.

The next morning, reality hit.

Mallory was up as soon as the sunlight hit his tent at 5.00 a.m., but when he went to rouse the Sherpas, he didn't get the response he'd hoped for. In an attempt to stay warm, they had fastened the entrances to their tents so tightly that they were almost hermetically sealed. Mallory opened them up and allowed some fresh air in, but of the nine men only four said they were capable of continuing. In one fell swoop half the support team was out of action.

If that wasn't bad enough, Norton was in the throes of an unexpected culinary crisis. The Everest team's provision list had included several tins of Heinz Spaghetti, an easily digested, carbohydrate-rich fast food particularly suited for high altitude – or at least it would have been, if someone had remembered to keep their two precious tins of spaghetti at the bottom of their sleeping bag rather than outside in the snow. Instead of easy-to-warm-up instant food, Norton had opened the tins to find the spaghetti frozen solid. The only way to thaw the contents out quickly was to pour over precious hot water from the thermoses that they had prepared the previous night. Eventually the spaghetti was ready to be eaten, but it cost them an hour of valuable time and Norton got very cold hunched over the stove warming the spaghetti up.

At around 7.30 a.m., Morshead led them out of camp and

through a labyrinth of crevasses and mounds of ice. Then, aided by the ropes he'd fixed with Somervell the previous day, they climbed up the slope that led to the North Ridge. In spite of their unhappy start, they were feeling positive and hopeful. Ahead lay a broad snow slope, but rather than kick or cut steps with their ice axes, they moved to the left where it was mottled with small, firmly embedded stones: a good grippy surface to ascend. To the right, the North Face dropped down 3,000 feet to the Rongbuk glacier; to the left, the equally vertiginous Kangshung Face fell away to the east side of Everest. But in spite of the exposure, it was more of an upward slog than a climb.

Each of the sahibs was carrying a small rucksack with spare clothing, but their sartorial choices were idiosyncratic. Norton was sporting a Burberry climbing suit, a pair of heavy Carter's boots, three pairs of socks, and some sheepskin-lined gloves loaned to him by Strutt. Mallory was dressed in his familiar Norfolk jacket, a pair of motoring gauntlets, and two hats to protect himself against the sun and the cold. Somervell also had two hats (and a Norfolk jacket), but Morshead had no head covering and, as he later wrote, no bespoke mountaineering gear. Official confirmation that he would be going on the expedition had come so late in the day that he'd had no time to order special equipment and clothing from London, and had to make do with what he could find in the Darjeeling bazaar.

At first the weather continued to be fine but gradually the wind increased, making them colder and colder until, after about 1,200 vertical feet, they stopped to don their spare clothes. Mallory put on two extra layers – a silk shirt and another Shetland pullover – but Morshead just added a scarf around his neck. He was, according to Edward Norton, the hardest man he had ever come across and 'seemed completely oblivious to heat, cold or discomfort'.

For the third time that day, bad luck hit when Mallory tugged on their climbing rope and inadvertently caused Norton's rucksack to tumble into the abyss. It was 'stuffed spherical' with all his spare woollen clothing, his camp moccasins, and a pair of pyjama bottoms that Mallory had loaned him. There was no way to retrieve it; they would just have to make do.

The wind grew more intense, causing them to move gradually eastwards – first towards the crest and then further onto the lee side of the ridge. With the cold biting into their fingers, Morshead finally admitted defeat and stopped to put on a windproof sledging suit. The others carried on up and by mid-morning had passed 24,600 feet, breaking the Duke of the Abruzzi's 1909 record. Even so, they were still around 1,400 vertical feet short of their goal for the day.

Higher up, the snow changed consistency, becoming harder and more slippery. They would have made swift work, Mallory later reflected, if they had brought crampons. Instead he led up, kicking and chopping steps with his ice axe. It was hard, exhausting work, but it didn't stop Mallory from trying to increase the pace. Finally, at 11.30 a.m. and around 25,000 feet, he stopped and lay back on the rocks to regain his breath.

They had been going for four hours. Morshead was below, detained for some reason with two or three of the porters, but the others soon caught up. With the temperature continuing to drop and no obvious places to pitch their tents higher up, they decided to stay put and set up their fifth camp. The plan was to send down the Sherpas as soon as possible, but it took another three hours of searching around before they built two small rocky platforms about fifty yards apart and pitched their Mummery tents.

Each one weighed around three and a half pounds, groundsheet included. Developed by the pioneering Himalayan climber A. F. Mummery, it was a compact version of the classic A-frame ridge tent with its roof and walls made from oiled silk. Unlike the heavier Whymper tents they had on the North Col, which required dedicated tent poles, a Mummery tent was designed in such a way that a pair of long-handled ice axes could act as support at either end, held in place by guy ropes. Camp 5, however, was anything but glamping. They had no mattresses or blankets to put underneath their sleeping bags and, as they later discovered, the stones that covered the slope were pyramid-shaped and uncomfortably sharp.

Once the tents were up, the sahibs bid goodbye to their porters, sending them down to the North Col with instructions to wait until the next day when they too would descend. Though in theory there was a rule that Sherpas were not allowed to climb by themselves and always needed to be guided up or down by a sahib, in practice this did not happen. The sahibs all had their 'eyes on the prize' and, having chopped a staircase of steps in the ice on the way up, felt confident that the porters could get down by themselves. The Sherpas for their part did not need a chaperone on the North Ridge. They reached Camp 4 safely and, ignoring their orders, went all the way back down the slope to Camp 3, at the foot of the North Col. At around 6.00 p.m. Norton spotted them descending. 'They apparently conceived a horror of N.Col,' he recalled in a letter to his mother.

Over at their tent, Somervell and Morshead were on hoosch duties, melting pans of water for the evening stew. In order to avoid setting fire to the tent, all cooking had to be done in the open, regardless of the cold. In spite of all the discomforts and the fact that they had not got as far as planned, they tried to cheer themselves up by reminding each other of what they had achieved – now breaking their own world record for the highest-ever mountaineering camp. As Mallory later wrote: '"Hang it all" we cooed, "it's not so bad."'

Then, with each pair returning to their tent, they settled in for what no one expected to be a comfortable night. In order to minimize the weight they had to carry and also to keep warm, each pair of climbers shared a single flannel-lined eiderdown sleeping bag. Six-foot George Mallory was reasonably well matched with six-foot-four Edward Norton, but half their tent had been pitched on a slab which sloped down, and the other half on a bed of rocks, causing Norton to roll onto Mallory and press him into the sharp stones below.

To add to their misery, both men were already showing signs of frostbite. Mallory had made the fatal mistake of swapping one of his gauntlets for a woollen glove when he was cutting steps, in order to grip his ice axe better, and now the fingertips of his right hand looked bruised and swollen. Norton was in an even worse state. His right ear had swelled up to three times its normal size and was suppurating yellow pus. Unsurprisingly, he found it impossible to sleep on his right, so both men lay on their left sides, with Mallory putting his boots inside his rucksack to use as a pillow.

Frostbite was an occupational hazard for the polar explorer and high-altitude mountaineer. During the First World War, it had regularly been seen in the trenches too, but apart from rubbing and massaging affected areas to warm them and promote circulation, there was no effective medical treatment. It is a condition that proceeds in stages, beginning with the affected areas turning numb. If a climber gets help in time or is able to find shelter, they might end up with nothing more than a painful bout of 'frostnip' with no long-term consequences, but if it takes hold and develops into 'deep frostbite', then both muscle and bone can become affected with painful blisters appearing on the surface of the skin. Eventually, affected fingers and toes turn black and, *in extremis*, gangrene sets in, leaving little alternative but to amputate.

Over in the other tent, Somervell and Morshead were equally uncomfortable. Morshead in particular had endured a bad day. Everyone had noticed his tendency, whether through machismo or habit, to wear the minimum amount of clothing even in the harshest of conditions. He had only reluctantly donned his sledging suit long after the others had put on extra clothing, and a restless night sharing a bag with Somervell did nothing for his general well-being.

Outside, the skies were hazy, with occasional breaks in the cloud revealing the stars above. At dawn it started to snow, fine grains that bombarded their tents like small hailstones. When they finally got out of their bags at around 6.30 a.m. they found themselves surrounded by mist, with a thin layer of snow on everything around them.

Norton and Somervell were very keen to get going quickly, but for once Mallory was not his usual energetic self. He had exhausted himself cutting steps the previous day, and had endured such a bad night that initially he didn't think he could continue. In the end, he forced himself out of his sleeping bag and into the cold air.

For the second time, disaster struck a rucksack, when someone inadvertently pushed one over. This time, instead of clothing, it contained all their food for the day. The bag tumbled down the slope towards oblivion until, miraculously, it came to a halt, snagged on a ledge. Ever eager, Morshead offered to retrieve it. He struggled down the slope and back up again, but when, following a quick breakfast, they started up the ridge, he stopped abruptly after just 100 yards. 'I think I won't come with you,' he said. 'I'm quite sure I should only keep you back.'

It was the moment that Mallory had always feared: what would they do if one person had an accident or felt too bad to continue? He knew Morshead well enough by then to realize that if he was turning back, it had to be serious. Fortunately, they were close enough to their tents to allow him to go back alone, and he insisted that he didn't need a nursemaid, but if it had been a two-man attempt, that would undoubtedly have been that. Donning his doctor's hat for a moment, Somervell checked Morshead over and agreed that he was not in any imminent peril and could look after himself until they returned. The others pressed on up. They had a small aneroid barometer to measure their final height, and Somervell carried a Vest Pocket Kodak to record their achievements – as well as his sketchpad.

When Mallory had first contemplated the North Ridge during the Reconnaissance expedition, he had imagined that he might be tackling rock chimneys and awkward protruding flakes interspersed with patches of granite, but instead it all seemed to be layer upon layer of sedimentary rock which sloped down like roof tiles, making it difficult to find any handholds. For the most part, though, the angle was relatively easy, turning their ascent into more of an uphill scramble than a full-blown climb. They roped up, but more because no one wanted to carry the heavy climbing rope than because they had any particular fear of slipping.

The real battle was with the altitude, which made any thoughts of a 'dash' for the summit impossible. Somervell discovered that if he stuck to a steady pace of roughly 300 feet per hour – very slow by Alpine standards – he could just about cope, but any faster and he had to stop to regain his breath. Mallory maintained the same technique that he had learned on the mountain in 1921, inhaling very slowly and deeply rather than taking shallower and more frequent breaths like the others.

Gradually they got into the rhythm of climbing for about twenty minutes, then stopping for three or four before getting under way again. One halt took a little longer when Mallory announced that one of his feet was becoming frostbitten. He was wearing four pairs of socks and, though theoretically warm, they made his boots so tight that they restricted his circulation, causing him to get colder. Ever the doctor, Somervell noticed that the higher they got, the tetchier they all became. Though no actual quarrels broke out, there was definitely a feeling of tension in the air, in spite of the dulling effect of the altitude.

Earlier that morning they had agreed that 2.30 p.m. would be their 'turn-around time'. Any later and they wouldn't be able to get Morshead back down the North Col in daylight. If it turned out that he was suffering from altitude sickness, then they all knew it would be vital to get him to a lower altitude as quickly as possible.

Down at Camp 3 – some 6,000 feet below, at the foot of the col – Edward Strutt had spent the morning looking out of his tent anxiously, worried about his men above. If anything, the weather was far worse lower down the mountain, with what seemed like a full-blown snowstorm raging outside. Strutt was a brave man who, at the end of the First World War, had led a daring rescue of the Austrian royal family from the country's new republican government, fearing that, like the Russian tsar and his family, they might be executed.

Accompanied by six military policemen and a non-commissioned officer (NCO), he had bluffed his way into releasing the royal train and rode it in style all the way to the Swiss border, his pistol at the ready. Afterwards Strutt was censured by Lord Curzon, the British Foreign Secretary, for what he saw as an ostentatiously rash act, but, as a staunch Catholic, Strutt was very proud to have rescued Charles I of Austria, one of the last Catholic monarchs of Europe.

There was no comparison with his current predicament, but Strutt was honest enough to admit that one trip to the North Col was his own personal limit. If he had to put together a relief party, then he would not be able to lead it himself. The porters who had helped the first party establish their first camp had, contrary to their orders, left the North Col altogether. Finch and Charles Bruce's cousin, Geoffrey, had arrived in the camp and, having spent the last two days testing and adjusting their oxygen equipment, were keen to climb up. But they could go nowhere until the weather improved, and by the afternoon over a foot of snow had fallen.

Mallory's party could not contact Strutt or any of the others below, but they were in better shape than Strutt feared. At around 2.00 p.m., Howard Somervell took out his Vest Pocket Kodak to capture Mallory and Norton climbing a forty-five-degree slope. In the photo they look confident enough: Mallory standing still but staring upwards; Norton a few feet in front of him, his ice axe plunged into the snow, poised to take another step upwards. But the image is deceptively positive. The end was in sight, literally; all three men knew by then that they would not reach the summit that day. They were at 26,985 feet, still more than 2,000 feet from the top, and if they continued at the same speed, they could not possibly summit before nightfall. Even if Morshead had been with

Mallory and Norton at 26,985 feet, 20 May 1922,
photographed by Howard Somervell

them, they knew that they had reached their limit. As Mallory later wrote: 'We were prepared to leave it to braver men to climb Everest by night.'

For a few minutes they stopped and untied, shovelling down a pocket's worth of dried fruit, chocolate and some stray pear-drops, along with Somervell's favourite hill food: Kendal Mint Cake. No one could eat too much with a dry mouth, but eventually Somervell or Norton – Mallory refused to reveal who in his 'official' account – fished out a flask of brandy and offered it round.

They had stopped a few hundred feet below the rock tower, or gendarme, at the top of the North Ridge. Because of the angle, they could not see the summit itself or the rock steps that led up to it, but looking in the other direction the view was stupendous. Changtse, at the other end of the North Col, was in Mallory's words 'a contemptible fellow beneath our notice', but far more impressive was Cho Oyu, the sixth-highest mountain in the world. According to their aneroid barometer, they were at 26,800 feet, just below its summit, but later on they used a theodolite to check their final position and were able to confirm that, as they suspected on the day, they were almost 200 feet higher. They had smashed the world altitude record set by Abruzzi, but as for reaching their ultimate goal, there was no prospect of that. To Mallory's amazement, Somervell asked if he could stay a little longer to make a final sketch, but when his request was refused he didn't argue.

The descent did not start well.

Mallory was in the lead, followed by Norton and then Somervell. He had noticed a long snow slope below, to the west of the ridge, which he thought might get them down more quickly, not realizing that in places there was just a very thin layer of snow

covering treacherously smooth slabs of rock. Mallory slipped and
had to be held by Norton. After that, they moved back onto the
same line they had used on the way up.

At four o'clock they reached their tents and roused Morshead.
It had taken an hour and a half to descend what had taken some
six hours to get up. If they continued at the same rate, they
should reach the North Col by six. There was no time to pack the
Mummery tents or their double sleeping bags, but they took some
smaller items and then continued on down. Mallory stayed in the
lead followed by Morshead, then Norton, and finally Somervell
playing the anchoring role at the back. If anyone in front of him
slipped, it would be his job to hold them on the rope.

Morshead had told them that he'd spent the day smoking his
pipe and that he felt much better, but it was obvious to everyone
that he was far from recovered. It wasn't long before he slipped
on some snow and had to be held by Norton. Rattled by the
incident, Morshead seemed to lose his nerve and began moving
ever-more slowly.

Mallory remained in the lead, climbing down over mixed
ground where patches of snow alternated with rock, and
occasionally having to cut steps where their old tracks had been
filled in with fresh snow. Then suddenly, just as they were crossing
the top of a long, icy couloir which swept down towards the
foot of the mountain, something caught Mallory's attention, a
kind of sixth sense kicking in. Norton had slipped and pulled off
Somervell.

As they slid past, Morshead tried to hold on but he too
came off and found himself flying down the mountain. Time
slowed down as Mallory instinctively plunged the pick of his
ice axe into the snow, wrapped the rope around the head and

pressed into the slope with all his weight. Experience told him
that either the ice axe would be ripped out or the rope would
snap, but there was nothing else he could do. As he later wrote:
'In the still moment of suspense before the matter must be put
to the test nothing further could be done to prevent a disaster
one way or the other.'

For Somervell, the experience was more numbing than
terrifying. As he flew down, he attempted to press the pick of his
axe into the ice below to arrest his slide. He was getting to the
point where he thought it was under control when the rope around
his waist suddenly jerked tight and he felt himself come to a halt.
The combined effect of Mallory's ice-axe belay and Morshead's
section of the rope snagging on some rocks had brought them all
to a halt. It was little short of miraculous.

After that, their progress became even slower, as they worked
their way down ever so gingerly, only moving one at a time.
Morshead tried to put a brave face on it but he was almost done
in and needed Norton's support for hour after hour. Once or
twice he suggested that they could all glissade down the snowiest
sections and sometimes Mallory was tempted, but as he later
recalled: 'We were not playing with this mountain; it might be
playing with us.'

Finally, after about three hours, they found themselves at a
point where they could look down on their camp below. There
was about an hour of daylight left, leaving them with what should
have been easily enough time to reach their tents. As distant flashes
of lightning seared the sky, they were all even more eager to reach
safety, but with Morshead continuing to struggle, the pace stayed
agonizingly slow. When the daylight was utterly gone, Somervell
pulled a lantern out of his rucksack and to everyone's amazement

was able to light it with one of the cheap Japanese matches that they had previously complained about so much.

Now, with Somervell in the lead, they worked their way through a dense labyrinth of crevasses and walls of ice. They had not put down route markers on the way up, so occasionally they lost their way and had to retrace their steps. Afterwards, none of them could explain why it had taken so long, but the combination of poor visibility, altitude, exhaustion and dehydration turned what should have been a fifteen-minute hike into a four-hour slog.

The final obstacle was an icy cliff about 10–15 feet high. Illuminated by moonlight, they could see the outlines of their tents now, just 200 yards away, down a snow slope along which Somervell and Morshead had fixed a rope a few days earlier. It was all so tantalizingly close, but after lowering Morshead they all had to jump down into the snow below. It was a nervous moment but they each made it intact.

'We're very near ex the end of our candle,' said Somervell. He was right, both literally and metaphorically, for within a few minutes their lantern burned out. To make things even worse, a foot of fresh snow had fallen and no one could locate the fixed rope even after trawling with their ice axes through the drifts. There was no alternative but to carry on without it, Morshead still insisting that he was perfectly all right, and everyone else knowing that he wasn't. Then suddenly, for once, their luck changed. Someone found the rope and within a few minutes they were in their tents. Later on, when they tried to remember, no one could agree when precisely they arrived: Somervell said 10.00 p.m., Norton 11.00, Mallory 11.30. Whoever was right, they were long over schedule.

One more small disaster awaited. They had hoped to find warm smiles and steaming tea, but no one had come up to replace the

Sherpas who had gone down the previous evening – and to make matters worse, they appeared to have taken all the cooking pots and camp stoves with them. Without these, the returning men could neither melt water nor cook. They did find a stash of ship's biscuits, which normally they would have devoured, but with parched throats the dry biscuits were impossible to swallow. It was a terrible end to a brutal day, but just after they had wriggled into their sleeping bags, Norton piped up with an unexpected proposal: why not make some ice cream?

Taking a tin of frozen jam, some frozen milk and a fistful of snow, he mixed the concoction in a pan and shared it out. Norton's patent recipe was not quite Ben and Jerry's. When he wrote to his mother, he said that it was 'rather good but not very sustaining'. Mallory was more critical: after swallowing a few mouthfuls he retired to his sleeping bag, only to find himself convulsed with cramps so severe they left him breathless.

Amazingly, Norton enjoyed a 'glorious' night's sleep, but the next morning, even when they eventually found the stoves and cooking pots tucked in the corner of one of the porters' tents, no one wanted to spend any more time on the North Col making breakfast. Down below at Camp 3 they would find their comrades and surely be feasted like kings – and after all, they told themselves, it was less than two hours away.

They were very wrong. The steps they had cut three days earlier on the way up had been obliterated, filled in by the recent storm, and the fixed ropes were impossible to find, so they had no alternative but to recut everything. Norton led them out, taking them first over a very exposed icy lip, with Morshead, Somervell and Mallory following. Morshead still looked very shaky. They worried that he could stumble or slip at any moment, so they had to be very careful. It took four long hours to reach the final snow slope that led down to the foot of the North Col.

Right at the end, Mallory heard someone suggest that they should all glissade together for the final few dozen feet, but before he could reply, he felt himself being pulled off his final step and sliding down the slope, with the others laughing uproariously. Mallory travelled eighty feet until he managed to arrest his slide at the bottom of the slope, only to find himself looking straight down the lens of George Finch's Kodak camera.

At the end of the previous evening, Strutt and Finch had spotted Mallory's party descending towards the North Col. It was a great relief for everyone at Camp 3 but, in case they were injured, Strutt had sent Finch and Bruce out that morning to greet the returning men, along with Arthur Wakefield, the team's unofficial second doctor. If they needed help, Finch and Bruce would escort them back to Camp 3, but if Mallory's party seemed okay, they planned to climb up to the North Col to give the oxygen sets their first proper field test.

Finch's first thought after he'd put his camera away was to hand over several large thermoses of tea laced with brandy. The four returning men had not drunk anything at all for almost thirty hours. They were unsurprisingly delighted and made swift work of all the refreshments on offer. Then, escorted by Wakefield, the four weary men trudged on down to Camp 3, leaving Finch and Bruce to carry on up to the North Col with their team of Sherpas. Mallory's party was exhausted, but before they reached the tents Morshead spotted a stream of meltwater and lay down to drink his fill. The water was ice-cold, but that didn't stop him from drinking mouthful after mouthful.

Back at Camp 3 one final surprise awaited: John Noel and his movie camera. He had set up his tripod inside the main tent to get some candid shots of truly flogged men, and was not disappointed. Quite what the returning party's reactions were is not recorded but can well be imagined.

Edward Strutt, as Norton had noticed, seemed particularly glad to see them. He went down on his knees to unlace Norton's boots and swapped them for a pair of soft moccasins. Strutt had given his all to reach the North Col a few days earlier, but he clearly felt guilty that he had not been able to accompany them on the attempt itself. Somervell's only thought was to drink as much tea as possible, knocking back seventeen mugs and still feeling thirsty.

The shots that Noel took inside the tent did not appear in the expedition film, but Noel did include footage of Wakefield tending to Morshead's hands, which showed signs of severe frostbite. Painful-looking blisters had already formed on three of the fingers of his right hand, and his left hand looked ragged too. Later, Morshead would conclude that his breakdown and subsequent frostbite were caused by severe dehydration, a diagnosis that many modern doctors would agree with – though also pointing to the inadequacies of his clothing and his strange reluctance to wear it.

Mallory too had damaged fingers, though they weren't nearly as bad as Morshead's. As for Norton, in letters home he played down his injuries, but his feet were badly affected and he would lose the tip of his right ear. Only Somervell, the youngest man in the party, had escaped without any injury, as did the porters.

Later that afternoon, Finch and Bruce returned with their party of Sherpas, buzzing with excitement. They had climbed up to the North Col in just three hours, and made it back down in a staggering fifty minutes. Their oxygen sets had worked perfectly, and the porters who had followed them, climbing under their own steam, had also performed well. Obviously they had been helped by the steps that Mallory's party had cut that morning, but Finch had no doubt that the three bottles of oxygen that he and Bruce consumed had contributed significantly to their speed, and, as he told Norton, he was sure that the positive effects lasted for several hours afterwards.

Mallory's party had set a new world record, but would pay the price in fingers and toes. Next up it was Finch's turn. Just how far he would get with a mountaineering novice like Geoffrey Bruce on the world's highest mountain remained to be seen.

The climbers of the first summit party, after their attempt:
(left to right) Morshead, Mallory, Somervell, Norton

George Finch demonstrating the oxygen he would use on his attempt

8

The Gas Offensive

When he first met Geoffrey Bruce in Darjeeling, George Finch wasn't that impressed. 'Good for 23,000 ft,' he wrote in his diary. 'Too young (lack of stamina) lung capacity not very pronounced (he is slightly narrow in chest from back to front). Not a climber.' When Geoffrey Bruce first tried one of Finch's oxygen sets, he was equally underwhelmed. 'Doing a bit of oxygen drill,' he wrote to his parents during the approach march. 'I find it quite easy to manipulate but have not much confidence in the apparatus. It is undoubtedly a step in the right direction, but not yet sufficiently perfected.'

Finch had always hoped that Edward Norton would be his partner on the 'oxygen attempt', but when he saw Norton walk out of Base Camp with Henry Morshead on 14 May he realized straight away that he would have to find an alternative partner if there was ever going to be an oxygen-fuelled attempt on Everest.

Over the previous week Finch had spent most of his time in his tent, suffering from dysentery. Several of the other climbers had also been affected but no one quite so seriously. To have endured rejection in 1921 and to have spent so much time working on the oxygen equipment and arguing for it, and then ultimately to be thwarted by his guts – it seemed such a terrible bit of bad luck for the man who a year earlier had told Sir Francis Younghusband 'you've sent me to heaven' when first offered a place on the Everest team.

In early 1918, towards the end of his service in the British Army, Finch had been felled not by a bullet, but by a severe case of malaria. He had spent several weeks in a military hospital and then gone to Paris where he was 'cured' by an experimental French treatment. His malaria never came back but for many years afterwards he had recurrent gastric problems.

By 14 May, two days after he watched Norton and Morshead leave Base Camp, Finch could feel his strength returning. He still wasn't fit enough to go up to the North Col, but knew that soon he would be. The only question was who would accompany him. In theory Arthur Wakefield or Ferdie Crawford were both strong-enough climbers to be his partner, but Finch didn't rate either of them. He had got to know Crawford on the approach march when they had waited in Kalimpong for the delayed consignment of oxygen cylinders. The two men had got on well and Finch had taught Crawford how to use the apparatus, but that was as far as it went. Wakefield, after his bad experience in London, was very dismissive of the oxygen equipment, and had argued with Finch about it on both the voyage out and the approach march.

With all of the other climbers up at Camp 3 and possibly already up on the North Col, Finch had no option but to consider taking one or both of the transport officers, Geoffrey Bruce and John Morris. They had been working hard, getting supplies and equipment up the East Rongbuk glacier, and both had done well. Ever-critical, Finch did not rate Morris, but he had come to like Bruce and admired his fitness and strength.

In order to make a proper attempt, Finch felt he needed a third man, but instead of Morris he decided to take one of the Gurkha officers, Lance Corporal Tejbir Bura. Tejbir was an experienced soldier from the same regiment as Geoffrey Bruce. He was unusually tall for a Gurkha, and like Bruce was athletically built. Though Finch himself was often accused of being serious and rather humourless, the qualities he appreciated in both men were their good humour and cheerfulness – vital to have, he thought, on Everest.

On 16 May, Finch, Bruce and Tejbir left camp, accompanied by ten porters and Arthur Wakefield, who somewhat to Finch's annoyance, had been sent up to look after them. The party reached Camp 1 in three hours, giving them plenty of time to examine the cache of oxygen cylinders that had been built up over the last few days. Back in London they had been filled at a slightly lower capacity than their maximum, and fortunately none of the cylinders seemed to have leaked.

The next day, for the sake of the porters, they took it easy. Finch and Bruce had brought skis with them, so they spent the day in the snow-filled bed of the East Rongbuk river, having fun and teaching the Sherpas the basics of the art. When they reached Camp 2 the following morning, Finch decided it was time to move on to ice-craft, showing his new partners and the porters how to use crampons and ice axes. The lesson went well until Tejbir overextended himself and fell from an ice cliff into a freezing lake below. Instinctively he managed to hold on to his axe and get out, but it was a tougher lesson than Finch had planned for. In order to dry out his clothes, which were literally frozen stiff, Finch stood them against some rocks in the sun and waited until they collapsed when the moisture evaporated – a perfect demonstration, he later wrote, of 'scientific' principles.

Tejbir fortunately suffered no ill effects from his dunking, and accompanied Finch and Bruce to Camp 3 the following day. It was the first time that anyone in the party had been so high, and Finch admitted in his diary that he could feel the altitude. They arrived in camp at around 12.30 p.m., in time to see Mallory and the others moving about, far above them on the North Col. They would try to set up camp at 25,000 feet, Strutt told Finch, from where the two fittest men would make their attempt, aiming to break the Duke of the Abruzzi's altitude record at the very least.

Finch's first thought was to check the oxygen equipment that was piled up at Camp 3. Up until this point, he had been working with just one set, which he had used for demonstrations on the ship and on the approach march, but he hadn't had time to unpack the main consignment. For his plan to work, Finch needed three good sets, but what he discovered appalled him: gauges that were broken, soldered joints that had come apart, and washers that had shrunken so much that the parts they connected were no longer airtight. It was not clear whether they had been damaged in transit or had been badly assembled back in London, but either way Finch had a big problem. The only good news was that the team's toolkit had made it up to Camp 3, so Finch was able to cobble together four useable sets – one for everyone in his party and an additional set for the expedition cameraman John Noel, who wanted to come up to the North Col to film Finch's progress up the mountain.

But when they tried them out at Camp 3, Finch got another shock.

The oxygen sets had come with two types of mask, but their first high-altitude test showed the limitations of both designs. The main mask was called the Economiser and was supposedly designed not to waste oxygen. In fact, at 20,000 feet it was so parsimonious that, in Finch's words, it was absolutely 'useless' – even when he cut a large hole in it. The second, a simpler set-up which pumped out oxygen continuously, was both very wasteful and very uncomfortable.

Fortunately Finch was well prepared. Just before he left Darjeeling, he had visited the bazaar and come away with a bag full of football bladders and a set of glass T-pieces. He connected the main shaft of the T to the oxygen delivery tube, and then attached a second rubber tube to one of the arms and a rubber bladder to the other. When a climber inhaled, the oxygen flowed through the main rubber tube, into the T-piece, and then via the second rubber tube into his mouth. When he exhaled, he bit the delivery tube, stopping the flow and diverting the oxygen into the bladder, which inflated, only to deflate when he breathed in again.

It was a Heath Robinson solution, but would it work? On the afternoon of 20 May, Finch found out, when he and Bruce climbed up the Rapiu La, the nearby 21,000-foot pass which overlooked the Kangshung glacier. They were accompanied by Wakefield and Strutt, climbing under their own steam. As Finch wrote gleefully in his diary: 'The effect of the O2 was remarkable – we two went ahead like a house on fire.'

On 21 May, after a heavy overnight snowstorm, they did not leave camp, but the following morning they donned their oxygen sets again when they went out to meet Mallory and the others at the foot of the North Col. If the returning party were strong enough to get back by themselves, they would give the oxygen sets their first big test and go all the way to the North Col.

Finch had lost all patience with Wakefield, who once again insisted on accompanying them but was unable to keep up with their oxygenated pace. 'He can barely crawl along,' Finch wrote scathingly in his diary, 'is always fussing and making a nuisance of himself and generally speaking he is a b---y old woman and good for nothing.'

When they met Mallory's party, Finch was thrilled to hear that they had done so well. Leaving them in Wakefield's hands, he and Bruce carried on up. Once again the results were everything that he could have hoped for. They were able to climb much more quickly than their Sherpas, and when they turned their oxygen off at the top to test how they would react, they did not suffer the sort of cataclysmic collapse that had been predicted by Tom Longstaff and by so many scientists back in Britain. Even the Sherpas were impressed by the sahibs' performance, which Geoffrey Bruce told them was down to their containers full of 'English air'. In order to further demonstrate its effectiveness, Finch held up a cigarette in a stream of oxygen released by Bruce from his set. It glowed with a bright white light and burnt down quickly. 'A better audience for this perhaps most beautiful of all laboratory experiments,' as he later wrote, 'could not have been desired.'

Having climbed up for three hours, they were able to get down in just fifty minutes, returning to camp 'fit and fresh' having consumed three bottles of oxygen each. That night, Finch sent down an exuberant note to General Bruce at Base Camp. He called Geoffrey Bruce 'a born mountaineer' and reiterated that he did not want to take Wakefield or Crawford with him, doubting their 'capacity for managing the apparatus safely'. Of that oxygen apparatus, he now felt utterly confident, though he added deferentially that 'after consulting Colonel Strutt, we are pushing oxygen for all it is worth, pending your approval'.

Whether he ever got that thumbs up from Bruce is not recorded, but on 23 May Finch and Bruce spent another day checking over their gear while Strutt escorted the first party down to Base Camp. Then at 8.00 a.m. the next day, they began the expedition's second attempt on Everest, heading back up to the North Col with twelve Sherpas and one additional tent. As promised, John Noel, another convert to the 'true faith' of oxygen, came with them – along with his dedicated camera porters, who like the other Sherpas had to climb under their own steam.

After the euphoria of the previous few days, Finch was brought down to earth by a terrible night's sleep. It was his first time on the col and the highest he had ever been, so perhaps it wasn't so surprising that he woke up the following morning feeling truly awful. Later he would put it down to a very uneven tent floor that forced everyone to lie with their feet higher than their heads, but for the moment all that mattered was how rotten he felt. After sitting around for a couple of hours in a semi-dazed state, Finch eventually sent the porters up at 8.00 a.m., promising to leave with Bruce and Tejbir an hour and a half later. Whether to stave off tiredness or to make up for all the weight he'd lost in the previous weeks, Finch gobbled down a second breakfast before they finally pushed off, confident that before long their cylinders of English air would enable them to overtake the porters.

On the way up they encountered one porter who could not continue and was on his way down, and then at 24,500 feet they passed the others, who were struggling on. After another 500 vertical feet, they passed the site of Mallory's high camp, but instead of stopping and installing themselves in the first party's tents, Finch pressed on, aiming to get a thousand feet higher in order to have less to climb on their summit day. Like Mallory a few days earlier, Finch didn't quite achieve his wish, and was forced to stop at 25,500 feet when the weather suddenly turned intensely cold and windy.

After a long wait, at around 2.00 p.m. the porters finally caught up with the climbing party. Finch had already gone a few hundred feet higher looking for somewhere to pitch their tent but had found nowhere suitable. There was nothing obvious on the leeward side, so with the wind continuing to roar, they cleared a small platform on the North Ridge itself and pitched a Meade tent – the third design in their armoury. It was taller than the lightweight Mummery tents used by Mallory and Norton, and big enough to hold all three of them. Then, leaving the climbers with one day's worth of food, the porters headed down, singing songs and undoubtedly glad to be descending to the comparative shelter of the North Col.

Unlike the first summit party, the climbers each had their own sleeping bag and soon wriggled into them. Ever the scientist, Finch noted how water boiled at a much lower temperature than at Base Camp, making it harder to brew a good cup of tea. Like the first party, they were running their Primus stove on solid Meta fuel which burned easily enough but did not have the satisfying roar – or the heating power – of a traditional paraffin-powered Primus. They made a quick meal and then hunkered down for the night.

At Base Camp, 9,000 feet lower down, Charles Bruce was writing his first letter for a long time to Sir Francis Younghusband. He had received Finch's note and was pleased to pass on the good news that the oxygen party had tried turning off their sets on the North Col and had survived the experiment. As to

Mallory's attempt, Bruce was surprisingly critical, noting how close to disaster they had come and revealing just how 'fagged out' the first party was by the time they reached the foot of the col. Morshead, he added, had suffered a lot because 'apparently he has some prejudice against wearing too many socks and gloves which very nearly brought him to a bad end'. As to the second party, he told Younghusband that he had high hopes that the oxygen sets would work in Finch's capable hands. John Noel, he finished, had climbed up with the second party to photograph 'the gas offensive'.

Initially Noel had not been able to do much. When Finch and the others left, he tried to track them through a telescope and then filmed them on a telephoto lens, but he found himself so breathless with the exertion that he too had to turn on his oxygen set. Noel's assistants weren't doing so well either. Of his five camera porters, three were ill with altitude sickness and one man, Songlu – his best assistant, and one of Alexander Kellas's favourites from the 1921 Reconnaissance – was so ill that Noel began to fear for his life.

Up on the North Ridge, the snowstorm intensified. Finch thought it his duty to stay positive and cheerful. He handed around cigarettes and discussed the plan for the next day, but with the wind eventually growing to gale-force, nothing could hide the fact that they were in a very precarious position. As the interior of their tent filled up with spindrift, the wind tore at the outside, snapping the guy ropes and threatening to rip off the entrance. It even got under the groundsheet, making them feel that at any moment the whole thing might be launched skyward like a paper plane. The only way to prevent this was to press their bodies into the ground and hold on for dear life.

At 1.00 a.m. on 26 May the storm reached a crescendo, with the tent canvas flapping so hard that it reminded Finch of a machine gun. They couldn't hear each other speak for what seemed like hours until the wind died down. Finch was so worried that during a pause in the storm he went outside and attempted to tie the tent down with climbing rope. The other two men took turns to copy him, but with the wind returning in vicious gusts, no one could stay outside for longer than five minutes. At 8.00 a.m. there was a brief lull, only for the storm to revive within half an hour, picking up a stone which flew into the tent and ripped a hole in the canvas. In quieter moments they went outside, retied the climbing ropes and attempted to build a protective wall of rocks, but it was obvious to everyone that for the moment they were trapped and could neither go up nor down.

Finally, at lunchtime, the wind dropped to a gentle breeze. If they were going to retreat they would have to go down straight away, but amazingly they all decided to stay. Having survived the storm they were willing to risk another night, in the hope that they would be able to get further up the ridge the following day. Their biggest problem was food – Finch had only planned to spend one night on the ridge, so they had carried a very small amount of provisions, and to make things worse, his cigarettes were running out.

Finch had come up with thirty and shared them out, rationing himself and his tent-mates to one every couple of hours, but after a day of waiting, there were very few left. Though to modern eyes the idea of smoking at high altitude seems very bizarre, most of the Everest 1922 team were smokers, though the majority preferred pipes to cigarettes. Tobacco in one form or another was a habit and a release, but as they sat in their tent at 25,500 feet, Finch became convinced that smoking actually improved his breathing.

His theory, which he elaborated on afterwards, was that at high altitude, increased respiration flushed the carbon dioxide out of a climber's blood, thus reducing one of the most important 'prompt signals' for regular breathing. When a smoker lit up, they raised the CO_2 level, causing their breathing once again to become more regular and less strained. The effect was strongest initially, but lasted for a few hours. Later, back at his laboratory in London, he would test his hypothesis, burning a cigarette in a variety of controlled conditions, but on the afternoon of 26 May, Finch was his own guinea pig.

At 5.00 p.m. they lit the stove again, cooked what they had left, and melted pots of snow with the remaining fuel. It ran out shortly afterwards, leaving them resigned to a long, freezing and distinctly parched night. Then, to his amazement, Finch heard the sound of voices approaching. He thought he was hallucinating but a few minutes later he heard them even more distinctly: it was a group of porters, sent up by Noel.

Down below, Noel had endured another bad day. Songlu had collapsed and his heartbeat was very weak. When Noel offered him food, he vomited it up over his blankets. Noel himself felt better, and in between bouts of nursing the Sherpa, he had gone out onto the col to peer through his camera. He was hoping that the weather would improve and allow him to film Finch's attempt, but instead it had got worse, with clouds covering the upper mountain and snow falling. He wrapped his camera in a tarpaulin and retreated inside.

By late afternoon Noel was convinced that Finch must have given up and he sent up his strongest Sherpa, Tergio, and a group of porters with thermoses of soup and beef tea, assuming that they would bring down Finch and the oxygen party. Instead, a few hours later, Tergio returned with the news that Finch and the others had decided to risk a second night on the North Ridge and were hoping to make their summit bid the following day.

As the night wore on and the warming effect of the soup diminished, the three men began to wonder if they had made the right decision. The weather had calmed down a little, but it was still windy and dreadfully cold. They moved their sleeping bags closer and draped all their spare clothes on top, but still couldn't warm up. Their cigarettes had gone, and with no new supplies of fuel, there was no way to melt snow for water.

Then, suddenly, Finch had a moment of inspiration. He rigged up an oxygen set and offered the mouthpiece to Tejbir. At first the Gurkha looked sceptical but then his expression changed. The oxygen made it easier to breathe and, crucially, warmed him up. Finch then delved into his bag of spare tubes and connectors and rigged up a system where each man was connected to an oxygen cylinder at a low flow rate for the rest of the night. Soon they were all nodding off, enjoying a few hours of desperately needed sleep. Finch later wrote that he had no doubt the oxygen saved their lives.

Down at Base Camp, the weather on the mountain did not seem nearly so bad. Tom Longstaff recorded in his diary that the night of 25 May had been windy, but when Mallory wrote to his wife Ruth, he told her that Finch's party had enjoyed much better weather than his party had on their attempt. He doubted that they would get to the summit on their first try but thought that they might get higher than he had.

For Mallory, who still felt proprietorial over Everest, team spirit fought a running battle with unspoken rivalry. His only comfort was the thought that his party had climbed unassisted.

'I shan't feel in the least jealous of any success they may have,' he wrote with a slightly hollow ring. 'The whole venture of getting up with oxygen is so different from ours that the two hardly enter into competition.' Had he seen what had happened on the North Ridge that morning, he would not have thought so much about competition.

They woke up at dawn when the oxygen ran out, but it took close to an hour for Tejbir and Bruce to thaw out their boots over a candle. Finch had slept with his footwear inside his sleeping bag, but the others had not taken the precaution and had paid the price. With no food they did not need to waste time making breakfast but, as Finch would later recall, one of the other effects of using supplementary oxygen was to make them feel even hungrier.

Finch had decided to use Tejbir Bura essentially in a sacrificial role. He and Bruce would leave camp carrying four cylinders each, their sets weighing thirty-six pounds, but Tejbir would carry an extra two cylinders, and if everything went according to plan would turn back when they reached the shoulder, handing over the extra oxygen to Finch and Bruce. This was asking a lot of Tejbir, especially when neither he nor Bruce really had any mountaineering experience whatsoever, but if the terrain continued to be relatively easy, Finch was confident he could pull it off.

He was wrong.

They left at 6.30 a.m., but after a few hundred feet the inevitable happened: Tejbir had to stop. Bruce managed to cajole him in Gurmukhi, appealing to his sense of regimental honour, but as Finch later admitted: 'Forty eight pounds is never a joke to carry at whatever altitude and at 26,000 ft it proved a decidedly cruel imposition.' After a few hundred more feet, Tejbir sank down and inadvertently damaged his oxygen mask. There was no alternative but to take his cylinders and send him back, but fortunately their tent was still within sight so they were sure that he could get down by himself. In order to move more quickly, Finch and Bruce un-roped, hoping that the ridge in front would continue to be an easy scramble.

In addition to their oxygen sets, they each carried a thermos of water and Finch had a Vest Pocket Kodak camera, but they had decided to use it only for summit shots rather than risk having to change rolls on the way up. They were following roughly the same line that Mallory had taken six days earlier, but when they reached the steeper section at around 26,500 feet it became so windy that Finch was forced into a diversion.

Instead of continuing up the ridge, he roped up to Bruce and traversed out onto Everest's huge North Face. At first the climbing was no harder than the North Ridge and decidedly less windy, but then Finch began to notice how dangerously slabby the rock was. With the strata continuing to slope downwards, it was tricky to find hand- and foot-holds. For Geoffrey Bruce, who before the expedition had never done any proper climbing at all, this was an amazing initiation, especially when carrying a heavy oxygen set.

As they continued on, the North Face became more uneven, with patches of scree mixed up with steep rock slabs covered with treacherously loose snow. That wasn't their only problem: even though they continued to make good speed, Finch realized that most of their progress was horizontal – across the face rather than up it. So, at 27,000 feet, he changed direction again, moving up diagonally and aiming for a point above the shoulder on the final summit ridge. It was hard technical climbing, an even-greater challenge for Bruce, but they continued to make steady progress even when they were deliberately economizing on oxygen.

At around 12.00 p.m., they stopped at about 27,300 feet to discard their used oxygen cylinders, the hollow bottles bouncing their way down the North Face ringing out like church bells. Then the two climbers started up again, with Finch in the lead and Bruce belaying him from below. Suddenly, when he was in the middle of climbing a steep slab, Finch heard a muffled shout from below: 'I'm getting no oxygen!'

Finch worked his way back down to the ledge where Bruce was standing and tried to steady him, but for one terrifying moment it looked as if he was going to fall backwards into the abyss. Turning him round, Finch got Bruce to sit with his back to the rock and then started to examine his set. First he attempted to remove the flow regulator in order to allow Bruce to receive oxygen directly from the valve that came out of the cylinder, but it didn't work. Finch was undeterred. He fished an extra T-piece out of his pocket and connected it to his own set in order to share his oxygen with Bruce.

After a few minutes, Finch figured out what had happened: Bruce's glass T-piece had hit a rock and was now cracked and leaking fast. In an outstanding piece of high-altitude repair work, Finch swapped the broken T-piece for a spare, allowing Bruce to breathe freely again as he paused to take in the view. They were now about 300 feet above the summit of Cho Oyu. Far below, Mallory's favourite peak, the 23,000-foot Pumori, looked like an insignificant bump. More ominous, though – in the distance Finch could see malevolent-looking yellow clouds, the first signs of a storm brewing.

They were about 1,700 vertical feet and half a mile away from the summit. It appeared to be so close, but suddenly, inevitably, the reality of where they were and what they were risking dawned

on Finch. For the last five or six hours, the mountain gods had
been kind. Whenever there had been a problem, Finch had found
a way to solve it, but however committed, however physically
fit his partner was, this was no place for a novice climber. They
had plenty of oxygen left and Finch knew that on his own he
could go further, but not with Geoffrey Bruce. As he wrote in his
memoir, *The Making of a Mountaineer*: 'Never for a moment
did I think we would fail; progress was steady, the summit was
there before us; a little longer and we should be on the top. And
then – suddenly, unexpectedly, the vision was gone.'

When Finch told Bruce that it was time to turn back, initially
he seemed angry and refused to go down. He too had become
utterly fixated on the goal, and for a moment could not accept any
kind of reversal, but Finch was experienced and careful enough
to know they had no choice. It was simply too risky to go on,
especially with the weather getting worse by the minute. Finch
put Bruce on a short rope and told him to head back down. By
2.00 p.m. they had retraced their steps and were back on the
North Ridge with Finch in the lead. The vicious west wind had
returned, blowing in damp mist, but it was much easier to move
quickly than out on the North Face. In order to lighten their load,
each man cached their two spare oxygen cylinders and marked
the location with a cairn.

Within an hour they had reached their tent, where they found
Tejbir lying fast asleep, swaddled inside all three of their sleeping
bags. In the distance they could hear the sound of a party of
Sherpas coming up from the North Col to help them descend,
so for the moment they left Tejbir as he was and continued on
down, telling the Sherpas to follow with their colleague and the
sleeping bags.

Noel knew none of this. He had been so worried that he had even lit signal fires, burning off his extra film stock in an attempt to reassure everyone that the North Col camp was still occupied. Now, as he watched Finch and Bruce come into camp, he warmed up some tinned spaghetti and plied them with mugs of piping hot tea. To Finch's bemusement, he saw that Ferdie Crawford and Arthur Wakefield had also come up to the North Col, limiting the amount of tent space available. Finch had no plans to stay the night, though. All he could think of was one thing: food, and lots of it. So after a brief pause on they went, racing down the slope towards Camp 3 with Noel acting as their anchor man, arriving at the tents in a record-breaking forty minutes.

Overall, it was an astonishing performance. In a single day they had ascended from 25,500 to 27,300 feet to set a new world altitude record – getting 300–400 feet higher than Mallory's party – before descending an unprecedented 6,300 feet in just a few hours. What came next was equally prodigious: Finch ate the camp out of house and home, devouring four tins of quails in foie gras and nine sausages before retiring to bed with a tin of toffee nestled in the crook of his arm. That night he slept for fourteen hours straight.

When they woke up, Finch and Bruce were examined by Howard Somervell, who had come up to Camp 3 to do what he could to help. Geoffrey Bruce was quite severely affected by frostbite – his left foot 'useless', to use Finch's favourite adjective. Finch's feet were in better shape but he had dark patches of frostbite on the soles. Neither man was really in a fit state to walk, but they wanted to get down to Base Camp as soon as they could, so the Sherpas rigged up an ad hoc sledge and began hauling them both down the glacier. When it got too rough, Finch dismounted and limped down while the porters took turns to carry Geoffrey

Geoffrey Bruce (left) and George Finch, returning to the North Col
after their attempt, 27 March 1922

Bruce. At Camp 2, they stopped for another huge meal before
continuing down to Camp 1, where they stopped for the night.
The next day they reached Base Camp in time for lunch, not quite
triumphant but deservedly proud of their achievement.

With a mail runner at the ready, Finch immediately set about writing an account for General Bruce, to be published in *The Times*. In his diary he downplayed everything, writing that it was a 'poor satisfaction' to have come back with altitude records rather than the ultimate prize, but he was convinced that they had done the right thing in turning back. 'Had we gone on even 500 ft further, Bruce would have pegged out and it might not have fared much better with me. Storm and weather were too much against us, and also two nights at 25,500 ft is hardly by way of being tonic.'

The second attempt was over, and remarkably had been even more successful than the first. They could all go home with their heads held high – but life, as it turned out, was not quite so simple.

9

Summit Fever

On 16 May 1922, just before Mallory set off on the first summit attempt, London's *Daily Mail* told the story of a previous race to the summit of Everest. According to Tibetan lore, Guru-pimbo-che, the mystic who introduced tantric Buddhism to Tibet, had once been challenged by the Pombo Lama, a holy man who lived in a monastery at the foot of Everest, to see who could reach the summit first. The next day, the Pombo Lama got up early, mounted a drum and began riding up the mountain. Guru-pimbo-che bided his time, even when his followers warned him that he was about to be beaten. He waited and waited until the first rays of the sun appeared. Then he too rose up, and mounted a ray of light which carried him all the way to the summit, flying past his rival below. Guru-pimbo-che was gracious in victory, and rather than claim the whole mountain for himself, he offered the Pombo Lama all the land up to the halfway point. It was a win-win outcome.

The *Mail* credited the story jointly to Colonel Laurence Waddell, a famous Scottish Tibetologist, and their own correspondent –

who supposedly was at that very moment in Yatung, close to
the Tibetan border, poised to scoop any news of the more recent
Everest expedition. The sad fact, though, was that no news had
come through, official or unofficial, for weeks. Today we expect
virtually instant communication from even the remotest parts of
the world, but in 1922 things were very different. The bare fact
that Base Camp had been established would not reach Britain until
over a month after it had happened; the more pressing reports
of Mallory and Finch's attempts took a little less time, but it was
still three weeks before the message got home.

In truth, the delays were not really that surprising, though
they were very frustrating for both the press and the Everest
Committee. In 1921, there had been considerable problems getting
letters and messages back from the Reconnaissance because of
extensive flooding during the monsoon. In 1922, initially the
mail service had been a little better, but as in 1921 the further
the team got from Phari, the nearest telegraph station, the longer
it took for cables and letters to get through. In early March, at
the start of the expedition, it took around a day to get a cable
from the expedition to 'Obterras', the telegraphic address for the
RGS, and two to three weeks to get a letter from Tibet to London;
by the beginning of May, when Bruce set up Base Camp on the
Rongbuk glacier, it was usually taking over a month to get any
news back at all.

The only recent expedition photograph showed Charlie Bruce
posing at a Darjeeling station months earlier – an image supplied
to The Times by his wife, much to the irritation of Arthur Hinks
at the RGS. Apart from his personal desire to always be in control,
Hinks was very conscious of expedition finances and distinctly
worried that too few dispatches and photographs were making

their way to England. By the end of May, he had written to Bruce several times asking him why there were so many delays, but his letters simply didn't get through.

Hinks became increasingly concerned. The 1921 expedition had come in below budget and there was no doubt that Howard-Bury was more parsimonious than Charlie Bruce. The Reconnaissance had cost £4,241 (roughly £200,000 in today's money), but the main expedition in 1922 was expected to come to two or three times as much. In 1921, the Mount Everest Committee had funded the expedition initially through public subscription, raising almost £6,000 from members of the Alpine Club and the RGS. That initial pot had been topped up by deals struck with newspapers and more recently the profits of lectures. When Bruce started work in the autumn of that year, there was about £7,500 in the Everest account, but he had very quickly spent it all, so Hinks and the Committee felt very dependent on newspapers to top up their funds. *The Times* and the Philadelphia *Public Ledger* had each agreed to pay the expedition around £1,500 for the rights to print exclusive expedition dispatches, and the *London Illustrated News* a smaller sum for photographs. All those deals, however, were paid in instalments, based on an agreed supply of words and images, and Charlie Bruce simply wasn't fulfilling his side of the bargain.

To make things even worse, throughout the early weeks of the expedition, Bruce had sent a succession of letters back to London asking for more money – requests that had always been granted, but not without regular tickings-off from Hinks. Bruce usually replied that the expenditure was absolutely necessary, insisting that John Noel's film and photographs would be a 'gold-mine' that would cover any shortfall. Hinks was not so easily fobbed off and was particularly annoyed to discover that, because of its later arrival, the oxygen had to be shipped in a separate convoy, significantly adding to the costs.

Hinks' other worry was that the party would come back early. This would not matter if they succeeded on their first attempt, as the publicity value would be obvious, but if they did not get to the summit in May, he wanted the team to sit out the monsoon in Tibet and try again in the autumn. According to the instructions given to Bruce, he was at liberty to call up reinforcements and extra supplies but was expected to remain: 'The Committee desire that the fullest possible use should be made of the present opportunity and that the whole open season should be used as far as may be for attempts to attain our object.' Hinks and Younghusband had legitimate worries that the Tibetan government might not allow another expedition after 1922, but Hinks's instinctive niggardliness also played a role. Even though he was a geographer and cartographer, he had no experience of fieldwork and had no feeling at all for the privations of expedition life.

Bruce, on the other hand, as a veteran of many military campaigns, knew all along that there was a limit to maintaining morale once they reached Base Camp, especially after a tough approach march. Throughout May the weather had been almost uniformly awful. At one stage Bruce had turned to Chongay La, the Tibetan official sent by the governor of Shekar Dzong to assist the expedition, to ask him what was going on. He had replied that it was all the fault of the lamas at the Rongbuk monastery. Their religious services were causing the demons that lived near Everest to roar loudly. When the lamas stopped in mid-May, he told Bruce, the demons would quieten down and the weather would improve. As he predicted, after the services ceased, the weather did cheer up towards the end of May, but only very briefly, and as the temperature gradually increased, it also became more unstable. The relentless, enervating wind never abated.

For the lead climbers like Mallory and Finch, the tedium of tent life was leavened by the anticipation of their long-awaited summit attempts – but for the others, who were committed to spending long periods at Base Camp, taking endless supply convoys up and down the Rongbuk glacier, it was a gruelling and repetitive experience, which by the end of May had lost its charm. The porters kept themselves amused by running a book on which climbers would get highest. Some backed Finch, some backed Mallory. Most of the other sahibs weren't even in the running.

For Arthur Wakefield, the Lake District climber, the expedition had been deeply frustrating. He had never been an Alpine mountaineer of Finch's standard but he was well regarded within the British climbing world. The Everest Committee had tried to enrol him first for the 1921 Reconnaissance and, when he couldn't make it, they persisted and invited him to join the 1922 expedition. But none of the younger climbers on the team had made him feel in demand, with both Mallory and Finch particularly dismissive of his capabilities.

Like virtually all of the climbers in 1922, Wakefield had been involved in the bitter fighting of the First World War. For the career soldiers – the two Bruces, 'Teddy' Norton and John Morris – warfare was part of their lives; and for those assigned to the North-West Frontier, it was often brutal and bloody. For Arthur Wakefield it was different. He was a doctor who had emigrated from Britain to Canada before enlisting in 1914; nothing had prepared him for the carnage of the Western Front. Bearded and grey, in photographs he's usually smiling benignly, but as his family and friends knew, he was a deeply troubled man.

On the journey out, Wakefield had taken over Tom Longstaff's medical duties when he fell ill, and was called upon regularly for 'sick parades' at Base Camp. Along with Morris and Bruce, initially he'd been in charge of supplying and resupplying the camps on the Rongbuk glacier, working mainly with local Tibetan day labourers rather than the more experienced Sherpas. It reminded him, as he wrote in a letter home, of the life of a 'Westmorland farmer', but here he was herding an unruly flock of Tibetan men, women and children up the glacier – assisted by the expedition's Gurkha NCOs, who played the role of sheepdogs, barking orders and delivering the occasional bite.

As Bruce noted, the Sherpas looked down on the local Tibetans – regarding them as 'jangli' or wild men – much as Londoners looked down on country 'yokels'. Wakefield made no comment, but he was amazed at the amount that both the Sherpas and Tibetans were prepared to carry, sometimes shouldering two loads of up to eighty pounds. Even today it's humbling to see the huge sacks carried by everyone from old women to primary-school children on paths around Sherpa villages, but to carry double loads on a surface like the Rongbuk glacier was simply astonishing.

As everyone knew, Wakefield was a staunch opponent of supplementary oxygen, but he recognized that the principal challenge of Everest was overcoming the altitude – not the technical nature of the climbing. When in early May he wrote home shortly after arriving at Base Camp, he was pleased to announce that he felt good, and though some of the others had suffered attacks of vomiting, he claimed that he could barely tell that he was above sea level and was sleeping exceptionally well. Wounded by not being invited to take part in either the first or second attempt, Wakefield decided, without the permission of Strutt or Bruce, that he would make a summit bid of his own with Ferdie Crawford, another member of the team who had been underutilized. On 24 May, when Finch went up to the North Col with Geoffrey Bruce and Tejbir, Wakefield remained below at Camp 3 – but shortly afterwards, he too climbed up to Camp 4 and settled in with Noel and his photographic porters.

Then, on 27 May, the same day that Finch and Bruce came down the mountain, Wakefield was joined by Crawford on the North Col. The two men stayed on when the others went down, planning their own ascent for the following day. Unsurprisingly, Wakefield had decided not to use supplementary oxygen, but he was confident that they could at least make a stab at it. The only problem was that neither man had slept properly for the previous four days. Fortunately, Wakefield had come up with his medical kit, so he offered Crawford a small dose of morphine: one milligram first of all, with a second milligram standing by should he need it.

Crawford took both doses and woke up the following morning feeling refreshed, he said, after a great night's sleep. The only problem was that it soon became obvious he was so fuzzy and befuddled that he simply could not get going. When Wakefield discovered that the porters had used up all the fuel in the camp and that there was hardly any food left, he reluctantly accepted that there was no point in staying any longer and the two men headed back down – a miserable climax to their attempt. In a letter to his wife at the end of the expedition, Wakefield would comment that Everest had not been 'by any manner of means a picnic' and that the only parts that he had really enjoyed were the voyage out and the time spent in Darjeeling. Like Howard-Bury the previous year, he concluded that Everest was not a place for middle-aged men, even though he was proud to have spent so many days on the North Col.

When Wakefield and Crawford arrived back at Base Camp, it seemed as if their abortive attempt on the mountain would be the last. Altogether, the team had been on the Rongbuk glacier for just over a month, the weather had not improved and the strain was beginning to show. During the Reconnaissance, the base camps at Tingri and the Kharta valley had not really been occupied for long periods of time, and there was constant traffic with the various climbers, surveyors and geologists coming and going, as well as Howard-Bury moving between his different parties. The 1922 expedition was necessarily much more static. Bruce always had plenty to do to deal with the logistics, but after developing a sore foot, he had not ventured up to any of the high camps. His deputy, Edward Strutt, was a very irascible character who rarely held back from venting his feelings, whether he was complaining about the food or the weather. John Morris called him the 'biggest snob' that he had ever met, but recalled that even though Strutt was prone to ill-tempered outbursts at Base Camp, like a good 'gentleman' he invariably apologized afterwards.

As for George Mallory, after coming down from the North Col, he had spent most of the time in his tent, fretting about how high Finch would get and writing to his wife and friends in England. In a letter to Ruth on 1 June, he painted a miserable and despondent picture of daily life in the aftermath of the two failed attempts. Morshead, he wrote, bore his frostbite 'wonderfully well but he's not a cheerful figure. Norton is even more depressed. Strutt is more than usually full of curses.' Crawford and Wakefield, Mallory reported, were both very eager to get back home, while

Tom Longstaff, who initially Mallory had a lot of affection for, had become 'tiresome, interfering, self-important'.

Part of his annoyance undoubtedly came from the fact that, as the official expedition medical officer, Longstaff had declared Mallory unfit for another attempt because of his frostbitten finger, and had gone as far as to hand in an official report to General Bruce and write to Younghusband in London. Even though Longstaff had warned everyone at the beginning of the expedition that he had never practised as a doctor, and Wakefield had taken over much of his day-to-day role, he had never stopped feeling a duty of care to the climbers.

As a veteran of many expeditions, Longstaff knew how seductive 'summit fever' could be. In 1905, two years after graduating from St Thomas' Hospital, he had gone on his first trip to the Himalayas. While attempting Gurla Mandhata in Tibet, his party had been caught in an avalanche which had carried everyone a thousand feet down the mountain. They had come back the next day to try again, and had only given up when heavy snows made movement impossible.

When Mallory's party had returned to Base Camp, Longstaff had been the first to congratulate them. The returning men felt deflated, having failed to reach either the summit or the shoulder, but Longstaff was quick to remind them that they had set two new world records, for the highest camp and the highest altitude. 'You've done absolutely splendidly,' he told them, instantly boosting their spirits. Their success did not, however, blind him to their poor state of health.

As for Finch's attempt, Longstaff remained ambivalent about oxygen: he recognized that it might not be possible to summit without it, but he thought the technology underdeveloped and potentially dangerous, and shared the instinctive feeling among several of the climbers that its use was not quite 'sporting'. As he wrote in his diary after the first attempt: 'Much better to 27,000 without oxygen than the summit with it... Bruce and I consider the expedition is successful even if nothing more is achieved.'

Like General Bruce, Longstaff hoped that the second attempt would get further, but he thought Finch's party too small to succeed. His overwhelming feeling by the end of May was that the expedition was over and everyone should go home. 'I have to admit that I am feeling the altitude and the constant cold wind. We all are,' he wrote in a letter to his wife. 'We hope Finch and Geoff Bruce will stand it. The rest of us are played out.' When the oxygen party finally returned to Base Camp, Longstaff was very disturbed to see that, like Morshead and Norton, Geoffrey Bruce had sustained serious frostbite injuries. The time has come, he wrote in his diary, to 'put my foot *(sic)* down: there is too little margin of safety. Strutt agrees.'

Bruce also thought that everything was more or less over by the end of May, but as the leader of the expedition, it wasn't quite so easy to call a halt. He knew that Hinks and everyone on the Everest Committee would be disappointed if they returned early without reaching the summit. It was the right thing to do, but it still felt uncomfortable.

At the same moment that Bruce was chewing over what to do next, Sir Francis Younghusband was giving his latest presidential address to the Royal Geographical Society in London. Much had been achieved on the 1921 Reconnaissance, as he told the fellows and their guests, but now a 'full-blown' effort was under way to reach the summit. The Committee, he said, had 'sent out the hardiest, pluckiest, and most skilful and experienced mountaineers we can find'. Expectations were high, even if he acknowledged how difficult it was going to be.

Though Younghusband also wanted the team to stay on until the autumn, he had known for a while that it was unlikely. In a private letter a month earlier from Shekar Dzong – halfway between the Base Camp and the Tibetan border – Bruce had warned him that a post-monsoon attempt was pretty much out of the question. 'No one here seems to think that it would be possible as we stand at the present moment,' he wrote. 'With regard to the personnel, it is very doubtful, as I pointed out before I left London, whether more than one or two of them would either be ready or fit for a further attempt.' If there was a completely new team, and if they could be trained in the use of oxygen, and if the whole expedition could be resupplied... then it might be possible to stay on; but far better, Bruce advised, to come back the following year. Bruce had finished his letter on a positive note, writing that 'this is only a warning as perhaps we are going to climb Everest after all', but the tone of the letter had not exactly been bullish.

Now, as May headed into June, Bruce had to make a final decision about when to leave and whether or not to allow one more summit attempt. Whatever Longstaff said or reported, Mallory was obviously keen and Somervell did seem to have recovered his strength faster and better than anyone could have expected. But who else could take part?

The three men with serious frostbite could do no further climbing. Norton had spent the first few days after his return in his tent – 'a complete worm', as he put it in his diary. More recently he seemed to have regained some of his old energy and had even done some surveying with his theodolite, but his ear was still badly affected and he was obviously not fit for anything strenuous.

Morshead was the worst case of all. With the marginally warmer temperatures at Base Camp his frostbitten hands had begun to thaw, making them even more painful. He tried to maintain a brave face but couldn't hide the agony, even when he was regularly taking two grams of opium – a very hefty dose of painkiller. During the day, he stayed out of his tent and walked about trying to avoid the others, but at night he could be heard weeping with pain. The priority, as Bruce realized, was to get him back to Darjeeling as quickly as possible.

As for Geoffrey Bruce, he was not in quite as bad a state as Morshead or Norton, but could barely walk on his frostbitten foot. Having invited him to join the team and having pulled a lot of strings to get him released from the army, Charlie Bruce undoubtedly felt a strong sense of responsibility towards his young cousin and would not be sending him back up.

Lance Corporal Tejbir had done exceptionally well, but he too did not look fit enough for another attempt, and Bruce didn't really rate any of the other members of the team.

The only possibility was George Finch.

Finch had returned to Base Camp on 29 May exhausted and wind-blown, but though he had patches of frostbite on the soles of his feet, he had been able to walk into camp. Bruce still had not warmed to Finch on a personal level, but he could see how ambitious he was and recognized that the oxygen party had done significantly better than Mallory's team. It was all down to Finch being so 'handy' with the oxygen equipment that they had got so far, as Bruce wrote in a letter to Hinks. The 'dream team' would be Mallory and Finch climbing together, but was Finch up to it?

Two days earlier, on 27 May, John MacDonald, the son of the British trade agent at Yatung, had arrived in camp with a sack full of mail and two Tibetans who offered to ride hard back to Phari with the latest news. Bruce composed two brief messages to be telegraphed immediately, along with detailed reports by Mallory and Finch that would appear later. Ultimately, Mallory's report got to Phari the fastest, with the outline of his record-breaking ascent published in *The Times* on 9 June, followed a week later by his full account. News of Finch's attempt did not get back to London until 16 June, because the second messenger fell ill and did not reach the telegraph station until several days after the first.

It was a relief for Bruce to finally be able to send some good news to London, but in MacDonald's postbag there was also the first of several letters from Hinks complaining about the parlous state of the expedition finances. On 29 May, Longstaff handed Bruce his official report, declaring Mallory and Norton unfit for any further climbing. Three days later, on 2 June, he examined Finch and reported that his heart had become enlarged and would not return to normal for two weeks. It looked as if that was that, but on the same day, Finch heard 'a pretty little plot concocted in the tent next to mine... Wakefield examines Mallory and me and finds both fit for another shot (yet Mallory's fingers are all frostbitten!)'.

Slowly but inexorably, the drums were beating for a final attempt on Everest, even though no one was utterly convinced. Bruce wrote to Hinks telling him that 'the flower of the men's condition must have gone', and even Mallory admitted in a letter to his close friend David Pye that he recognized the danger. 'Perhaps it's mere folly to go up again,' he wrote. 'But how can I be out of the hunt?' To his wife, Ruth, he tried to sound more positive, acknowledging that going back up meant risking further damage from frostbite, 'but the game is worth a finger and I shall take every conceivable care of both fingers and toes.'

As for climbing with Finch, Mallory remained ambivalent. 'I'm afraid he will get on my nerves a bit before we're done,' he wrote to Ruth, 'but I hope we shall manage our climb without serious friction.' Mallory was very critical of what he saw as Finch's cavalier treatment of his porters. 'Finch seems to have an altogether different standard of caring for the coolies from mine,' he said, adding: 'I'm determined we will not risk their lives during this next venture.'

That was unfair. Mallory criticized Finch for allowing a party of Sherpas to come up to relieve his high camp – 'the idea of coolies wandering about up there in the dark with none of us to look after them fills me with horror' – but forgot that it was John Noel who had dispatched the porters, and that during Mallory's own attempt they had sent a party of unaccompanied porters down the North Ridge once their tent had been pitched.

Finch for his part was nervous, but like his rival Mallory could not turn down the chance, especially when they would be using oxygen and he nominally would be in charge of the party. Unlike Mallory, however, who had been at Base Camp for ten days, Finch had been there for just four and was still far from fully recovered. He didn't really think that Mallory was fit enough for another attempt, though like everyone else he was amazed at Howard Somervell's resilience.

To add to the risks, Finch could see that, if anything, the weather was getting worse rather than improving. When he wrote to his wife on the night of 2 June, Finch didn't mention the latest plan, but the next morning he left camp with Mallory and Somervell. The lure of Everest – and his rivalry with Mallory – was too great for good sense to prevail.

The British team was living on its wits. On the first and second attempts Mallory and Finch had set new world records, but both parties had narrowly avoided disaster. The third time round they would not be so lucky.

10

Trouble in the Sanctuary

I t was just so unpredictable.

On 8 June, the Everest Committee had met for the first time in several months. Nothing was going well. The treasury had just informed them that there would be no tax relief on Captain Noel's film, the 1921 Reconnaissance photographs were not selling, and they had just sent out another £2,000 to Bruce, whom they had not heard from for two months. If worse came to worst, they would have to take out a bank loan to cover their overdraft.

And then everything changed overnight.

On the morning of 9 June 1922, *The Times* published a brief report on the first attempt, and a week later printed Mallory's detailed account. On the same day, 16 June, they also had a short report of the second summit bid led by Finch, which had done even better. The other newspapers all echoed *The Times*, praising the climbers fulsomely – and to add to the excitement, four days later, on 20 June, there was yet another short article in *The Times*, from their correspondent at Yatung, announcing that a third attempt was under way.

Arthur Hinks could not contain himself. He wrote to Mallory on 15 June: 'What pleased us as much as anything was that it was done without oxygen. Some of us never really liked the idea of oxygen, and consequently we felt sure that the record could be beaten without it.' On the following day he wrote to Edward Norton that breaking the altitude record was 'a great feat and one that we shall remember all our lives'. When the news came in that Finch had managed to get even higher, Hinks was so thrilled that he forgot his opposition to oxygen and wrote to his least favourite climber to send his 'hearty congratulations on your successfully beating the record', adding that 'things are moving so fast and the telegrams coming at such irregular intervals in such funny order that we have some difficulty in sorting out events'.

Not only were Bruce and his team achieving great things on Everest, but they were finally sending back cables and dispatches. If everything went well and the narrative of progress continued, they would honour the *Times* contract and might even reach the summit.

Then it all became just so confusing.

On 23 June, a week after Mallory's long article in *The Times*, Hinks was rocked by two telegrams from Strutt and Longstaff, from Gangtok in Sikkim. The first, from Strutt to Sydney Spencer, the Honorary Secretary of the Alpine Club, repeated the altitudes achieved on the first two attempts and then announced that 'monsoon broke June third... Longstaff, Finch and self returning England immediately, rest of party proceeding Kharta Valley June fourteenth before homeward journey... Longstaff considers whole party played out.'

The second telegram from Longstaff to the Everest Committee was shorter but equally perplexing: 'Returning with Strutt, Finch, Morshead...Latter's frost bites doing well... hoping sail July first... Cable Bruce whether leave heavy baggage at Phari Jong for another expedition.'

Hinks was thrown into an angry panic. What had happened to the third attempt? Why was Finch coming back early? What exactly did Longstaff mean by 'another expedition'? A few days later, Sir Francis Younghusband appeared again in front of the fellows of the Royal Geographical Society, but he did not mention either telegram. He told his audience that the Committee had viewed the first two attempts that year as 'reconnaissances' and had hoped that the third and final effort would be 'the real attempt'. That belief had been thrown into question by the news that the monsoon had broken on 3 June. It would in all probability bring an end to any further hopes. Nevertheless, Younghusband said that he had been thrilled by the results and he finished his talk with a quote from 'a certain father Ratti', better known as Pope Pius XI: 'Mountaineering proper is not necessarily rashness, but is entirely a question of prudence and of courage, of strength and steadiness, of a feeling for nature and her most hidden beauties, which are often awe-inspiring but for that reason the more sublime and to a contemplative spirit the more suggestive.'

Arthur Hinks was less forgiving. He wrote to Bruce to say that he had been 'staggered' by Longstaff's telegram. He was now very worried that because of the dearth of dispatches, they would lose £1,300 worth of sponsorship from *The Times*, and he warned Bruce that from then on they would have to conduct themselves as economically as possible. There would be no 'upper-deck' tickets and no question of taking a train from Marseille to Calais. So what was really going on with the third attempt? Had it taken place? Would it ever?

In fact, the *Times* report from Yatung had been correct. On 3 June, the third attempt had got under way, with Mallory, Finch, Somervell and Crawford leaving Base Camp with fourteen porters. John Noel and his team of camera assistants had accompanied them, and so had the long-suffering Arthur Wakefield, who was planning to stay in support at Camp 3 when the others went up to the North Col. John Morris, the Gurkha officer, also joined them, but he was not intending to play any role in the climbing, having been ordered by Bruce to start bringing down all the unused supplies and equipment. If everything went perfectly, Mallory and Finch would climb Everest and then strip the high camps on the way down, while Morris got everything out of Camps 1 to 3.

The unknowable factor was the weather. Today's climbers take it for granted that they will have access to high-quality weather data; and even in the early 1950s, with massive improvements in forecasting coming during the Second World War, the British expeditions to Everest and Kangchenjunga were able to organize bespoke weather forecasts to be transmitted on Indian radio. In 1922, neither the radio nor the meteorological technology was available. The idea of anyone waiting for the perfect 'weather window' was inconceivable.

Instead, Bruce and his team relied on local knowledge and guesswork. The monsoon generally hit the Indian subcontinent somewhere between the end of May and the middle of June, but precisely when seemed to change from year to year. The lamas at the Rongbuk monastery had told the team that they thought it would not arrive until around 10 June, but it was clear that conditions were very unstable and there were increasing amounts of snow.

To complicate matters, tea planters in Darjeeling had noticed that sometimes after the first monsoon downpours there was a week or so of fine weather. If this was the case, then maybe they were about to enjoy a perfect few days of their own. The harsh west wind which had made their lives such a misery during the first and second attempts seemed to be abating, replaced by much warmer and more humid currents from the south.

So even though the weather did not look particularly promising when they left Base Camp on 3 June, they put a brave face on it. It soon became obvious, however, that Finch was just not well enough to take part. On the way to Camp 1 he marched very slowly, and repeatedly had to stop. He did manage to reach 'Villa Never-Sweat', but that night as he lay in his 'flea-bag', listening to the snowstorm swirling outside, he found it impossible to sleep.

At 2.00 a.m. on 4 June, according to Finch's diary, the 'monsoon broke', depositing a heavy layer of snow all over Camp 1. The next morning, when he finally emerged from his tent, it was clear to Finch that he could not continue, so after giving Somervell a final lesson on the oxygen sets, he set off back to Base Camp. When Finch arrived a few hours later, Bruce was shocked to see him but accepted that he had done the right thing. Longstaff concurred; when he examined Finch, he found that the returning climber's heart was 'all over the place'.

By this point, Bruce had already decided that the weakest men should leave for Darjeeling as soon as possible. Morshead was still very badly affected by frostbite, and fearing that his fingers might have to be amputated en route, Longstaff had agreed to

escort him – along with Strutt, who also seemed to have 'shot
his bolt' and was not a good man to have around camp. When
Bruce offered Finch the chance to join the returning party, he
readily agreed.

Two of the slightly less badly affected men, Edward Norton
and Geoffrey Bruce, would leave Base Camp at the same time,
heading for the nearby Kharta valley. The hope was that once
they reached the comforts of lower altitude, their frostbite would
improve. Charlie Bruce intended to join them with the remaining
members once the third attempt was over. Together they would
spend a few weeks resting up before the long march back to
Darjeeling and then the journey to Britain. If they had the supplies
and the inclination, there was time to do a little bit of exploring
of the local valleys, but Bruce was not too concerned about doing
any more work, whatever Hinks expected.

In the late afternoon on 5 June, both parties moved out of
camp, leaving Bruce with just a handful of Sherpas and Gurkha
NCOs to await the return of Mallory and the others. Judging
from the weather, he expected they would be back soon.

As predicted, up at Camp 1 on the Rongbuk glacier, things
were not good. Mallory and the others had been pinned down
in their tents by a blizzard which showed no sign of stopping.
No one was optimistic but, as Mallory later wrote, he felt that if
they turned back straight away they would always regret it. So
on 5 June they carried on up, passing Camp 2 but not stopping
until they reached Camp 3 at the foot of the North Col.

It was an even less inviting sight. Around a foot of snow
covered everything, and new snow was still falling. The previous
party had collapsed the tents in order to stop the poles from
snapping, but they were filled with snow and ice. After a lot of grim

work, they re-pitched the tents and got ready for the night. Once again they discussed the idea of abandoning the third attempt, but before finally saying goodbye to Everest, they decided to spend one more day at Camp 3, in order to see what the weather would do.

The next morning, to make things a little more complicated, it dawned fine and bright and stayed like that for most of the afternoon. The porters were tired after a long day carrying, and everyone was happy to stay in camp and watch the snow melt and consolidate around them. For once their tents seemed to be sheltered from the wind, but they were glad to see how, high above them, the snow was being blown off the North Ridge. Somervell and Mallory planned out the next few days of their campaign.

Even though Finch was no longer with them and Mallory had previously been a staunch opponent of supplementary oxygen, they decided to stick with it but, modifying Finch's plan, would only use their sets for the final stage of the attempt, intending to climb to the North Col under their own steam. Then, taking the fittest porters, they would endeavour to get ten cylinders to a high camp, ideally at 26,000 feet on the North Ridge. Mallory had budgeted for just one bottle of oxygen to be used between 25,000 and 26,000 feet, leaving them with four cylinders each for the final summit push. Ferdie Crawford would climb with them up to the North Col and then stay in position to look after the porters coming down from the high camp. Ever the bridesmaid, Arthur Wakefield would most likely remain at Camp 3.

Though by now they had been up and down to the North Col several times, Mallory decided to be cautious and carry the stores up in two stages: on the first day they would hump everything to a point a few hundred feet below the col, and then on the second day they would return to take the loads to the col itself.

On the morning of 7 June they were up early. It had been a cold night and it took a long time and a lot of shouting to get everyone mustered. Wakefield had had a bad night, so he decided to stay in camp and await developments. Everyone else was nervous about the snow conditions, but excited to get away. As Mallory later wrote, 'You may read between the lines how anxious I was about this venture. I knew enough about Mount Everest not to treat so formidable a mountain contemptuously. But it was not a desperate game I thought with the plans we made.'

At 8.00 a.m. they left their tents, and immediately found themselves ploughing through deep snow. In some places it was topped with a hard crust but it quickly broke, causing them to sink through into the softer layer below. Somervell took the lead, followed by Mallory, then one of the porters, then Crawford and then the other thirteen men, carrying their supplies and precious oxygen cylinders. It was such hard going that it took a full two hours just to get to the slope leading up to the col.

Mallory and Somervell were by then familiar with the 2,000-foot slope leading up to the North Col, but neither their nor Finch's tracks were still visible. When Mallory had first climbed it, about a month earlier, it had been hard ice and compacted snow, requiring a lot of step-cutting, but now it appeared to be covered in a thick layer of soft snow. There was a real danger that it might avalanche, so first of all they stamped out a series of trenches at the foot of the slope to test the stability of the snow. Nothing happened so they started to climb, but as a precaution they roped up into four separate parties.

John Noel wanted to go with them to film their ascent, but his heavily burdened camera porters found it too hard to carry the equipment through the deep drifts. Realizing that it would be futile to persevere, Noel ordered them to turn back after about 150 feet and returned to Camp 3, from where he planned to film the ascent with a long lens.

Further down the mountain, everything was proceeding as expected. Charlie Bruce had sent down a message to the headmen of local villages, asking for the porters and yaks that would be needed to evacuate everyone from Base Camp. John Morris was busy at Camp 2, looking after the Sherpas who had begun to strip the Rongbuk camps. Further to the east, the two parties that had already left had just separated, with Longstaff, Finch and the others hurrying back north towards Darjeeling while Norton and Bruce headed for the Kharta valley.

At 11.30 a.m., Mallory's team halted on the final section of slope to regroup. They were now about 600 feet from the crest of the col but they were not quite high enough to create a useful supply dump. The weather seemed to be holding and the angle of the slope had eased off. There was ample time to return to Camp 3 once they found the perfect site and cached everything.

Somervell was still full of energy. He un-roped and went ahead to kick steps in the snow to make it easier for the others to follow. After a few minutes everyone else began to move up. Then Mallory thought he heard something: a low boom that reminded him of the sound of untamped gunpowder exploding. At the same time, Somervell looked up and saw a crack in the snow, about twenty feet above him.

Mallory reacted almost instantly, heading up towards the break, but before he reached it, he felt himself being submerged in snow and carried down the mountain. Somervell was also sucked into the avalanche and flung upside down. He lost his hat but managed to hold on to his ice axe. Strangely, he felt no fear. The moment of his death had come, he realized; the only question was how long it would take.

Mallory had never been in an avalanche before, but instinctively he tried to turn around to avoid being carried down headlong and backwards. After a few seconds, he managed to right himself, only to be overwhelmed by another wave of snow. Like Somervell he was sure that 'the matter was settled', but remembering what other mountaineers had told him about avalanches, he tried to keep his arms above his body. Then, after a few seconds, just as suddenly as the avalanche had begun, Somervell felt the rope tighten around his waist as he came to a stop.

Somehow he managed to get back upright and claw his way to the surface. He looked around and saw Mallory and Crawford and one group of porters below. He assumed that the other two ropes were somewhere in between and that soon they would come to the surface, but then he noticed the porters pointing at something below them.

Down at Camp 3, Noel and Wakefield had been having lunch. Every five minutes or so, Noel would leave the tent to watch the team's progress through his camera, but they had been moving tediously slowly. Noel didn't hear anything, but when he went out shortly after 2.15 p.m., to his amazement the slope that his camera was trained on appeared to be totally clear. Wakefield came out to check and could see nothing either. Then the awful truth dawned on them.

Noel immediately called to his camera porters to fill thermoses with soup and gather up any blankets and sleeping bags they could find. In order to move more quickly, both he and Wakefield grabbed oxygen sets and began running towards the col. They saw huge balls of snow and chunks of ice at the foot of the slope, but in their haste and in spite of their oxygen sets, found themselves running out of puff and had to stop to catch their breath.

When they eventually reached the foot of the slope, at first they could see no one, but then they noticed a group of porters huddled together at the top of an ice cliff. About sixty feet below, Noel spotted Mallory and Somervell, using their hands and ice axes to claw at the snow. Close by were the bodies of several porters.

When the avalanche ended, initially Mallory and Somervell had thought that group at the top of the cliff was the last of the three ropes, and that the two intervening parties would soon emerge from the snow. In fact, the four men below them were from the closest rope and had been dragged 150 feet down the slope. The other nine porters had been carried over the edge of the cliff by the avalanche and flung down towards a large crevasse. Some of them had smashed into its hard outer lip and died instantly but others had been buried under a mass of snow – some on the outside of the crevasse, several deep within.

When they reached the site, Mallory and Somervell had frantically begun digging. The first man they found was still alive, the next three were dead. Then, following the trail of ropes, they climbed down into the crevasse to continue the search. The first man they hauled out was dead, but to their amazement the second man was still alive, even though he had been buried upside down in tightly packed snow. Hoping against hope, they kept on going and retrieved the corpse of one more porter but they were unable to pull out the last man and eventually had to give up. In total seven men were dead: Thankay, Sangay, Temba, Lhakpa, Pasang Namgyn, Norbu and Pema.

Mallory was devastated. Having promised himself that above all he would look after the porters, and after criticizing Finch for taking too many risks with them, it felt as if he had led seven men to their deaths. Somervell was equally appalled by the death toll and the fact that so many porters had died. 'Only Sherpas and Bhotias [Tibetans] killed,' as he later wrote, 'Why, oh why could not one of us Britishers have shared their fate? I would gladly at that moment have been lying there, dead in the snow, if only to give those fine chaps who had survived the feeling that we had shared their loss, as we had indeed shared the risk.'

The surviving porters removed the religious tokens and jewellery from the dead men to return them to their families, but told the sahibs that the bodies should all be placed within the crevasse, rather than taking them back down the glacier. As everyone trekked back to Camp 3, one porter was sent down to Base Camp to deliver the terrible news. Meanwhile, Somervell and Wakefield began work on a large cairn at Camp 3 to commemorate the deaths. Mallory later commented that he was glad that the Sherpas had chosen to leave the bodies on the mountain: 'What better burial could they have than to lie in the snow where they fell?'

The next morning, Mallory was the first climber to return to Base Camp, coming down on his own. He was very tired and visibly distraught. Bruce tried to comfort him as best he could, but he couldn't quite understand why the attempt had taken place at all. As far as he was concerned, the previous days' weather had been so bad that no one would have risked an ascent to the North Col. He sent a runner up to Morris, telling him to abandon everything above Camp 3; no one would take any more risks for the sake of a few tents and sleeping bags.

Wakefield, Crawford and Somervell came down on 9 June with some of the lighter equipment, followed a few days later by John Morris and the last few porters. Morris was amazed at how quickly Everest was changing; the warm south wind was melting the seracs on the Rongbuk glacier, causing many of them to topple over. With the west wind gone, the whole of the North Face was covered in snow, giving the mountain a very different look. Morris's porters brought down three oxygen sets but several had to be left behind, along with food and other supplies.

For the next five days they stayed at Base Camp, awaiting the yaks that would take them to the Kharta valley where they would join Norton and Geoffrey Bruce. The Rongbuk Lama had been notified of the accident, and services were being held for the dead men in the nearby monastery. It was an awful time for everyone and Morris noticed a palpable air of depression settling in over Base Camp. When Noel wrote to Arthur Hinks on 12 June, a few days after he had returned to Base Camp, he confided that they were all still very distressed by the accident and the thought that the porters whom they all admired had perished. 'Everest is a tough mountain,' he concluded, 'and has knocked out our party with hard blows such as nobody expected. In fact it is a terribly dangerous mountain with its fearful wind, cold, misty weather and avalanches.'

Mallory wrote a long letter to his wife, worried that the news of the accident would reach her first via the press. 'My dearest Ruth,' he began, 'I will answer what I imagine to have been your first thought – it <u>was</u> a wonderful escape for me and we may indeed be thankful for that together. Dear love when I think what your grief would have been I humbly thank God I am alive.' Though he had never formally been appointed the leader of the third attempt, Mallory clearly felt responsible for what had occurred. 'It's difficult to get it all straight in my mind,' he admitted. 'The consequences of my mistake are so terrible; it seems almost impossible to believe that it has happened forever and that I can do nothing to make good. There is no obligation I have so much wanted to honour as that of taking care of these men; they are children where mountain dangers are concerned and they do so much for us: and now through my fault seven of them have been killed.' The main part of the letter was a detailed account of the accident, which he later asked her to circulate among his friends.

Mallory also wrote a separate letter to his mentor, Geoffrey Winthrop Young, reiterating how guilty he felt about the accident but insisting that 'it was not the result of any spirit of recklessness or any carelessness of coolies' lives'.

Young was sympathetic, replying that, though it was a natural response to feel guilty, Mallory had done nothing wrong: 'The proud man's instinct is to dispute that chance could have produced all those grim effects; the very magnitude of the pain he suffers forces him to bite on the aching tooth, to blame himself with a larger share in the responsibility for it than is rightly his to claim.'

When he heard of the incident, Sir Francis Younghusband was equally insistent that Mallory should not take it all on himself: 'I certainly am not one to blame you, for I have done precisely the same thing myself in the Himalaya, and only the purest luck can have saved me and my party from disaster.'

Edward Strutt took a rather dimmer view. On 11 June, Mallory sent him a brief letter, hoping it would reach him before he returned to Britain. He repeated in brief what he had told his wife and Young but, sensing how the story might play out in Britain and the questions that might be asked as to why he had risked an ascent to the North Col after heavy snow, he pleaded with Strutt to support him in public: 'If you can say anything to excuse our being there please say it. To me half the tragedy lies in the fact that these men were so ignorant of mountain dangers – like children in our care, I blame myself wholly. But I fear the accident will stultify the expedition in the eyes of the public – in public we must make the best of it.'

The letter did not reach Strutt until he was back in London. In his reply, Strutt was characteristically blunt. He told Mallory that, though he felt sorry for him, he should not have taken the porters up: 'After the great fall of fresh snow, seventeen persons on the North Col was fifteen too many, even after two days' perfect weather. Don't think these are criticisms: the man on the spot must be the sole judge, and he gets the reward or pays the penalty.' Strutt finished his letter on a more cynical note, mocking the press and the public's appetite for mountaineering disasters. 'As for the British Public, the middle classes, shop-keepers, gillies, etc., who alone show a real interest in the expedition, these rather welcome the accident (dead bodies always appeal to them) and think us real 'eroes in consequence…'

Mallory was throughout his life an instinctive risk-taker. As his friend and first biographer David Pye wrote, he was someone who could not get behind the wheel of a car without wanting to overtake the vehicle in front. As a child, he frightened his parents climbing trees and church roofs; as a youth, he amazed his friends with daring solo escapades on British crags. On Everest, as he had admitted to Geoffrey Winthrop Young in 1921, he sometimes worried that he had become too obsessed: 'Geoffrey, at what point am I going to stop?'

It would be a mistake, though, to focus on the avalanche and forget how close the other two attempts came to disaster. On the first summit bid, Mallory had been the hero of the day. If it hadn't been for his quick response when Norton slipped, the whole party might have perished. On the second attempt, the inexperienced Geoffrey Bruce came close to collapse when his oxygen set broke, and he would have fallen all the way down the North Face if Finch hadn't held him. On the third attempt, the team's luck ran out. They had managed to climb most of the way up to the North Col when the avalanche hit. Arguably Mallory should not have pushed for a third attempt and should have recognized the dangers posed by the snow conditions, but there have been many top climbers since 1922 who have been killed in avalanches, regardless of their experience. Whether the British public would blame Mallory for the accident or whether, as Strutt suggested, they would be thrilled by the danger remained to be seen, but it would be several weeks before Mallory returned to Britain

On 14 June the team finally left Base Camp and headed back up the Rongbuk valley. When they reached the monastery, Bruce made sure to seek a second audience with the head lama. Dzatrul Rinpoche was very sympathetic, blessing all the porters and paying particular attention to those who had lost relatives. He presented Bruce with sacred images to take away and even remembered to have Western-style milk tea prepared for him.

John Noel was brave enough to drink some of the more regular yak-butter variety, but was disturbed to discover that the lamas had painted a new image on one of the monastery walls. It showed the angry deity of Everest surrounded by demons, lions, yetis and barking dogs and, at the bottom of the image, 'speared through and through, lies the naked body of the white-man who dared to violate the ice-bound tempest-guarded sanctuary of Chomolungma – Goddess Mother of the World'.

The message was clear.

11

A Terrible Enemy

They strapped his hands to his shoulders and put his feet in improvised stirrups and rode hard – the first members of the 1922 expedition to be heading for home. On the way out, it had taken over a month to get from Darjeeling to the Rongbuk glacier, but everyone was so worried about Morshead's frostbite that they made the 324-mile return trip in just twenty days. Tom Longstaff looked after him as best he could, dosing him regularly with opium, and thanking his lucky stars that he did not have to do any amputations on the trail. Finch's feet had also suffered frostbite damage and Strutt was the worse for wear, but everyone was very glad to be leaving the bitter winds of Base Camp behind.

Though sorely afflicted, Morshead never complained, even when he had to get off his pony and walk over several 18,000-foot passes. Ultimately, once they reached Darjeeling he would go under the surgeon's knife, but it didn't stop him from dreaming of a return to Everest. Within a few weeks of getting back, he dictated a letter to his wife for Hinks asking about the next expedition.

'I sincerely hope to have an early opportunity,' he said, 'of getting my revenge on the old mountain. My fingers and toes are going on splendidly and I am only losing joints on the tips of a couple of fingers, it won't cause any inconvenience.'

The other three – Finch, Strutt and Longstaff – kept on moving, aiming to get the first ship back to England. They had no idea that Mallory and Somervell had gone ahead with the third attempt or that it had ended in tragedy. After their first telegrams back to London announcing their plans to return, Strutt sent a second cable from Darjeeling on 26 June: 'Bruce will require fifteen hundred pounds by middle August. Account now overdrawn. Remit Alliance Bank Darjeeling immediately.'

Hinks was apoplectic. He too had no idea that the expedition had come to a climax on the North Col with the death of seven men. The news hadn't reached London, and once again the letters and dispatches from Base Camp had dried up – everything that was, apart from the telegrams from Longstaff and Strutt asking for money. So what on earth was going on? Not only was half the party returning early, but now General Bruce apparently needed another £1,500.

The Everest Committee's financial problems were very real. All the money left over from 1921 had been used up, and the slow trickle of dispatches meant that *The Times* and the *Public Ledger* had not made their second payments. The RGS had already posted a £2,000 guarantee to the bank against the Everest account, but the Alpine Club had not been forthcoming, prompting an angry note from Hinks to their Secretary, J. E. C. Eaton: 'If you Alpine Club people cannot somehow publicly or privately guarantee a thousand pounds of an overdraft I fear that some of your eminent members will have to be left in India or work their passage home.'

Hinks wrote an equally tetchy letter to Charles Bruce, though he knew by now that it might not reach him for several weeks. Once again he reminded Bruce that the Everest Committee had hoped that the expedition would stay until the autumn, and warned that it would cost extra to bring team members back early. He even went so far as to criticize the planning of the first two summit attempts which had ended in failure, forgetting for a moment that two new world records had been set.

More immediately, he sent a telegram back to Strutt aiming to reach him in Mumbai before he embarked for London with Longstaff and Finch: 'Committee require strictest economy cannot afford upper deck or overland passages.' He followed it up with a letter intended to reach Strutt in Port Said, on the voyage back to Europe, in which he told him bluntly about the Committee's money problems and how confused they all were. 'Everyone was tremendously bucked up by the two successful climbs and we were waiting with high anticipation of a final success when we got Longstaff's cablegram from Gangtok quickly followed by yours. This was an unpleasant disillusionment... it was impossible to understand why the second in command [Strutt], the chief oxygen climber and the surgeon and naturalist had suddenly left the expedition and were coming home without giving a reason.'

Strutt was not impressed. Hinks simply had no idea of what they had endured and how tough it had been on Everest. When they reached Port Said, he sent a cable back from his ship, the SS *Macedonia*, reiterating that he had been ordered to take Morshead and Finch back because of their ill health and that Longstaff had accompanied them in case he had to operate on Morshead's frostbitten hands. Strutt finished tersely: 'Idea of staying till September ridiculous.'

As the crisis continued, the Everest Committee met again on 5 July. Hinks reported that the expedition account was £1,068 overdrawn and that they should expect a further £2,000 in costs. He had been forced to accept that there was no chance of anyone ~~staying until the autumn, but if there was ever going to be another~~ attempt, he was determined they would write into the official instructions a firm commitment to stay for both the pre- and post-monsoon seasons. Sir Francis Younghusband even offered to go out to India himself and organize things, if no one could be found of sufficient mettle.

Hinks grew even more jittery. On 13 July he wrote to Bruce yet again, reiterating his complaint about the lack of dispatches for *The Times* and insisting that 'something must be done if possible to save the contract'. He repeated his order to Strutt that no one should come back on an upper-deck ticket, and advised Bruce to send a small exploring party to search for the head of the West Rongbuk glacier. If no new geographical knowledge was gained by the expedition, Hinks warned, 'this society will have a real grievance'.

On 15 July the SS *Macedonia* reached Marseille, on the very same day that news of the avalanche below the North Col was published in *The Times*. Longstaff and Strutt read about it on the train from Dover to London. It was a sobering moment for the returning men. They had left Base Camp a month earlier and had assumed that the early arrival of the monsoon snows would have put paid to any idea of making a third attempt. Instead, as they discovered, Mallory and Somervell had tried to lead yet another party up the North Col, triggering an avalanche that killed seven porters.

The report in *The Times* began on a plaintive note. 'I regret to have to chronicle a disaster,' wrote Charlie Bruce, 'a terrible ending to what, up to the time when my last dispatch was written, had been an exceptionally successful expedition.' He then went on to explain the sequence of events: how the party had split, with the injured men heading down to lower altitude while a final attempt was made on the summit. The summit party had started, he wrote, 'in glorious sunshine', but halfway up the slope below the North Col, an avalanche had hit. The events, he said, had 'shown what a terrible enemy the great Himalaya is... Its sun is hotter; its storms are worse; the distances are greater; everything is on an exaggerated scale.'

Bruce's main thoughts, though, were with the dead porters and their families. 'It is terrible to think', he concluded, 'that no fewer than seven splendid porters lost their lives in this tragedy. No expedition which ever travelled in the Himalayas, or, for that matter, in any part of the world, was better served by its subordinates than we have been. The work done by the porters was prodigious and unparalleled. Thus ends the first attempt to conquer the greatest mountain in the world.'

On 17 July, the day after the first party reached England, Hinks arranged a special meeting of the Everest Committee to find out why they were coming back early and what had gone wrong, but instead of being able to tick them off, he found himself confronted by three angry men who partly blamed him. As far as Tom Longstaff was concerned, Bruce had been an excellent leader and had only reluctantly agreed to the third attempt after being constantly harassed by Hinks and Younghusband, who had demanded endless dispatches and tried to pressurize him into staying on until the autumn.

As he wrote in a letter to his old friend Sandy Wollaston, the expedition doctor in 1921, the Committee 'had consistently treated Bruce meanly; had not appreciated his difficulties; had quite unnecessarily and most ungenerously urged him to repeated attacks on the peak and hence landed us in an accident which made us all feel humiliated'. With regard to the specific cause of the avalanche, Longstaff was equally critical of Somervell and Mallory, who he called 'a very good stout hearted baby... quite unfit to be in charge of anything including himself... Mallory cannot even observe the conditions in front of him. To attempt such a passage in the Himalaya after new snow is idiotic. What the hell did they think they could do *on Everest* in such conditions even if they did get up to the North Col?' Longstaff admired Somervell for his toughness but thought him reckless, describing him as someone who was 'honestly prepared to chuck his life away on the most remote chance of success'. Bruce had warned everyone to be careful and not to take excessive risks, but as Longstaff concluded, 'By their ignorance and unwillingness to take advice Mallory and Somervell have brought discredit on old Bruce.'

These were angry words, but it would be wrong to underestimate how shocked the returning men were – both at the behaviour of Hinks and at the expedition news, which they had barely had time to digest. Strutt had spent eight nights at 21,000 feet, Longstaff had been ill for much of the expedition, Finch had put in a heroic performance by anyone's standards, and here they were hauled up in front of the Committee, forced to justify their actions. As for the third attempt, though Finch had initially agreed to take part, he had never been enthusiastic and Longstaff and Strutt had both opposed it.

In an editorial published on the same day, *The Times* struck a less judgemental note. General Bruce's report, it said:

... is only too familiar in the annals of mountaineering. Once more brave men have lost their lives in the effort to penetrate the secrets of the eternal snows. Once more their surviving companions did their utmost for hours to rescue the poor bodies from an icy tomb... It may be that they or others will someday once again try to conquer this terrible mountain. But in any case, apart from the mighty feat which they have actually accomplished, there is no more glorious chapter in the history of mountaineering than the courageous efforts of this band of Mount Everest pioneers.

It was all very different from the paper's most famous editorial on mountaineering, published in the wake of another tragedy – the deaths on the Matterhorn in Switzerland almost sixty years earlier, in 1865. Back then mountaineering had been in its infancy, and the news that three British climbers and one French guide had died in a single climbing incident had sent shockwaves through the British establishment.

The men had been part of an ad hoc team of four British climbers and three guides, led by the brilliant young mountaineer Edward Whymper, making the first ascent of the Matterhorn, the striking mountain on the border of Italy and Switzerland, then known as 'the last great prize in the Alps'. Whymper's party had reached the summit ahead of a rival party climbing from the Italian side, but on the descent the youngest member of the team, Douglas Hadow, slipped, pulling off four men. Whymper and two Swiss guides survived only because the rope connecting them to the others had snapped.

One of the dead climbers, Lord Francis Douglas, was the brother of a peer of the realm, prompting *The Times* to thunder, 'Why is the best blood of England to waste itself in scaling hitherto inaccessible peaks, in staining the eternal snow and reaching the unfathomable abyss never to return?... Is it life? Is it duty? Is it common sense? Is it allowable? Is it not wrong?' The deaths had even come to the notice of Queen Victoria, who mentioned them in her personal diary. At one stage, after another Alpine season in which several British climbers died, the Queen had even instructed her private secretary to write to the prime minister, William Gladstone, to ask if she should publicly register her disapproval of 'dangerous Alpine excursions'.

Gladstone persuaded her not to. Instead, the great and good of the Alpine Club spoke out, arguing that the new sport of mountaineering was no more dangerous than hunting or sailing – and that, as member T. E. Buxton put it, 'There is besides in every sport that commands the love of Englishmen a danger that is unavoidable.'

By the end of the nineteenth century, reports of deaths in the Alps had lost their power to shock, and as British mountaineers made their first ventures into the Himalayas, it was not so unexpected when they too ended in tragedy. In 1895, the great A. F. Mummery, one of the finest British Alpinists of his day, had disappeared in a suspected avalanche along with two Gurkha soldiers, Ragobir Thapa and Goman Singh, while attempting Nanga Parbat, the world's ninth-highest mountain.

Ten years later, death came once again to the Himalayas, when three porters and a novice Swiss climber, Alexis Pache, died in an avalanche on Kangchenjunga, the world's third-highest mountain, at almost the same altitude as the 1922 Everest avalanche. The 1905 climbing leader was the maverick mountaineer Aleister Crowley. The dramatic end to this expedition and the bitter arguments that followed generated a lot of sensational press coverage, but by then no one condemned mountaineering outright as a sport. Himalayan climbing in particular had been subsumed into bigger narratives about the exploration of cold places – narratives in which British heroes like Scott and Shackleton were willing to give their all for national glory.

After a lot of work from Younghusband and the Everest Committee, the 1921 and 1922 Everest expeditions had also been elevated to the status of 'national' enterprises, like Scott's attempt on the South Pole, rather than mere 'sporting' trips to the Alps. This didn't mean that the expedition was thought to be more risky, but if it was, then at least there was a 'great' purpose to it.

And it would be wrong to think that British climbers were reckless. On the contrary, they had a reputation both for upholding standards of 'fair play' and for being cautious and safety-conscious. In the 1930s, when he was elected President of the Alpine Club, Edward Strutt would become famous for his condemnation of German 'suicide climbers' who took what he declared were unnecessary and gratuitous risks on the north faces of the Matterhorn and the Eiger.

Of course, there is another way to look at the end of the 1922 expedition and the muted press reaction that followed. The simple fact was that none of the sahibs had perished. The Sherpas' names weren't featured in any of the *Times* reports and they weren't even recorded in the official 1922 account. As London's *Daily News* pointed out, the porters had been 'enlisted in a cause which cannot have meant as much to them as it did to their employers'.

If Howard Somervell had also been killed, or if the whole
British party had been wiped out, would the press have been
more condemnatory? Would they have questioned the purpose
of the expedition and seen the deaths as a waste of life? Perhaps,
but it is equally possible that if Mallory, Somervell and Crawford
had also been killed, their deaths would have been added to the
roll call of British mountaineers and explorers who had died in
the field. The sympathy for the dead Sherpas and Bhotias was
undoubtedly genuine on behalf of both the team and the British
press. The porters had been not treated as cannon fodder, and as
Mallory and Somervell made clear, if it hadn't been for a lucky
escape it was quite possible that everyone on that slope below
the North Col would have died.

At the very least, the avalanche did remind the world that
Everest was a very tough proposition. In early June, when news
had come in of the altitude records that were being broken,
it might have been easy to underestimate the world's highest
mountain, but the accident on the North Col showed just how
dangerous Everest could be. The next day, *The Times* continued
their coverage with a report on the Committee's meeting, recording
how everyone had now come to realize that 'the accounts which
have so far reached this country from the expedition have erred
considerably on the side of modesty and that Mount Everest is
a much more formidable mountain than has so far appeared'.

Charlie Bruce had known that all along, and though in his
dispatches to *The Times* he had not pointed the finger of blame,
he did not believe that the avalanche was inevitable and, like
Longstaff and Strutt, thought that Mallory and Somervell should
not have attempted the North Col at all. In a private letter to Sir
Francis Younghusband written on the same day as his dispatch for

The Times, he confided: 'I have no information or suggestion as to how on that day and under those conditions they had intended to take their great caravan of three climbers and 14 loaded coolies across this place… Mallory is of course very cut up over the whole episode… the whole thing turns on an error of judgement.' As far as Bruce was concerned, they should not have gone ahead, especially after Finch was forced to retire. 'It is altogether a rather humiliating and I am sorry to say, I consider, a quite un-necessary ending to the Expedition.'

In a long second page, Bruce gave candid assessments of his team's strengths and weaknesses. The great successes of the expedition were Norton, a 'first rate' climber, Somervell, 'a wonderful goer', and Finch, who was 'probably the best snow and ice man on the expedition'. Mallory was second to Somervell in 'going capacity' but was too chaotic, or as Bruce put it: 'He is a great dear but forgets his boots on all occasions.' Morshead he dubbed another 'first rate goer' but he was scathing about Crawford, an 'entirely useless' transport officer, and Wakefield, calling him 'a complete passenger'. Longstaff and Strutt had done their jobs well; Bruce's only regret was that Strutt had not been around to call off the third attempt.

Looking forward, Bruce had two main concerns: how to compensate the families of the dead porters, and what to do with the equipment and any surplus supplies. The Everest Committee sent him a cable asking him to award the families 'fitting recognition of their splendid services' but did not specify the precise amount or confirm what was happening next. If there was going to be a third expedition in 1923, it would make sense to leave a certain amount of material in storage in Tibet – but would it go ahead? He wrote back to the Committee asking for guidance, but he knew that with all their postal problems it would take a while to get an answer.

In the meantime, as planned, Bruce had decided to take what remained of his party to the Kharta valley. Notionally there was still some exploration to be done, but Bruce's main motive was to give everyone a rest in a more comfortable location before they began the long and gruelling trek back to Darjeeling. Howard-Bury had waxed lyrical about the beautiful meadows and pastures of Kharta, and at the very least it would be several degrees warmer and sheltered from the harsh winds that still tore up and down the Rongbuk valley.

On 17 June the main party met Norton and Bruce, and two days later they all celebrated the end of the expedition with what Bruce called an 'epicurean feast' of sardines, Gruyère cheese, truffled yak and three bottles of Champagne. The porters began searching out the local hooch from nearby villages, determined to enjoy their own escape from the Rongbuk. Charlie Bruce was phlegmatic, accepting the fact that they would 'go on the spree', his only rule being that any man who was so drunk he could not lie down, never mind stand up, would face a penalty.

Bruce had hoped that at the end of the expedition he might make a brief foray into the forbidden kingdom of Nepal, returning to Darjeeling via the spectacular Arun valley, but the Maharajah of Nepal sent him a polite but firm message turning down his request. Instead, Bruce sent John Noel and John Morris off to explore and photograph the Arun gorge from the Tibetan side, while he and the others took it easy. They didn't have enough food or transport to carry out any further exploration, but they were happy simply to enjoy the scenery.

For Mallory, the move to the Kharta valley was initially the tonic he needed. After spending so many weeks utterly focused on climbing, for the first few days he found himself revelling in the natural beauty all around him. Like many other climbers of his era, he had a genuine interest and love of flowers and took great pleasure in walking through what he called the 'ravishing' array of irises, rhododendrons and primulas of a Tibetan summer. Soon he was writing home to Ruth, planning how he would expand his own flowerbeds back in Cambridge and plant new shrubs, and maybe even bring back some seedlings from the Himalayas.

But for all the release that Kharta offered, Mallory could not quite shake off the depression that had gripped him since the accident. When a post runner arrived with a copy of the recently published book of the 1921 Reconnaissance expedition, all he could do was complain about the quality of the photographic reproductions and reiterate his dislike of his former expedition leader, Charles Howard-Bury. 'Life is aimless,' he wrote. 'I can't really enjoy things at present in spite of the lovely flowers and scenery. We're not quite the jolly company we were – a slightly strained and indefinably ungraceful air has come over us even though we are so well rid of Finch.'

As ever, Mallory's disdain towards Finch was never too far below the surface, but his priority now was to get home to Ruth. Somervell and Crawford were planning to do some climbing around Kangchenjunga on the way back, and would have undoubtedly wanted him to join them, but his only desire was to get to Darjeeling as quickly as possible and then take the first boat back to England.

After a rapid trip through Sikkim, Mallory reached Darjeeling at the end of July, and stayed with Morshead and his family for a few days. His teammate, Mallory was glad to find, was in characteristically cheery spirits. Morshead's left hand was more or less recovered but his right hand and one big toe were still looking very unhappy. Eventually the top joints on three fingers would have to be amputated, but Morshead seemed genuinely stoic about it and was determined not to let it affect him – though he confessed in a letter to Hinks that it did make it a little harder to hold a tennis racket. In the face of such resilience and good humour, Mallory cheered up and began looking forward even more to getting back home. He signed off his last letter to Ruth on a horticultural note: 'I hope I shall find you as blooming as I am.'

General Bruce and the main party returned to Darjeeling via a slightly longer and more staggered route than Mallory, reversing the path of their outward journey. John Noel was very aware that he hadn't got quite enough footage for his expedition documentary, so he stayed busy, shooting more monasteries and images of Tibetan life. As in the previous year, the sahibs encountered a Buddhist pilgrim, this time a Mongolian, on a solo journey from Lhasa to Kathmandu, prostrating himself hundreds of times a day. Though ragged, he looked remarkably well and was duly filmed by Noel.

On 8 July, Bruce wrote what would be his final dispatch of the expedition for *The Times*, ignoring Hinks's pleas for seven more. Overall he was happy, though he bitterly regretted the deaths at the end. With regard to oxygen, he wrote, though initially he had been sceptical, after Finch had made such a success of it, Bruce was now convinced of its value. He claimed that 'with a properly instructed and trained personnel and the correction of the few slight mistakes in the oxygen apparatus, a very great hope, practically amounting to a certainty, remains that with the assistance of oxygen men can reach the summit'.

He had also been very impressed by the carrying power and stamina of their Sherpas and Bhotias, and believed that they could do more next time. 'However,' Bruce concluded, 'it must further be impressed upon all that the Himalaya are a desperate enemy; no chances are ever taken with them. There is only one motto for the Himalaya: "When in doubt, don't." With this little aphorism I bring to a close the account of this year's attempts.'

On 20 July, Bruce and the rear guard arrived at the Dak bungalow at Phari, and a few days later crossed from the border at the Jelep La pass. Sikkim was, as expected, much mistier and wetter than Tibet, but even on the way home, Bruce still took immense pleasure in the landscape. From one ridge they were able to look all the way down onto the plains of India and get an unrivalled view of Kangchenjunga, 'a perfectly marvellous vision of ice and snow', which looked immeasurably high. It was, Bruce later recalled, 'a moment to live for' before the inevitable clouds and mist rolled in, obscuring their view.

Almost two weeks later, on 2 August, Bruce finally reached Darjeeling, to be followed a few days later by Crawford and Somervell on the way back from their final spurt of climbing. As the *Times of India* reported, it was a low-key affair rather than any kind of triumphant re-entry. After leaving their baggage at the railhead in Kalimpong, they had started walking towards Darjeeling until they were intercepted by a small fleet of cars. As he was driven into town, Bruce was recognized by more and more people but he had given no advance notice of the return date and there was no official reception or cheering crowds. The *Times* correspondent noticed unsurprisingly that, after their weeks recuperating in the Kharta valley, Bruce's party looked considerably fresher and healthier than Strutt and Finch, who had rushed back to Darjeeling over a month earlier.

Bruce had by then caught up with most of his mail – a disagreeable process. He had been depressed by all the letters sent by Hinks in May and early June, pestering him for dispatches and trying to persuade him to stay for the autumn season. 'To tell you the truth,' he wrote to Francis Younghusband, 'from the terrific strafes we have been receiving we thought that the expedition was not considered to be a very great success, in fact I was contemplating a flight to South America.'

Hinks, however, was by then in a much more conciliatory mood, apologizing to Bruce if his letters had been 'taken as complaints', but once again excusing himself on the grounds that the breakdown in communication in May and June had left him feeling mystified and anxious. Hinks was very pleased to announce on 15 August that *The Times* had told him that nine out of the promised fifteen field dispatches was good enough for them to send the final payment, and that overall the newspaper was very pleased with what it had received.

There was still no certainty about another expedition in 1923. Bruce was pushing for it, telling Hinks that the Tibetan authorities were amenable and the Sherpas keen to return, but the Committee refused to commit to anything. In the end they fixed up a grant of 250 rupees for the families of the dead porters – the equivalent of eleven months' wages. In the future, the Everest Committee would insure the lives of their hired Sherpas, though the climbers would be left to make their own arrangements and pay for their own policies. The *Times of India* reported that several of the expedition Sherpas had camped around Bruce's temporary house in Darjeeling, taking note of his movements while playing cards and generally amusing themselves. 'He is their general Sahib,' the reporter added, 'who has accomplished more in their mountain fastness than any other living man.'

In mid-August, Bruce moved on to Kolkata, where he had officials and friends to meet before taking the boat back to England. When a reporter from the *Daily Telegraph* caught up with him, Bruce was in a loquacious but contemplative mood. He told their man that he couldn't say for certain, but he thought that Everest could be climbed, though next time round it would need a combination of experience and youth, along with the vital good weather. 'In his opinion,' the reporter noted, 'it would be a great pity to abandon the project after the very valuable experience they had gained in the recent expedition.'

As for the avalanche, on 4 September, a couple of weeks after his return to England, Mallory's complete account of the events was finally published in *The Times*. Though he was still very distressed over the deaths of the porters, he insisted that he and the other sahibs had not been reckless. General Bruce, he said, had agreed that after the first snows there was likely to be a period of good weather. On the day they tried to reach the North Col, he said, they had taken all possible precautions, but: 'A mountaineer is bound to take some risks; not every possible occurrence is under his control to prevent or foresee... I need hardly say how grievously the loss of these men, who served us so faithfully, affected the whole party.'

By the time Bruce reached London on 3 October, the gloomy mood that had engulfed the end of the expedition had finally begun to lift. When he appeared in front of the Everest Committee two days later, the official minutes recorded that Bruce got a 'cordial welcome' and was congratulated for his organizational skills and for keeping everyone in 'good health and spirits'. When asked about the possibility of a 1923 expedition, Bruce repeated his belief that the Tibetans were very friendly at that moment and would permit another attempt. The Committee were still not convinced that there was enough time to organize things, so they sent instructions to the expedition's shipping agent in Darjeeling to sell off all the remaining perishable food and send back the valuable oxygen sets.

The big excitement among Committee members was the series of lectures that would take place over the following months to tell the tale of the summit attempts. The first, an official reception attended by various dignitaries – along with the combined members of the Royal Geographical Society and the Alpine Club – was held at the grand Central Hall in Westminster on 16 October. Lord Ronaldshay, the former governor of Bengal who a year earlier had feted the members of the Everest Reconnaissance at Government House in Darjeeling, had by then been elected President of the RGS. He opened the proceedings by making a formal announcement that the Tibetan government had given permission for a third expedition. Though everyone was confident that the summit could be reached, he added, they still had not decided precisely when the next attempt should take place.

After Ronaldshay's introduction, Charlie Bruce took to the stage. He spent much of his time praising the great work that the porters had done and emphasizing how keen they all were to return. 'I do not think ever before in the history of Himalayan exploration have men been called on to do harder, or even as hard, work,' he said. 'I think their performance was absolutely without precedent... in Darjeeling on the return every single man volunteered for next year.'

Next, Mallory stepped up to the podium.

For someone who has always been marketed as a romantic figure, he began in a surprisingly analytical frame of mind. Everest, he declared, had become for him 'a problem' that had to be solved. When he thought of getting to the summit, he no longer imagined 'panting efforts up the final slopes' or conjured up the mountain as a 'symbol of adventure'. Instead, he now saw a series of slopes, punctuated by groups of tents and piles of equipment, and parties of men, each with their own role to play.

As for the first attempt, he remembered how the principal factor governing their ascent was sheer lung power. 'From the Alpine point of view,' he joked, it was so difficult to breathe that 'our lungs made us pause to admire the view oftener than is correct in the best circles.' Like Bruce, he emphasized that the key to reaching the summit was getting the most out of the porters. 'They showed astonishingly little signs of fatigue,' he remembered, and said he was confident that next time round if they could get the final camp up to 27,000 feet, then it was possible the sahibs could get to the top.

Mallory still felt guilty about the avalanche that had ended the third attempt, putting it down to 'imperfect knowledge of snow in this part of the Himalayas', though he added that 'one could never know enough'. As for supplementary oxygen, he remained ambivalent: he and Somervell had planned to use it on the third attempt, having seen how well Finch and Bruce had done, but nevertheless, Mallory remained convinced that it might be possible to summit without it. Showing how far he had come since 1921, when after the Reconnaissance, Mallory had quoted partner Guy

Bullock's assessment that the odds of reaching the summit were fifty to one against, he declared, 'If any gambler had been laying odds on the mountain, he should very considerably reduce his ratio as the result of this year's Expedition.' He finished on a more cautious note: 'Man may calculate how to solve his problem, and ... you may finish the sentence.'

Next up was Finch. He had no doubt about the value of oxygen, but rather than talk about the climbing itself, he remembered the incident when, after spending two nights trapped in their tents on the North Ridge, he had offered Geoffrey Bruce and Tejbir some reviving oxygen. 'Tejbir took his medicine reluctantly but with relief I saw his face brighten up. The effect on Bruce was visible in his rapid change of expression. A few minutes after the first deep breath, I felt the tingling sensation of returning life and warmth to my limbs. We connected up the apparatus in such a way that we could breathe a small quantity of oxygen through the night. The result was marvellous.'

With the following day's press full of articles about Britain's heroic deeds on Everest, the Westminster event was the perfect curtain-raiser for the programme of public lectures that took place all around the country. In the 1920s, before the era of television and mass media, there was an active public lecture circuit in Britain which the Committee knew could be very lucrative. They engaged Gerald Christy of the Lecture Agency, one of Britain's leading impresarios whose previous clients included Earnest Shackleton and Fridtjof Nansen.

Hinks wanted the lectures to be fronted by as many members of the team as possible, but Christie instinctively understood that Mallory and Finch were by far the best attractions for the general public, especially if he could play up their competitiveness. As the flyer advertising the October lectures announced: 'The keen rivalry between the exponents of high climbing with and without oxygen adds great interest to the story of this year's expedition.' Both men were charismatic, experienced speakers who enjoyed being in front of an audience.

Over the next few months, Finch and Mallory would give over 100 lectures. Outside of London they rarely appeared on the same platform. Finch travelled the length of Britain and made a foray into Switzerland, while Mallory was tasked with selling the Everest story to America, sailing in style on a White Star Liner in early January 1923. When he reached New York he was put up on the twelfth storey of the Waldorf Astoria. He joked to local pressmen that he liked to keep fit by getting to his suite via the stairs rather than the elevator.

In late November, Captain Noel's film had its first showing in London before also going on tour, first in Britain and then in Europe and America. In truth, neither the foreign lectures nor the expedition film were as successful as the Committee had hoped, but combined with the profits from the official book and the belated payments from *The Times* and the *Illustrated London News*, the Everest Committee's finances were soon looking much healthier.

As 1922 ground to an end, it became obvious that there would be no return to the Himalayas in 1923, but preparations were soon under way for a third expedition in 1924. If they could get the weather, the team, the equipment and a bit of good luck... everyone was convinced that Everest could be climbed. As Finch had told the audience at the reception in October, on their way down the Rongbuk glacier, after making their record-breaking attempt, his frostbitten partner Geoffrey Bruce had bid Everest, the Mother Goddess of the World, an irreverent adieu: 'Just you wait old thing, you'll be for it soon.'

The Rongbuk monastery, 1922

12

2020 Hindsight

Almost 100 years on, the impact of the 1922 expedition can still be felt in the Himalayas. It set the style for the huge expeditions to come, created the founding myths of high-altitude climbing, and turned Everest into by far the most famous mountain in the world. Even if ultimately the British team did not achieve everything that the expedition organizers had wanted, for a first attempt it was remarkably successful, setting new world records for the highest point reached and the highest camp ever established.

It also ended with a notable, and today largely forgotten, disaster. Seven men died on an ill-conceived final attempt that really should not have taken place, however inevitable. In its very oscillation between triumph and tragedy, 1922 is the archetypal Himalayas expedition, crystallizing that strange mixture of glory and futility that sums up so much of mountaineering and exploration history.

By comparison, the first attempts on the world's second- and third-highest mountains, K2 and Kangchenjunga, were far less effective. In 1902, Oscar Eckenstein led a small party of British and Swiss climbers to K2 in the Karakoram, but they barely got above the glacier at the foot of the mountain. Three years later, in 1905, Eckenstein's friend Aleister Crowley returned to India with another Anglo-Swiss team, aiming to climb Kangchenjunga. They did better, reaching approximately 22,000 feet but there was still a further 6,000 feet to go before the top.

The achievements of the 1922 expedition were not totally surprising, of course. Charlie Bruce, for all his bluff and bluster, was a seasoned and successful soldier, able to utilize the skills that he had learned on the battlefield and the parade ground to run an exemplary mountaineering campaign. He understood the importance of logistics, was willing to spend money when needed, was not afraid to delegate power and understood the crucial importance of maintaining morale, particularly among his untrained porters.

As climbers, the 1922 team exceeded expectations. George Mallory, Howard Somervell, George Finch and Edward Norton all proved themselves to be powerful, determined and fearless. Aside from Mallory, none of them had previously been to high altitude but they all coped amazingly well, and with a little more luck could have gone even higher.

The Sherpas and Bhotias, too, were far more effective than anyone could have predicted. None of them had any formal mountaineering training and hardly any of them had ever been on an expedition, but they were able to reach altitudes of more than 25,000 feet and were able to move on the mountain independently, disregarding the so-called rule that they always had to be chaperoned.

Today's Himalayas, of course, would barely be recognizable to those porters or anyone on the 1922 team. If the ghosts of

Mallory or Bruce or Pema or Gyaljen were to return to Everest, instead of a small cluster of drab-coloured tents on an isolated glacier, they would find what looked like a medium-sized tented village, with brightly coloured prayer flags jostling with equally vivid tents and mess tents containing climbers from all over the world – male and female, young and old.

The same forces that have transformed every aspect of twenty-first-century life – globalization, computers, jet engines – have transformed the Himalayas. Perhaps, a century later, the rather more surprising thing is how important Everest remains in the global consciousness, and how much its summit is still an object of desire for so many people. In spite of all the negative press and all the stories of queues, corpses and high-altitude refuse, there are still many thousands of people out there who are willing to spend their life savings and risk their necks to get to the top.

The biggest and most profound change is geographical: in 1922, the only way to get to Everest was via Tibet, but today, though many climbers do still attempt Everest from the Rongbuk glacier, the standard approach is via the other side of the mountain, from Nepal. The first ascent was made in May 1953 by Edmund Hillary and Tenzing Norgay, two members of a thirteen-man British team supported by twenty-two Sherpas and several hundred local porters. Seven years later, a Chinese team and their Sherpas reached the summit, following the North Ridge route pioneered in 1922.

After that, the most significant event in Everest's history – and one that would have undoubtedly pleased Arthur Hinks – was the first ascent without supplementary oxygen, by the Italian climber Reinhold Messner and his Austrian partner Peter Habeler, in 1978. The great oxygen debate, which was such a feature of the 1922 expedition, had run throughout the 1930s and the post-war years. Even in the 1970s there were some in the scientific and climbing communities who initially doubted that Messner and Habeler were telling the truth. Just to prove them wrong and re-emphasize his credentials as the world's pre-eminent mountaineer, Messner repeated the feat two years later, this time climbing solo from the north side – again without oxygen.

Messner's ascent initiated a new era of lightweight 'Alpine style' ascents of Himalayan peaks by the world's elite climbers, but the next most important ascent in Everest's history was by the fifty-five-year-old American businessman Dick Bass, who in 1985 became the oldest man to climb Everest and the first to ascend the highest mountain on each continent – the Seven Summits, as it came to be known. The 1921 and 1922 Everest expeditions had ended with declarations from various team members that Everest was no place for old or even middle-aged men, but Bass proved that age was no barrier and that you didn't even have to be an elite climber to reach the highest point on earth, especially if you were very rich and could afford to hire some of the world's best guides.

Prior to Dick Bass's ascent, most Everest expeditions had been financed through a mixture of private and public sponsorship, but that traditional model was soon looking very outdated. Instead, professional guiding companies took over, staging expeditions that were directly funded by the assorted team members. Whereas Francis Younghusband had boasted in 1922 that his Committee had assembled the world's best team for the first attempt, in the new commercial era you no longer had to be a top mountaineer to get up Everest. Commercial clients were required to be competent and fit and have some experience of high mountains, but with the right amount of Sherpa and mountain guide support, any decent mountaineer could do it, provided they could come up with around $50,000 in peak fees and guiding charges. Before long there were several American and New Zealand-based companies offering guided commercial expeditions and in spite of the significant costs and obvious risks on what was still considered a very dangerous mountain, every year there seemed to be more people wishing to take up the challenge.

The growing commercialization of Everest generated some disquiet, but it didn't come to international attention until 1997 when, following a disastrous year in which eight people died in a single storm on Everest, the American writer Jon Krakauer wrote *Into Thin Air*, a damning critique of the modern 'Everest industry'. Suddenly the world's highest mountain was no longer depicted as the pinnacle of mountaineering prowess. Instead Krakauer presented it as a rich person's playground, populated by socialites and businessmen cramponing their way past the dead and the dying in order to be able to boast about 'conquering' Everest.

Paradoxically, Krakauer's lurid tale and all the negative press did nothing to diminish the attraction of Everest. Far from putting anyone off, it only increased the number of people wanting to take on the world's highest mountain. In the spring of 2012, a record-breaking 683 climbers from thirty-four countries made attempts on the mountain, with no less than 234 of them and their Sherpas and guides reaching the summit on 19 May 2012.

It seemed as if Douglas Freshfield's prediction might come true: the Himalayas had not quite become the 'playground' of the world, but they were getting there. In 2016, China completed the much-trumpeted 'highway to Everest' to bring tourist buses to within a mile of the mountain and climbers all the way into

Base Camp. On the other side, Nepal has begun a new road to Lukla, the traditional jumping-off point for Everest treks and climbs, which until recently has only been properly accessible by plane. In 1922 it took the British team two weeks to get from Britain to India, and a further month to get from Darjeeling to their Base Camp. Today's climbers can fly into Lhasa, spend a few days acclimatizing and then drive to Base Camp in around three to five days, depending on the time of year.

It is even possible to arrive at Everest in a pre-acclimatized state. For almost two decades, the Altitude Centre in London has been running 'hypoxic' workout sessions and hiring out equipment which enables climbers and athletes to train in a low-oxygen environment. The keenest will even spend several weeks sleeping at home in a special tent which simulates high altitude.

When it comes to the equipment and the nitty-gritty of expedition life, that too would be unrecognizable to the 1922 team. Mallory and Somervell carried long-handled ice axes and wore nailed leather boots. They kept themselves warm with layers of waxed cotton and Shetland sweaters, supplemented with the occasional silk shirt. Today, with the exception of Botany wool underlayers, synthetic materials dominate. The introduction of Vibram rubber soles revolutionized climbing footwear in the late 1930s, and more recently plastic mountaineering boots have become the most common high-altitude footwear.

The great equipment innovator on the 1922 expedition was of course George Finch. His theories on the beneficial effects of smoking at high altitude have not gained any traction, but the down suit that he commissioned for Everest has become the uniform of the high-altitude mountaineer. Ever the good scientist, Finch also understood the importance of nutrition, but in some ways modern high-altitude food – dried rather than tinned, and high in carbohydrate – is more akin to the Sherpa rations from 1922 than the Army & Navy Stores delicacies that Finch enjoyed on the mountain, courtesy of that great bon viveur General Bruce.

The most significant development in terms of nutrition, however, is the recognition of the importance of liquid intake at altitude. In 1922, the inefficiency of the British team's stoves meant that it was virtually impossible to melt sufficient snow for drinking water. When in the early 1950s the physiologist Griff Pugh was recruited to work with British Himalayan expeditions, he pored over reports and accounts from the 1920s and noticed how many climbers, not just Henry Morshead, had confessed to going for long periods without urinating because they were simply not drinking enough. As a rule of thumb, Pugh advised that any climber going to high altitude should down at least six pints of liquid – or 2.8 litres – per day. Modern advice is to drink about a litre more.

Though Messner and Habeler's 1978 ascent ended the debate about whether or not it was possible to get to the summit without supplementary oxygen, the vast majority of Everest climbers still depend on it. Modern-day sets are much lighter and more efficient than the very primitive equipment that Finch and Bruce had in 1922, allowing clients on commercial exhibitions to use 'English air' from early on in their ascent. For the world's elite mountaineers, however, climbing without oxygen remains a badge of honour.

The other oxygen controversy is one that was not foreseen by George Finch or Arthur Hinks: what to do with the used cylinders? In 1922, Finch and Geoffrey Bruce gaily tossed their empty bottles down the North Face. In a similar way, George Mallory had been happy to throw his excess food and fuel supplies off the Lhakpa La in 1921. For obvious reasons, these actions would not be condoned today. The first 'Everest clean-up' expedition took place in 1990, and there have been several others since then. Modern-day expeditions have to leave a substantial deposit to guarantee that they will take away their trash – and avoid being named and shamed.

Modern-day communications systems have revolutionized many other aspects of the mountaineering experience. In 1922 it took between two and four weeks, and occasionally even longer, for news to get from Tibet to London; nowadays, messages and phone calls can be made virtually in real time. At the end of the twentieth century, the first satellite telephones started to appear on Everest, with Peter Hillary famously speaking to his father Ed Hillary via a radio patched into a sat-phone at Base Camp in 1990. The first conventional mobile telephone call from the summit was made in 2007, the first tweet in 2010 and the first video call in 2013.

Equally, or perhaps more importantly, the technology that enables climbers to keep in touch with their friends and sponsors also offers them access to up-to-the-minute, increasingly accurate weather reports. In 1922, the British team were very aware that they were racing against the monsoon, but they had no means of predicting the weather and were dependent on local knowledge and guesswork to decide when best to climb. Almost a century later, in 2021, teams at Base Camp anxiously await the latest satellite-derived weather news to be emailed to their tents, aiming to make their summit bids within the ideal weather window. This can paradoxically add an extra layer of danger when there are several different teams on the mountain. If there is just one decent weather window, then everyone goes at the same time and Everest's infamous high-altitude queues are more likely to occur.

Of all the non-technological changes over the last century, perhaps the most profound has been to the role of Sherpas. In 1922 there was a clear distinction between the sahibs and the porters when it came to climbing: the British stayed in the lead, finding and fixing the route and staging the summit attempts, while the Sherpas and Bhotias were there principally to do the carrying.

Today that role has been reversed, with Sherpas looking after and leading the way on commercial expeditions, as well as organizing their own attempts. In January 2021, an all-Nepali team made the first winter ascent of K2, one of the very 'last great prizes' in high-altitude climbing and a feat that for many years had been thought impossible. It is unthinkable to imagine anyone ever again comparing Sherpas to children, as George Mallory did in 1922. Whether ultimately Everest has been a curse for the Sherpa community or a blessing is a different question.

Though they can earn far more on Western expeditions than in typical Nepali jobs, many do not work in the mountaineering industry and do not want their children to have to, regarding Himalayan work as far too hazardous. Some prefer to send their children abroad to be educated at American and European universities, and over the last few decades there has been a significant Sherpa diaspora – with several famous guides choosing to split their lives between Nepal and the United States, where they have established their families.

The last decade in particular has not been good on Everest. In 2013 there was an infamous brawl in which a Swiss climber and his support team became embroiled in a violent argument with a group of Sherpas over who had precedence on the mountain.

The following year, a huge avalanche killed sixteen Sherpas in the Khumbu Icefall, and in 2015 at least ten more Sherpas were killed on Everest along with several Western climbers when a 7.8-degree earthquake struck Nepal. There were bumper seasons in 2016 and 2017, but then it was reported that the Hillary Step, the iconic feature close to the summit on the Nepali side, had collapsed. A superstitious person might wonder if the warning image of a wounded white man painted on a wall at the Rongbuk monastery should long ago have been heeded, and that perhaps after almost a century of expeditions, it's time to leave Everest alone. That, however, is very unlikely to happen, and would have been equally inconceivable to Mallory and the other leading members of the British team who arrived back in London in the autumn of 1922.

Even if in the future, Everest would start to feel like a long, drawn-out slog of a campaign, almost like the First World War that preceded it, there was a freshness and a sense of excitement about the 1921 Reconnaissance and the first attempt in 1922 that kept both the public at home and the climbers in the field engaged and enthusiastic. The only important question was when would they get another crack at it.

A few – like the two doctors, Arthur Wakefield and Tom Longstaff – had no intention of returning. Wakefield resettled in Cumbria, where he lived and worked as a general practitioner for the next two decades. He took part in no further big expeditions, though he did remain an active member of the Fell and Rock Club. Tom Longstaff followed a different trajectory. He did return to the Himalayas in 1927 for an expedition to the Garhwal mountains, but gradually he turned his attention northwards towards the

Arctic, exploring and climbing in Greenland, Spitsbergen and Baffin Island. Unlike Wakefield, he remained very involved in future Everest expeditions, becoming a member of the Everest Committee and President of the Alpine Club in 1947. He died in 1964 at the venerable age of eighty-nine, demonstrating that mountaineers who don't die young frequently live to a ripe old age.

Like Wakefield and Longstaff, Edward Stutt, the expedition's climbing leader, realized that he was too old to return to Everest, but he remained very involved in the Alpine Club, becoming both the editor of the *Alpine Journal* and club's President in the late 1930s. He never mellowed, being well known for his 'Struttisms' in print and in person, as he denounced everything from 'artificial' climbing aids such as crampons and pitons to the conduct of young German and Italian climbers.

Strutt, Longstaff and Wakefield were out of the running, but, for the two Georges – Mallory and Finch – and the eternally young Charlie Bruce, there was no question of not getting back into the fray. Everest remained the supreme challenge; it still held the promise of fame for the first person to climb it, and for all of them it was now 'unfinished business'. Finch was convinced that he had turned back early for Geoffrey Bruce's sake, and with a different partner, or climbing on his own, he might have reached the summit. Mallory was equally sure that he could have gone higher if it had not been for Morshead's breakdown.

Charlie Bruce had been publicly in favour of returning in 1923 and had held out for as long as possible before selling off the expedition's unused supplies, but as 1922 rolled on towards the New Year, he came to accept that there would not be another expedition until 1924. The only issue was when precisely it would take place, and who else might be involved?

Norton had lost part of his ear to frostbite but was very keen to get back to Everest, and he remained convinced that it was possible to climb it without oxygen. His character and his climbing ability had impressed everyone in 1922 and Bruce was keen to have Norton on any further attempts.

Howard Somervell had also performed exceptionally well for a first-timer and was well liked by everyone on the team and the Everest Committee. He had decided to stay on in India after the expedition to see more of the country. When he finally returned to England later that autumn, he was very much involved in the aftermath of the 1922 expedition. He finished several paintings and, good to his word, sold them at the Alpine Club to fund further expeditions. If that wasn't enough, Somervell also wrote the music for John Noel's film and delivered dozens of accompanying lectures when it went on tour.

Then, in early 1923, Somervell announced that he was going back to India to work in a hospital, tending to the poor and destitute. His family were deeply religious, so it perhaps wasn't totally surprising, but his colleagues and bosses were shocked that he was prepared to give up what looked set to be a glittering career as a top London surgeon. The only thing that would divert him, albeit temporarily, was the promise of a place on a further Everest expedition. It was coming ever closer.

In the spring of 1923, the Everest Committee began official preparations for a return to Everest the following year. First things first, they began canvassing for new members of the climbing team. Francis Younghusband mooted the idea of sending the team to the Alps for six weeks of winter training before they embarked for India. George Finch promised to carry out a programme of experiments to ascertain the best high-altitude ration. *The*

Times were approached to see if they were willing to support the expedition for the third time in a row, but with money flowing in from lectures and the royalties from Howard-Bury's book on the 1921 Reconnaissance, the Committee were not really so worried about funding. Having given themselves an extra year, they felt confident that they could build on the success of 1922 and, with fresh blood on the team, finish the job that Bruce had started.

The extra time also gave space for new arguments and for old debates to be rekindled. Who ultimately should choose the party, and who was really in charge – the Alpine Club or the Royal Geographical Society? General Bruce had done well in 1922 but would his health really hold for another two years? Was Mallory the right man to be his deputy? And what about Finch, the team's odd man out? At the end of the 1922 expedition Edward Strutt had nominated him for membership of the Alpine Club, an honour that he duly accepted, but Finch was never as 'clubbable' as the other members of the team, and it did not take long before he was once again wrangling with Hinks, this time over lecture fees and expenses.

The 1922 expedition had been ground-breaking but it had ended with a brutal reminder of the sheer elemental struggle of Himalayan climbing. In 1924, a new British expedition would be coming back to Everest. There would be new personalities, new equipment and ultimately an equally dramatic outcome. If anyone thought that the controversies were over, they would be proven to be very wrong as the next chapters in Everest's history were written.

But that, as they say, is another story.

Bibliography and Sources

The principal source for this book was the vast number of documents, letters and diaries collected together in the Mount Everest Foundation's archive, which is housed at the Royal Geographical Society. The material pertaining to 1921 and 1922 is contained in twenty-two file boxes, with headings ranging from 'Correspondence mainly with India Office' to 'Seeds, plants etc.'. The second principal source is the Alpine Club's archive and library in London, which contains diaries, newspaper cuttings and letters, as well as original documents. Other important sources include the National Library of Scotland, where George Finch's Everest diary and photographic albums are housed; the Blakeney Collection at the British Library, which includes much original material collected by a former member of the Alpine Club; and *The Times* newspaper, which covered both the Reconnaissance and the first expedition from beginning to end.

Though I have prioritized the primary and archival sources, it is not always the case that everyone agrees on the precise details. There are frequent small discrepancies between the climbers and other participants over altitudes and dates. The majority of these are minor and I have taken the most common view. Occasionally the disagreements are slightly comical. In George Finch's book, *The Making of a Mountaineer,* he writes how after coming down from his attempt he had stuffed himself full of sausages and quails, and then gone to bed with a tin of toffee nestled in the crook of his elbow. In the English translation of Finch's other book *The*

Struggle for Everest, which was originally published in German, that tin of toffee is transformed into a flask of coffee! More significantly, most writers have assumed that on their descent from the first attempt, it was Morshead who slipped pulling off Norton and Somervell. In fact, Norton's diary, which was not published until 2014, reveals that it was Norton who slipped, dragging Morshead and the others off with him. John Noel's recollection of their first audience with the Rongbuk Lama is very different from anyone else's and so are a few other details in his Everest book. Ultimately the discrepancies are small, and with differing accounts appearing at different times after the events, it's not so surprising that recollections occasionally diverge.

Published Sources

For anyone researching Everest, Walt Unsworth's monumental book *Everest: A Mountaineering History*, and Wade Davis's excellent *Into the Silence* remain key texts. For Everest 1922, I have stuck wherever possible to the primary sources – the books and articles published at the time, and later accounts by the team members and protagonists of the drama.

Books

Bell, Charles, *Portrait of the Dalai Lama*, London, Collins, 1946.

Bruce, C. G., *Twenty Years in the Himalaya*, London, Edward Arnold, 1910.

—— et al., *The Assault on Mount Everest 1922*, London, Edward Arnold, 1924.

Buchan, John, *The Last Secrets*, London, Thomas Nelson and Sons, 1923.

Finch, George Ingle, *The Making of a Mountaineer*, London, Arrowsmith, 1924.

——, *The Struggle for Everest*, ed. George W. Rodway, Trowbridge, Cromwell Press, 2008 (originally published as *Der Kampf um den Everest*, Leipzig, F. A. Brokhause, 1925).

Howard-Bury, C., et al., *Mount Everest: The Reconnaissance, 1921*, London, Edward Arnold, 1922.

Longstaff, Tom, *This My Voyage*, London, John Murray, 1950.

Mallory, George, *Climbing Everest*, London, Gibson Square Books, 2012.

Morris, John, *Hired to Kill*, London, Rupert Hart-Davis/Cresset Press, 1960.

Noel, J. B. L., *Through Tibet to Everest*, London, Edward Arnold, 1927.

Norton, Christopher, *Everest Revealed: The Private Diaries and Sketches of Edward Norton 1922–24*, Stroud, The History Press, 2014.

Somervell, T. H., *After Everest: The Experiences of a Mountaineer and Medical Missionary*, London, Hodder and Stoughton, 1936.

Younghusband, Francis, *The Epic of Mount Everest*, London, Edward Arnold, 1926.

Journals and Newspapers

The Alpine Journal (various): the key reference source, both during the 1920s and beyond.

Geographical Journal (various): another key reference, for the 1921 Reconnaissance and the 1922 expedition.

The Himalayan Journal (various): established in 1929, several years after the first Everest expedition, but another key archive source.

Films

Climbing Mount Everest, dir. John Noel, Royal Geographical Society, 1922.

Galahad of Everest, dir. John-Paul Davidson, BBC, 1991.

Selected Secondary Sources

Band, George, *Everest: 50 Years on Top of the World*, London, Collins, 2003.

Breshears, David, and Audrey Salkeld, *Last Climb: The Legendary Everest Expeditions of George Mallory*, London, National Geographic Society, 1999.

Conefrey, Mick, *Everest 1953: The Epic Story of the First Ascent*, London, Oneworld, 2012.

——, *The Ghosts of K2: The Race for the Summit of the World's Most Deadly Mountain*, London, Oneworld, 2015.

——, *The Last Great Mountain: The First Ascent of Kangchenjunga*, Michael Conefrey, 2020.

Davis, Wade, *Into the Silence*, New York, Alfred A. Knopf, 2011.

Douglas, Ed, *Tenzing: Hero of Everest*, Washington, DC, National Geographic Society, 2003.

Gillman, Peter, and Leni Gillman, *The Wildest Dream: Mallory, His Life and Conflicting Passions*, London, Headline, 2000.

Hillary, Edmund, *High Adventure*, London, Hodder and Stoughton, 1955.

Holzel, Tom, and Audrey Salkeld, *The Mystery of Mallory and Irvine*, London, Jonathan Cape, 1986.

Hunt, John, *The Ascent of Everest*, London, Hodder and Stoughton, 1953.

Irving, R. L. G., *The Mountain Way: An Anthology in Prose and Verse*, London, J. M. Dent and Sons, 1938.

Krakauer, Jon, *Into Thin Air*, London, Macmillan, 1997.

Lowe, George, *Because It Is There*, London, Cassell, 1959.

Morshead, Ian, *The Life and Murder of Henry Morshead*, Cambridge, Oleander Press, 1982.

Murray, W. H., *The Story of Everest*, London, J. M. Dent and Sons, 1954.

Noel, Sandra, *Everest Pioneer: The Photographs of Captain John Noel*, Stroud, Sutton, 2003.

Norton, Hugh, *Norton of Everest: The Biography of E. F. Norton, Solider and Mountaineer*, Sheffield, Vertebrate, 2017.

Ortner, Sherry B., *Life and Death on Mount Everest: Sherpas and Himalayan Mountaineering*, Princeton, NJ, Princeton University Press, 1999.

Pye, David, *George Leigh Mallory*, London, Oxford University Press, 1927, republished Orchid Press, 2002.

Robertson, David, *George Mallory*, London, Faber and Faber, 1999.

Shipton, Eric Earl, *The Mount Everest Reconnaissance Expedition 1951*, London, Hodder and Stoughton, 1952.

Tenzing Norgay, *After Everest: An Autobiography*, London, George Allen and Unwin, 1977.

—— (in collaboration with James Ramsay Ullman), *Tiger of the Snows: The Autobiography of Tenzing of Everest*, London, Putnam, 1955.

Unsworth, Walt, *Everest: A Mountaineering History*, Boston, Houghton Mifflin, 1981.

Venables, Stephen, *Everest: The Summit of Achievement*, London, Bloomsbury, 2003.

Wainwright, Robert, *The Maverick Mountaineer: The Remarkable Life of George Ingle Finch: Climber, Scientist, Inventor*, London, Allen and Unwin, 2016.

Ward, Michael, *Everest: A Thousand Years of Exploration*, Hayloft, 2013.

Photograph credits

Front and back end papers panoramic shot: The Everest 1922 team, with their high altitude porters, cooks and camp followers. Photo: J.B. Noel/ Courtesy of the Alpine Club.

Page 8: John Noel kinematographing the ascent of Mount Everest from Chang La. Photo: J.B. Noel/Royal Geographical Society via Getty Images.

Page 48: The Everest Reconnaissance Team, Darjeeling, 1921: Photo: Royal Geographical Society via Getty Images.

Page 66: The Abbot of Shekar Chöte, by Charles Howard-Bury. Photo: Royal Geographical Society via Getty Images.

Page 74: Mount Everest from the Rongbuk glacier, with Changtse in foreground. Photo: Royal Geographical Society via Getty Images.

Page 84: The 1921 Everest Reconnaissance party. Photo: Apic/Getty Images.

Page 106: Charles Granville Bruce. Photo: Lord Elibank/Royal Geographical Society via Getty Images.

Page 130: The Everest Team, March 1922. Photo: Royal Geographical Society via Getty Images.

Page 156: The head lama, Dzatrul Rinpoche, of the Rongbuk monastery. Photo: Royal Geographical Society via Getty Images.

Page 193: Mallory and Norton. Photo: T.H. Somervell/Royal Geographical Society via Getty Images.

Page 201: The climbers of the first summit party, after their attempt. Photo: J.B. Noel/Royal Geographical Society via Getty Images.

Page 202: George Finch demonstrating the oxygen he would use on his attempt. Photo: J.B. Noel/Royal Geographical Society via Getty Images.

Page 220: Bruce and Finch descending from their record climb. Photo: Royal Geographical Society via Getty Images.

Page 276: The Rongbuk monastery. Photo: J.B. Noel/Royal Geographical Society via Getty Images.

Acknowledgements

This book could not have been written without the help and assistance of many friends and colleagues. At Allen and Unwin, I'd like to thank my editor, Ed Faulkner, for commissioning the book and for all his work on it, and Mike Harpley at Atlantic for initiating the project. I'd also like to thank my agent, Leah Middleton, and her colleagues at Marjacq for their work and encouragement. Copious thanks also to Gemma Wain, my patient and assiduous copy-editor, and Kate Ballard, my senior editor.

This book is primarily based on research contained in the archives of the Royal Geographical Society and the Alpine Club, and I would like to thank them heartily for giving me access to their material in the especially difficult era of Covid. I'd particularly like to thank Alasdair MacLeod at the RGS, for being so positive and helpful with this project, along with Eugene Rae, the principal librarian. At the Alpine I'd like to thank Glyn Hughes, the honorary archivist, and Nigel Buckley, the former librarian. I'm very grateful also to the staff of the British Library and the National Library of Scotland and to Catherine Sutherland at Magdalene College, Cambridge, and to the Master and Fellows of Magdalene for permission to quote from Mallory's letters.

A special word of thanks for Tim Jordan, my former writing partner at the BBC, for his close reading of the first draft and all his advice and good humour, and to Jerry Lovatt for reading and commenting on the text. I'd also like to thank Stephen Venables, Anthony Bard, Jonathan Westaway, Peter Hansen, Lord Aberdare, Barbara Grigor-Taylor and Adam Lloyd.

Last but never least, I'd like to thank my children, Frank and Phyllis, and my darling wife, Stella, for all her love and support.

Mick Conefrey
Oxford 2021

Index